Preaching
and
Cultural
Identity

Preaching and Cultural Identity

Proclaiming the Gospel
in
Africa

JOHN WESLEY
ZWOMUNONDIITA
KUREWA

Abingdon Press
Nashville

PREACHING AND CULTURAL IDENTITY:
PROCLAIMING THE GOSPEL IN AFRICA

Library of Congress Cataloging-in-Publication Data

Kurewa, John Wesley Zwomunondiita.
 Preaching and Cultural Identity: Proclaiming the Gospel in Africa / John Wesley
 Zwomunondiita Kurewa.
  p.   cm.
 Includes bibliographical references.
 ISBN 0-687-09031-8 (alk. paper)
 1. Preaching—Africa, Sub-Saharan. 2. Christianity and culture—Africa, Sub-Saharan.
 I. Title.
 BV4208.A357   K87   2000
 251'.0096—dc21   99-044306

00 01 02 03 04 05 06 07 08 09 — 10 9 8 7 6 5 4 3 2 1

MANUFACTURED IN THE UNITED STATES OF AMERICA

*To Isaac and
Rebecca, my parents, who feared God from
the time they believed, introduced their
children to the Way, and lived an exemplary
Christian life of prayer and unwavering
faith in God to the end of their
earthly pilgrimage*

Contents

Preface

As a student of theology in the United States in the 1960s, I became good friends with a fellow African student from Nigeria studying anthropology at the same university. During one of our frequent discussions on African religion and culture, my Nigerian friend asked, "When an African is converted to Christianity, does he or she abandon his or her beliefs and practices in African religion? Or would it not be true to say that many of the Africans who become Christian remain committed to African religion?" He went on to explain, "I say this because it appears that in times of personal or family crisis, like illness, some Christians easily revert to beliefs and practices of African religion, and then they return to Christianity when everything has been put right." That question has haunted me through the years, demanding a review of genuine Christian identity in the African situation.

For almost three centuries now, a number of churches in Africa have been worshiping (including preaching the gospel) and singing in strange ways. I say "strange ways" because more often than not, when we sing in our Sunday worship services we still mostly sing the songs that missionaries brought to Africa—songs with Western tunes. Consequently, while we do not sound like Africans singing, neither do we sound like westerners singing. As African Christians who now worship God through our knowledge of him in Christ, we must worship God with the splendor of African cultures:

- with buildings of worship whose architecture portrays the congregation as a family or an extended African family—

9

round buildings that provide the atmosphere of oneness, togetherness, and face-to-face relationships with no one pushed into a corner;
- with some of the songs that have the African tune and beat, and singing that is accompanied by some of the African musical instruments;
- with liturgical design that provides the African swing, characterized by the spirit of celebration of joy and victory even in times of death; and with the kind of preaching that has roots not only in the Bible, but also in African rhetoric.

As cultural awareness increases in Africa, the Christian gospel and its cultural identity in sub-Saharan Africa should be critically examined by the African church as we enter the new millennium.

Some examples will illustrate the situation and the dilemma. Especially in the rural areas of Africa where such culture still prevails, when a child is born into a family, the person who would normally attend to the birth of a baby is a midwife. The midwife is always in the company of the relatives of the father and mother of the newborn baby. Immediately following the birth, traditional rituals are often performed, and these may include herbal ointment as a way to protect the newborn baby from the evil ones. These are traditional rituals that the young parents of a newborn baby may not be familiar with, and are often performed in secret. Even if the parents know about the rituals, they might not be in a position to do anything to prevent them, because at that moment neither of them is in control. It is often the midwife and relatives who take control.

Even more controversial would likely be a situation where a Christian may go to a *n'anga*—a traditional healer, medicine man or medicine woman, herbalist or diviner—either with a child or for himself or herself. That would also usually be done secretly: there are times when a Christian parishioner walks "through the valley of the shadow of death" (Ps. 23:4) alone—without any other member of the church or the pastor knowing, because the parishioner knows that the churches condemn such African practices.

Such secrecy arises because the churches have preached against their parishioners going for traditional healing without looking at the plight of their Christians and the communities from which they come. Once in a while, to their surprise, they meet some of the very people who preach against traditional healing at the quarters of the traditional healers. When the Christians' problems have been taken care of by the traditional healer, they go back to church and never share those experiences with other members of the congregation or with their pastor. Such experiences remain family secrets. Some pastors could testify about members of their churches who have died hundreds of miles away from home when the family was seeking traditional healing for their relative. Such pastors could also testify about the horrible stigma such death has brought to the bereaved family because of what the other Christians were saying about them seeking help from a traditional healer, instead of the church.

I am fully aware of some of the shortcomings of our traditional practices of healing, and I am not advocating that people go to traditional healers who cast lots and deceive people. Rather, I am suggesting that the church ought to openly discuss what we consider the limits of acceptable traditional healing. I am also advocating that the church discuss African culture, including African religion and the role of traditional healing in it, in such a manner that the church will be able to give guidance to parishioners today. Like any other culture, African culture should be subjected to and judged by the gospel. What is condemned should be done away with; and what is redeemed by our new faith should be preserved and used to glorify God.

Today, Asian traditional practices of healing are being used in some Western countries. There seems to be an interest in herbal healing worldwide. Africa should not once again have to wait until we are taught by outsiders what is Christian and not Christian about our own ways of life. The church must take a lead in condemning the attitude that whatever is African is of the devil, and whatever is Western is of God. That is the issue my Nigerian friend was raising with me. It remains the problem of the gospel and cultural identity in Africa.

The focus of this book is on preaching, and its purpose is to use preaching as an instrument that will invite the African church once more to take a closer look at our African culture as God-given. It is God-given because no one can choose to be born in a particular culture. When missionaries used Western culture and Western practices to introduce Christianity to Africa, they probably did not consider other cultural alternatives. But that should not be an excuse for the African church to enter the new millennium still worshiping, singing, preaching, and counseling our parishioners like African-westerners who continue imitating missionaries; neither do we still have a good reason to keep blaming missionaries for mistakes they made during their era. Missionaries used their own cultures, the cultures they knew best, to propagate the faith. What is preventing the African church today from using its own cultures to communicate the same gospel even more effectively? Would Christianity have no concern in protecting our newborn babies from the evil forces of the day? Would Christianity sacrifice a person's life just because the only source of healing is at the hospital or a clinic that could be miles away? Is the African church making its people hypocrites? Don't Jesus' words "And if anyone causes one of these little ones who believe in me to sin, it would be better for him to be thrown into the sea with a large millstone tied around his neck" (Mark 9:42) also apply to us in this situation?

Christian cultural identity does not in any way erode the Christian faith; instead, it entrenches the faith in the social fabric of a people, with the gospel always remaining the judge of culture. I hope the reader begins to perceive the magnitude of this issue of Christian cultural identity, and begins to develop an honest and sincere desire to be involved in the discussion. It is my hope that some of the traditional practices and customs in African culture could be Christianized and adopted into the church without doing harm to the Christian faith.

In this light, this book approaches the subject of preaching from the African situation with the African preacher in mind. Its purpose is threefold: (1) that the church in Africa continue to affirm the preaching of the gospel of Jesus Christ, "the power of God for the salvation of everyone who believes" (Rom. 1:16); (2) that the church in Africa learn afresh to indigenize itself to the point that Christianity truly becomes the African religion; and, (3) that preaching in Africa increasingly utilize African historical, cultural, and religious concepts, as well as imagery and idiom, in order to communicate the gospel more effectively in the new millennium. Thus the book is written with the deliberate intention of convincing the African pastor that African cul-

ture that was once viewed by foreigners as heathenish and therefore spoken and written about disparagingly, is to us not only
God-given, but the only authentic human voice that the African
people and the African church have when we respond to God's
calling in worship. We must not be ashamed of it.

Chapter 1

African Cultural Background

One day, as associate pastor of a United Methodist church in Zimbabwe, I was called upon in the pastor's absence to lead a burial service for the first and only child of a young couple. Having finished leading the Christian burial service, according to The United Methodist Church burial ritual, I heard an elderly woman who sat next to the bereaved young mother giving instructions to the latter, saying, "Do it! Do it now!" Wondering what was going to happen, I decided resolutely that, because as the officiating pastor I had finished the Christian burial ritual, whatever traditional ritual the family wanted to add was entirely up to them.

Immediately, the lay leader of the congregation came to me and whispered rather loudly: "Pastor, these people are about to perform a traditional ritual—a heathen ritual. Please, stop them."

"Let's sit back and observe," I responded.

"The pastor does not allow people to add anything after he has conducted the Christian burial service. And this is not the first time that people have tried these things; and the pastor always stops them," the lay leader insisted.

"Today, I am the pastor; so leave everything to me," I resolutely assured the lay leader.

Undisturbed by the rather loud, whispered conversation, the bereaved young mother followed the instructions exactly as she had been told. Quietly and mournfully she got up and loosened her *mbereko* (a special tailored cloth in which women in Africa carry or cover a baby on their back) that had been tied around her waist. She struck the child's grave with her *mbereko* once, and then walked around the grave, making a complete circle around her child's grave, while at the same time pulling the *mbereko* behind her. It was fascinating to observe the performance of that ritual, although I did not think that many of the congregation (including me) understood the meaning of the ritual. The elderly woman then gave her last instructions to the bereaved young mother: "Go straight home," she said. "Don't look back until you get home," she emphasized.

According to a traditional custom among the Shona people in Zimbabwe, mourners are not encouraged to disperse to their homes from the cemetery after a burial service. It is customary that they first go back to the house of the deceased; and after washing their hands ceremonially, they can leave if they so wish or stay around for a while. As is the custom, I went to sit with the men under a big tree that was in the yard of the house. When I asked the men sitting next to me about the meaning of the ritual that had been performed, they did not seem to know, but offered some suggested interpretations.

I returned to college to attend to my other duties as a lecturer, but determined to find out the meaning of the ritual. When I returned to the family that evening to lead a prayer meeting, several members of the extended family and some of the church members were still there. I was particularly pleased to discover that the elderly woman who had been in charge of the traditional ritual at the graveside that morning was among them, and after the prayer meeting, I asked her to interpret what had occurred.

The ensuing conversation reminded me of the one between Jesus and Nicodemus. She began, "I understand that you teach at the theological college."

"Yes, I do," I answered.

"And you tell me that you do not know the meaning of the ritual that was performed this morning?" the woman asked. She appeared amazed. She thanked me for allowing the bereaved young mother to perform her ritual, and also testified to the fact that most pastors of mainline churches did not allow people to perform their African rituals at such occasions. She thanked me again for being open-minded about the whole thing. Then, with a deep sigh, the woman started explaining.

"In our African communities—in the villages where we come

16

from, not here in town—we believe that the death of the first child, especially when it is still the only child in a marriage, is critical. And that was the reason we came. We knew that young couples in towns do not often know the traditional customs pertaining to death, which if properly followed, would avoid problems in the future. These days, young couples often don't perform certain traditional rituals because they live in town, or because they think they are educated, or because they are Christian, or whatever excuse they come up with. Traditional customs are ignored as being insignificant or treated as mere superstition. Later in life, when all sorts of problems occur in their marriage or family life, such couples are not able to solve those problems, neither are they able to trace their source.

"In the case of the couple today, the death of the first child can cause the mother not to have other children. So, when the young mother struck the child's grave with her *mbereko*, she was giving her last instructions to her child, and the instructions were as follows:

My little child, *Nyadenga* (He who dwells in heaven) has not made it possible for me to see you grow up, and look after you. But where you are going, your uncles and aunts will look after you, just as I would have done here.

Therefore, as I go back home, I want you to understand that you now have a new home for yourself.

I have just marked your new home (grave) with your *mbereko*. Do not leave this place, as I will come and see you from time to time."

I asked the old woman why she had instructed the young bereaved mother to walk straight home without stopping on the way or looking back. She laughed for a while, and then went on to explain: "Again, I must say that death is cruel; it is the most vicious enemy of humankind. Death brings unbearable grief to families and it leaves irremovable scars to the human soul. But one has to learn to handle death and its resultant grief so that one minimizes the inflicted damage. Young couples and those staying in towns nowadays, and especially the young, bereaved mothers, are often left completely paralyzed by death. A young bereaved mother would spend most of her time mourning over

17

her deceased child, forgetting that it was time to have other kids. Certainly, one must mourn one's child but for how long is one to mourn? Therefore, the ritual of the bereaved mother walking without looking back was simply a way of dramatizing the message to her that she would have to quickly learn to forget mourning the deceased child, and begin thinking about having another child, or even many more, if that was the wish of *Nyadenga*."

That encounter with African traditional culture and wisdom overwhelmed me. For the first time in my study of African religion, I had a commitment to the hidden beauty, richness, and wisdom of African culture that for years had been condemned and, to this day, is still misunderstood, often in the name of Christ. I left the home of that bereaved couple that evening more educated about the situation of the people we serve and to whom we preach the gospel and also about how we, as African pastors, remain culturally alienated from the knowledge and worldview that they hold. Although that worldview may sound imperfect by our Western philosophical and theological orientation, the African people still want to affirm it, especially in times of crisis. Further, I was impressed by the wisdom of African traditional life in the manner it handles grief through such rituals.

What was important to me was less the traditional belief that the deceased baby has the power to stop its mother from having other children, but far more the issue of how Christian pastoral care handles a bereaved young mother and family who hold that kind of belief. Such traditional rituals, which are performed corporately, have a way of generating tremendous healing power for an individual or member of a family as well as unifying the family so that they bear together whatever burdens individual members may suffer (Gal. 6:2). Such corporate or communal practice of traditional rituals in Africa is likely to produce better results in terms of generating a capacity for healing and restoring the needed sense of unity to a family in grief than any Western or so-called modern forms of psychotherapy.

African practical theology could learn to adopt that kind of traditional ritual in order to express the caring love of God through Christ, instead of adopting Western methods of pastoral counseling, which in many cases may not communicate the healing power of the gospel for our people in time of need. In fact, that incident often takes me to that passage of scripture that talks about the burial of Jesus, when Joseph of Arimathea, accompanied by Nicodemus, approached Pilate for the body of Jesus for burial; and in reporting all that happened, John, the evangelist, took pains to explain that the burial "was in accordance with Jewish burial customs" (John 19:40). Often, when a people are deprived of their innocent and meaningful cultural practices that are in accordance with their traditional customs, they feel lost and devoid of help and comfort. What it means, actually, is that they have been deprived of their cultural identity.

Christianity in sub-Saharan Africa must learn from the mistakes of Christianity of Roman North Africa, which was established fairly early during the first century, and even demonstrated to be very strong to the extent of producing great church leaders that included Tertullian, Cyprian, Augustine—all leaders of reputation and international recognition in their influence on the life of the church and Christian thought. An observation has been rightly made that one of the reasons the church in North Africa became an easy prey of the Vandals in the sixth century was because the church in North Africa did not identify with the common people—the church was not indigenized; it was a Latin church, a point we will observe again later. Originally, Carthage had been a Phoenician city and a great rival of Rome. As Kenneth Latourette points out, Carthage, having been destroyed by the Romans, was rebuilt as a Roman city with immigrants, with a large Latin-speaking element emerging.[1] Therefore, the church in North Africa became and remained a Latin church that did not identify with the indigenous people, the Berbers. Those Berbers who became Christians spoke Latin and remained more connected with Rome than they did with the common people of North Africa. All efforts to indigenize the church in North Africa were heavily suppressed with Latin theological perceptions and rhetoric. In contrast, although it took time for the native Egyptians to accept Christianity, by the beginning of the fourth century

> parts of the Scriptures had been translated into more than one of the non-Greek vernaculars and the foundations had been laid of a native Egyptian (Coptic) church. This is the land, according to Matthew (2:13-18), Joseph and Mary were forced to take the baby Jesus into exile, fleeing away from Herod who sought to kill Jesus.

And the Coptic Church has continued its existence to this day, claiming and holding on to a tradition that it was the Apostle Peter and his interpreter, John Mark the Evangelist, who brought the church to Egypt in A.D. 42.[2]

According to Henry Chadwick, the "fourth-century historian, Eusebius of Caesarea reports that Mark was the first Bishop of Alexandria."[3] Coptic tradition also teaches that subsequently Mark suffered martyrdom in Egypt. A church that refuses to indigenize itself runs a risk of being rejected. When the church anywhere comes into existence, it is meant to be the church of God for the people—for the salvation of the people. The church must therefore accept the culture of the people, which at the same time the gospel judges. One culture should not judge another culture; rather, in the life and history of the church, the gospel judges culture because it needs that culture for the propagation of the faith. And culture always represents the human voice—the human response as a result of finding its fulfillment in Jesus Christ. That is where and when the new Christian cultural identity of Africa comes into existence.

Compared with mainline churches, the African independent churches seem to be doing very well in terms of moving toward a new African Christian cultural identity. For the purpose of planning for effective proclamation of the gospel on the continent of Africa in the twenty-first century, preachers may want to take a fresh look at what the national cultures of the continent are able to offer that might make African conceptualization of the faith and the propagation of the good news more relevant, enriching to the total life of the church, as well as yielding meaningful and more lasting results. The African church cannot afford to perpetuate the thinking of the past two millennia, which considered Africa void—a continent without history and civilization of its own, and a continent without culture or religion of its own. Nor can it enter the new millennium without an experience of a renaissance of our Christian and cultural identity as the African church.

With the collapse of Communism in Eastern Europe and apartheid or separate development in South Africa, African nations are in search of a new socioeconomic identity that will become the basis and springboard for both political and eco-

20

nomic development. This is also an opportune time for the church in Africa to ask itself if it has not been thriving through the use of religious cultures of other people; whether the church has fully identified with the masses of the people; or whether the church still worships as Western or missionary communities on African soil.

Any preacher who plans to proclaim Christ more effectively in the new century needs to attend to some topics about Africa, such as African history and its civilization, African culture and African religion, and socioeconomic development. These topics form the context within which the gospel will be preached in the new millennium, and that is the same fertile sociocultural environment that will make Christianity the fastest growing religion on the African continent.

African History

It is now common knowledge that "Africa was the birthplace of the human race."[4] This latest discovery in the disciplines of archaeology and anthropology about the origin of humankind on the continent and the ensuing Stone Age cultural-technological development, in which Africa was in the lead,[5] comes as a providential boost to the image and self-esteem of the African continent, and as an act of enlightenment to all who search and cherish knowledge. That discovery came as a result of the archaeological excavation carried out by Louis and Mary Leakey at Olduvai Gorge in northern Tanzania. Because of that discovery, historians Oliver and Fage write, "The earliest men were, once again, East African, the earliest dated examples occurring around 2.5 million years ago."[6] It was also from East Africa "that human populations spread northwards into the Sahara and North African latitudes and so across the Isthmus of Suez into Asia."[7]

Further, historians of Africa now tell us about the ancient Sudanic civilization, which stretched "right across sub-Saharan Africa from the Red Sea to the mouth of the Senegal, and right down the central highland spine of Bantu Africa from the Nile sources to Zimbabwe."[8] Within this geographical area, several kingdoms that existed before colonialism have been established as historical. The Arab traders, the European explorers, and even the earliest colonialists found those kingdoms in existence before

21

PREACHING AND CULTURAL IDENTITY

the fifteenth century; and they engaged in trading of gold and ivory before slave trading. Those Sudanic kingdoms, which were found in East, West, Central, and Southern Africa, had many similarities. For example, they all had kings whose title was changed to "chief" by the colonialists; and it was the king "to whom divine honors were paid and to whom divine powers were attributed."[9] The spreading of such kingdoms in the sub-Saharan region, including along the Nile River and down to Egypt, is a good indication of the widespread presence of the Bantu people and their civilization—the Sudanic civilization. Therefore, those who denied Africa her history and civilization had hidden agendas, which revealed themselves in the ensuing catastrophic events of slave trade and the partitioning of Africa.

The church in Africa must assist the African continent in restoring its self-esteem by taking a special interest, not only in African church history, but also in the precolonial history of the continent and its ancient civilization. One of the ways the church can effectively achieve that goal is through preaching that has interest in the dignity of its people—preaching that takes seriously both the history of the African people and African church history.

African Religion

When the colonialists and missionaries got to Africa in the fifteenth century, they believed that Africans were a people who lacked not only a history and civilization of their own, but also a culture or religion of their own. Missionaries who worked with the African people failed to get close enough to the African people to discover that traditional religious phenomenon. At least Africans knew something about the God that the missionaries sought to introduce to Africa. One is surprised that even those missionaries who came to Africa out of the Wesleyan tradition were blinded, though John Wesley's teaching on prevenient grace had been very clear. Indeed, Wesley taught that every individual had a measure of prevenient grace to the extent that no one could ever claim to have a purely natural conscience. That teaching in Methodism could have acted as a guiding post to a new inquiry about the religious beliefs of the African people. It is true that our forebears did not know Jesus Christ, but we cannot say that they were equally ignorant of God. It may be true that they might not have perceived of God as love, but there are many other characteristics that they attributed to God, including the same one God that the missionaries were talking about.

Maybe the time is already overdue for the African Christians—and I really mean African Christians—to be proud, and not ashamed of our culture, including the inherent religion, namely, the African religion. For too long, we have been made to think and believe that the African religion, and anything else related to it, was heathenish or the work of the devil. Consequently, we have vigorously campaigned against our own culture and religion through the preaching of the churches. Ultimately, as Christians, we find ourselves completely alienated, not only from our culture, but even more so from our own people as a whole. It would appear that African Christians, especially those of us in the mainline churches, have placed ourselves in a position where we are cut off from the many sources that would have enabled us to gain knowledge about our own culture. Or we have built walls in the name of Christianity that are against our own culture that deprive us access to the riches of our own heritage.

True, not all that we find in a culture is good; nor is everything that we find in a culture bad. For example, in the Shona culture, there are traditional and religious concepts that would enrich the preacher's theological reflection as well as one's vocabulary in the communication of the Christian faith in proclamation. Take, for example, the concept of *unhu* in the Shona culture. The concept begins with the word *munhu,* which means a person. Therefore, *unhu* is the totality of all that makes up a person qualitatively. When people say that your son or daughter has *unhu,* it means that your son or daughter has been well brought up, and has that special or expected quality of one's being that makes one a good son or daughter. And *unhu* is a quality of life that one acquires because one belongs to—one lives in, and comes from—a good family, and a good community or a good people. People perceive and understand *unhu* in relation to how an individual relates to other individuals and to the community as a whole. Therefore, *unhu* becomes "the organizing principle of the African mind, defining the pre-eminence of the interests of the community over the individual, the duties and the responsibilities the individual owes the community, the obligation of the individual to share what he has with the community."[10]

What a beautiful concept! It raises one's imagination beyond limits—the ideal type that one would want to see in one's son or one's daughter, and indeed, in many others in the community. The beauty about the concept of *unhu* is that it is not self-achievement; rather, it is provided by one's family and the community. It is the family and the community that have the potential to make people. In considering this concept of *unhu* as Christians, we would therefore say that it has now been fulfilled in Jesus Christ, in whom God revealed his righteousness (Rom. 1:17); and that genuine and perfect *unhu* is no longer just man-given, but now given through Christ in the community of faith in the fellowship of the Holy Spirit. Such traditional concepts like *unhu* would naturally quicken genuine African theological reflection and expression of the Christian faith in the African church. That is one way the African church could do theology uniquely; and that is one way it could make its own contribution to the rest of Christendom.

Even more important, in the Shona culture, as in the other African cultures, there has always been a strong belief in the one Supreme Being or God. There are many similarities in African religion to the Old Testament. For example, in addition to the belief in one Supreme Being, there are several names attributed to God, like *Musikavanhu* (Creator of the people), *Nyadenga* (He who dwells above), *Chidzachepo* (the Stump that has always been there), *Muwanikwapo* (He who was found already there), and many others. Also, as in the Old Testament, where God is referred to as "God of the patriarchs," in Africa God is referred to as "God of the ancestors." Students of African religion do confirm that throughout Africa—East Africa, West Africa, Central Africa, and Southern Africa—that is, among the Bantu people, those who fall under the same Sudanic civilization, all believed and still believe in the one Supreme Being. This is not a book on African religion, but suffice it to say that the belief in the one Supreme Being by the whole of sub-Saharan Africa (regardless of what would be considered as other minor differences in beliefs) is strong and fundamental enough for the Africans to claim that they have always had one religion, namely, African religion.

It has been interesting to observe how other people who have had an interest in writing about African religion have had difficulties in trying to figure out what to make of African beliefs. In the beginning, the assumption was that Africans did not have any religion at all. Later, as John Mbiti, a renowned scholar in African religion pointed out, in 1886 E. B. Taylor wrote an article in a book entitled *Primitive Culture,* in which he coined and used the term *animism,* referring to African religious beliefs and practices.[11] More recently, a number of scholars have referred to African religion as African traditional religions. At times, the argument given for "religions" is because Africa possesses so many ethnic cultures. Others have said that there are as many African religions as there are ethnic language groups in Africa. I find that argument illogical, and I also interpret that view as a continuous attempt by some people to judge and reject Africa more by what they do not know than what they know about Africa, as has been the case in the past.

Ironically, Christians who confess God through Christ do not all come out of the same culture. The battle to work toward a united Africa, and to perceive of Africa as a unit, is not just a political and economic issue; it is also a matter of pride and self-esteem by everyone who is proud to be African. Because the African church labors vigorously to make disciples from all the African nations, it is also the hope of the church that the African nations will join hands with nations from other continents, walking together, all with their heads high, into the new city of God as one humanity in Christ (Rev. 21:22-27).

Further, as much as I have had immense interest in African religion, which I often referred to as "African traditional religion," I have become convinced that any religion that exists in the context of a living culture is bound to be a living and dynamic religion. After an interesting and revealing discussion about African religion with Sundah Sanganza, I was convinced that the term "traditional" in African traditional religion ought to be dropped, for I realized how limiting and restrictive the term could be in one's perception of African religion. That is the reason in this book I prefer talking of African religion instead of African traditional religion. I am convinced African religion is dynamic, and many of our African people are strong adherents of the religion. I close this discussion with the words of a Shona

(African religion) prayer, as recorded and presented by Geoffrey Parrinder, a renowned scholar in African religion.

> Great Spirit, piling up the rocks like mountains, sewing the sky like cloth, calling forth the branching trees, You bring out the shoots so that they stand erect. You fill the earth with mankind, the dust rises on high. O Lord, wonderful one, You live in the midst of the sheltering rocks, You give rain to men. You are on high with the spirits of the great. You raise the grass-covered hills above the earth and you create the rivers. Gracious one.[12]

Socioeconomic Development

The dream of the founding fathers of the Organization for African Unity, which envisioned the whole continent rid of colonialism, was superbly accomplished when, at last, South Africa came under majority rule in 1994. The political struggle against foreign dominance took sub-Saharan Africa thirty-seven years from the time when Ghana took the lead in becoming independent in 1957. When one considers all the obstructions that Africa has had to overcome throughout the years—slave trade and slavery, which deprived the continent of millions of lives that perished during the slave capturing struggle, those who perished en route to the ocean, and those who died before reaching the Americas; the partitioning of the continent that left several ethnic groups divided by boundaries of colonial convenience, which continues to be a problem to this day in some of the countries; and the colonial occupation itself that deprived the citizens of the country of their good land, accompanied by the exploitation of the natural resources and their labor with the use of oppressive and harsh methods of control, which led to detention and imprisonment, and included executions— Africa has every reason to congratulate itself and to celebrate its independence.

As we congratulate ourselves, as the survivors of the captivity ordeal, jointly those on the continent and those in the diaspora, our thoughts and memories often take us back to the history of our struggle when many of our people lost their lives. The victims included a wide range of dedicated leaders, like politicians, pastors, teachers, doctors, nurses, businesspeople, and other innocent ordinary citizens. Knowing, as we do, that many of these people were outstanding community leaders, and some of them our outstanding Christian leaders at the same time, we can paraphrase what the early church said of its martyrs, "their blood became the seed of nationhood." That was a sacrifice of real life for our countries to become independent, and with the hope that the dream for our freedoms would be fulfilled. "Africa consists of fifty-two countries that are often grouped into four regions: the Maghreb in North Africa, which comprises the six Arab states . . . Francophone Africa, made up of the former French colonies; Anglophone Africa, comprising the former British colonies; Lusophone Africa which consists of the former Portuguese colonies."[13] One hopes and prays that in this new millennium, Africa will be known increasingly by a new image of its own creation and projection than by what others have done to it. Again, it is our prayer that the regional communities of West Africa, East Africa, and Southern Africa will provide a new character and determination for our continent pertaining to its economic development and freedom, for that is what the masses have been awaiting for a long time.

The total population of Africa today is estimated at about 750 million. An interesting statistic about the population of Africa is that, while in 1987 it was estimated at 559 million, 50 percent of the people were less than fifteen years old. That is a very good indication that the African population for a while will consist of young people, and will continue its fast growth. However, the question that seems to be in the minds of people today is, Whitherto, Africa? In the past millennium African countries, both during and after colonial struggle, may have legitimately embraced and used the socialist ideology, both to be rid of and to scare away colonial capitalism. At the same time, it became clearly evident to most of our people, including the leaders themselves, that foreign socialism as a guiding ideology for the development of Africa was not a better substitute, especially when it came to the economic development of Africa.

Therefore, people still raise the question, Which way is Africa going to take? People are ready to move, and that move is toward progress. The people are tired of African countries that fight internally and against one another over issues that could be settled through diplomatic channels. They are tired of empty promises, political slogans, and becoming exiles and refugees when their own countries already have the political power and freedom to avoid suffering for thousands of people. Who is in charge now? Is the Organization for African Unity strong enough to give direction and chart the way for member nations to take for the development of their own people? Or is that the responsibility left to the regional organizations or institutions, such as the Central African Economic and Customs Union (UDEAC), founded in 1966; East African Community (EAC), formed in 1963; the Economic Community of West Africa (CEAO), founded in 1972; and Southern Africa Development Co-ordination Conference (SADCC), founded in the early 1980s. These are all questions that are in the minds of those who want to see independent Africa take its rightful place among other successful continents of the global community today.

At the beginning of a new millennium, one wants to think that our African political leadership by now would have envisaged the need, and developed the political will, for greater unity. The new millennium will require that African nations, like nations of the other continents, concentrate on developing their own national economies. Africa is not poor. Africa is rich in natural resources that are at the same time widely diversified. Historically, we read about Arabs and several European explorers who traded with African countries, especially those that were near the ocean, in ivory, gold, and many other natural resources. It is so exciting to learn from some of our scholars who are in the relevant areas of potential development in Africa that Africa has 40 percent of the world's potential hydroelectric power supply; the bulk of the world's diamonds and chromium; 30 percent of the uranium in the noncommunist world; 50 percent of the world's gold; 90 percent of its phosphates; 40 percent of its platinum; 7.5 percent of its coal; 8 percent of its known petroleum reserves; 12 percent of its natural gas; 3 percent of its iron ore; millions upon millions of acres of untilled agricultural land; 64 percent of the world's manganese; 13 percent of its copper; and vast bauxite, nickel, and lead resources.[14] What a blessed continent! These are God-given natural resources that Africa was endowed with millions and millions of years ago. What is needed is to convince our African leaders that there is no reason for Africa to remain hungry, let alone to suffer from poverty in this day and time. In Shona we have a saying that captures this untapped affluence well: *Kufangenyota makumbo arimumvura,* which means, to be thirsty when one's feet are in the flowing waters of a river.

Again, I want to emphasize the importance of the opportunity to preach the gospel of Jesus Christ, especially to our younger generations as they enter the dawning century. Africa is once more at a crossroads, searching for a new face or new identity. It is always good news when one reads about some of the African countries making changes, especially constitutional changes in order to accommodate democratic and progressive principles. It is always encouraging when young people who have received training from developed countries return to their countries, determined to take the role of leadership for the economic development of their own nations. And those are some of the countries where leaders are becoming open-minded in relation to democratization, liberalization, and pluralization. Indeed, those are some of the African countries that are beginning to experience growing economies. All this is refreshing and encouraging. And we want to urge our leaders to persist on these new trends, and to assure them of our support. The people of Africa deserve to see and witness a new day of the continent's rebirth of its political and economic development. They have been waiting for such a day for too long. But such crucial decisions will have to be made in the context of faithfulness to the people of Africa.

Although the church cannot enter the political arena to make political decisions, the church in Africa, through effective preaching of the gospel, can assist toward creating a new socio-economic conscience in the minds of our young leaders aspiring for high offices in both public and private enterprises—a new conscience that accepts a sense of stewardship, responsibility, and accountability of the God-given resources, both natural and human.

Rapid Growth Rate of the African Church

One of the most noticeable and interesting social phenomena in sub-Saharan Africa today is the rate at which Christianity is growing. Some church leaders have quoted growth rates that range between 10 and 30 percent. For example, we are informed that "about 87 percent of the Anglicans worldwide reside in eight countries. . . . The greatest growth has been concentrated in Africa and in a few spots in Asia. In Nigeria, for instance, the number of Anglican dioceses has increased 35 percent from 26 a decade ago to 61 this year [1998]."[15] Also, according to the report of the Africa–Church Growth and Development of the General Board of Global Ministries of The United Methodist Church, during a period of eleven years, the African Central Conference of The United Methodist Church reported a total membership of 435,000 in 1982 and 1,240,500 in 1993.[16] The Central Conference is constituted of thirteen annual conferences in the following countries: Angola, Burundi, Liberia, Mozambique, Nigeria, Sierra Leone, Zaire, and Zimbabwe. Even in the absence of actual statistical evidence for the other African churches, one is tempted to generalize that this common phenomenal growth of the church in Africa would be true with most of the mainline and independent churches. Thus, Thomas Best of the World Council of Churches in Geneva shared the same observation in his paper, "Turn to God, Rejoice in Hope," when he said that in the Southern Hemisphere churches were growing, and were acting increasingly as if their historic divisions had been healed. According to David Barrett, in the year 2000, the population of Africa is estimated to reach 813,390,700 people; and the population of Christians is estimated to reach 393,326,210 (48.4 percent).[17] No wonder, reporting on the Eighth Assembly of the World Council of Churches, Patricia Lefevere wrote, "Africa may well be Christianity's biggest 'house' in the next millennium."[18]

It is always gratifying to observe the kind of people who are joining the church in Africa today, especially in the urban centers. They include young executives, medical doctors, professors and lecturers, lawyers, engineers, teachers, nurses, and many others who are in the majority—those who would be identified simply as faithful disciples rather than by any profession. Some of these people would represent a new middle class that is emerging in most of the urban centers throughout Africa. These people seek new meaning to life in relation to total human existence, experience, and development. The church in Africa today consists of a new generation of Christians who are enlightened in terms of formal education; and yet they still seek even greater enlightenment on a number of issues concerning life in its fullness, through the preaching of the gospel and the teaching of the church. Such a generation of Christians is part of the young breed of Africans searching for a new image or new cultural face, but in relation to the Christian faith. They want to know how Christianity relates to Africa on matters of culture, African religion, political and economic development, modern technology, business ethics, and many other issues. It is a generation that is exuberant with hope and pride in the potential that African nations are likely to bring for their generation. What a claim it is when some of them say that, if ever there was a historical Garden of Eden at all, then that garden must have been in East Africa, which would make Adam and Eve East Africans.[19] While such discoveries are made about Africa, and while many young men and women have dreams and visions about life, an opportunity is being presented for the preaching of the gospel that will provide responsible, Christian leadership and guidance needed at such a crossroads of faith and cultural identity.

It is, therefore, important that the church in Africa remain true in holding to its faith in Jesus Christ, and to preach "Christ the power of God and the wisdom of God" (1 Cor. 1:24) "in season and out of season" (2 Tim. 4:2). One would even dare pray, God forbid, that Christianity will not be wiped from the face of Africa or any part of Africa again, simply because the church is unwilling to indigenize itself for the sake of reaching out to and identifying with the common people—the "sinned against," for whom Christ also died. The church will have to cease being perceived as a Western religion, or a white man's religion in Africa. It must become truly an African religion. That ought to be the thrust of the ministry of the African church, and the impact of its message as Christ is preached in this new millennium.

——————————— *Chapter 2* ———————————

Preaching
in the Early Church

The history of Christian preaching is as old as the history of the Christian church itself. One is reminded that Jesus Christ, the capstone of the church that had been rejected by the Jews (Mark 12:10; Acts 4:11) had himself come preaching "the good news of the kingdom" (Matt. 4:23; Luke 4:43). It was through the preaching of Peter on the day of Pentecost (Acts 2:14-41), in the name of Jesus Christ, and through the power of the Holy Spirit, that God caused his church to be born into the world. We are reminded a few years later, when Paul wrote to the church in Corinth, that "since, in the wisdom of God, the world did not know God through wisdom, God decided, through the foolishness of our *proclamation* [my emphasis], to save those who believe" (1 Cor. 1:21 NRSV).

This chapter will discuss preaching in the early church, from the time of Jesus' earthly ministry A.D. 30, up to the time that Augustine died, A.D. 430, by reviewing the following: (1) historical roots of preaching; (2) preaching of Jesus of Nazareth; (3) apostolic preaching; (4) preaching of the apostolic fathers; and (5) schools of biblical interpretation.

Historical Roots of Preaching

Vernon Stanfield wrote, "The science of homiletics had certain historical antecedents, i.e., Hebrew preaching and ancient rhetoric."[1] If we are going to understand and appreciate the role and function that preaching has played in both the history of the church and the life of Christendom, homiletics needs to go back to those two roots of preaching.[2]

Hebrew Preaching

First, as one reads the Old Testament with its many discourses or materials presented as preaching or speeches, it begins to make sense that the Old Testament faith was one that was preached. Repeatedly, one comes across speeches made or supposedly made by Moses, Joshua, judges, prophets, and others. Gerhard von Rad, a renowned Old Testament scholar, points out that Levite preaching activities actually preceded cultic changes that took place under the reign of Josiah 640–609 B.C.[3] He goes on to say:

> Deuteronomy is in fact a hybrid: it contains, on the one hand, a great deal of legal material, both sacral and secular; while, on the other hand, the way in which it presents these old traditions is altogether paranetic, that is, it presents them in sermon form.[4]

We should note that these early preachers in the history of Israel did not have authoritative religious scriptures for exposition. Therefore, they were more exhorters than exegetical preachers who proclaimed the will of Yahweh to the extent they could understand the traditions of Israel.[5]

Second, prophecy developed into a very important institution in Israel. The list of great prophets of Israel includes personalities like Moses (the Exodus 1290 B.C.), a prophet "whom the LORD knew face to face" (Deut. 34:10); ninth-century B.C. prophets like Elijah and Elisha; and several eighth-, seventh-, and sixth-century prophets. Long before the canonization of the Old Testament, those Hebrew preachers had developed a formula to announce the proclamation of Yahweh's message, which was, "Thus saith the LORD" (Amos 7:17). They were great preachers who discerned the revelation of Yahweh through Israel's traditions, world or international political events, observation of nature and creation, worship and meditation, and other ways that Yahweh chose to reveal himself to them. Although they did not have scriptures, those prophets knew the historical acts of salvation that Yahweh had done in the history of Israel: the calling of the patriarchs (Isa. 51:1-2); the Mount Sinai covenant (Jer. 31:31-32); deliverance from slavery in Egypt (Amos 3:1).

Third, another essential event that enhanced Hebrew preaching was the canonization of the Hebrew Scriptures, with the Pentateuch accepted as being religiously authoritative for Israel around 400 B.C.; the Former and Later Prophets, in about the year 200 B.C.; and the Writings and the official closure of the Jewish Bible in a small Palestinian town of Jamnia when a rabbinic assembly was held in A.D. 90.

Fourth, as more Jews scattered in the Diaspora, especially around the Mediterranean countries, there emerged the new institution of the synagogue in the life and history of the Jews. No one seems to know exactly the period in which synagogues came into existence. For a long time, it was believed that synagogue was instituted during the Babylonian exile; now it is also recognized that the later period of the Persians provided the necessary conditions for the institution to flourish. Here, we are reminded that Ezra and his successors, the scribes, were actually products of the Persian era.[6] In Jewish worship, "While sacrifice could be offered only in the Temple, the reading and interpretation of the O.T. and prayer could be carried on in the synagogues even in Jerusalem itself."[7] Therefore, with so many Jews in the Diaspora, the institution of the synagogue flourished in all centers where Jewish population was found. These synagogues served primarily as places for the "reading of the Law"—centers to teach and interpret the Jewish faith for those who were Jews. One can begin to understand the reason why it is believed that Christian preaching has its roots in Hebrew preaching. This point will be even clearer when we discuss Christian preaching itself.

Ancient Rhetoric

Christian preaching also had its roots in ancient rhetoric. The fact that the task of preaching is communication means that understanding and acquiring related verbal and literary skills takes on an added importance.

First, as Stanfield points out to us again, the development of the theory of rhetoric in the Greco-Roman world started with Corax and his pupils, who first recorded what became known as the principles of rhetoric in 465 B.C.[8] But the study of such rhetorical principles found their greatest effectiveness in Greco-Roman culture, culminating in the writings of Aristotle, 384–322 B.C.; the Latin rhetoric of Cicero, 106–43 B.C.; and Quintilian, A.D. 35–95.

Second, every culture has produced some people who have not only the talent but also the learned skills for public speaking. Before colonial domination, African cultures thrived on organized informal education in the arts, including singing, dancing, and beating the drum, and the presentation of cases at village council meetings, family gatherings, and many other similar occasions. Although the African societies did not formalize this in writing, they have always known who to turn to to present important issues to the public. This is especially the case when the presentation is to be made to the chief. There have always been some people in African traditional life who knew that they had the talent for public speaking. Some of these persons have done all they could to develop the talent by insisting on the habit of speaking clean vernacular languages—using acceptable vocabulary, practicing the use of traditional ways of presenting cases or issues in family gatherings or when speaking to elders in the community. Effective use of vernacular idioms—not mixing one's vernacular language with European or other vernacular language in a speech—seems to be difficult for many these days, including preachers in the pulpit. The root of preaching that Stanfield traced back to ancient rhetoric could equally be traced back in the African cultures for African rhetorical and preaching purposes.

Both Hebrew preaching and ancient rhetoric of the Greco-Roman world and culture shaped the understanding and practice of preaching in the early church. We shall see how some of the preachers used both traditions or leaned more on one than the other. However, there is no way a preacher can ignore either one altogether. Just as most of the preachers in both the eastern and western parts of the Roman Empire benefited from both Hebrew preaching and ancient rhetorical principles in their preaching during the initial years of Christianity, a number of our own early African preachers were skillful enough to adapt Christian preaching to the African situation. This was true even of African preaching in eras when Western missionary presence was strong. It is unfortunate that oral tradition is all that has survived of their preaching.

Preaching of Jesus of Nazareth

The author of the Letter to the Hebrews provides an appropriate introduction for this section when he writes, "Let us fix our eyes on Jesus, the author and perfecter of our faith, who for the joy set before him endured the cross, scorning its shame, and sat down at the right hand of the throne of God" (Heb. 12:2). Preaching is a gift from God, and it is, at the same time, a task that needs to be carried out diligently, faithfully, and obediently. Every preacher who aspires to be the servant of the Word would do well to observe Christ, the preacher who became the proclaimed, as is reported in the memoirs of the apostles and the early church who shared their witness of him as reflected in all the pages of the New Testament.

First, Jesus is introduced by the evangelists as a preacher (Mark 1:14; Luke 4:21), who announced his message as follows: "The time has come. . . . The kingdom of God is near. Repent and believe the good news!" (Mark 1:15; see also Matt. 4:17). "I must preach the good news of the kingdom of God to the other towns also, because that is why I was sent" (Luke 4:43). To believe in the good news as Jesus requires of his listeners, "is loyalty to him as to the representative of the kingdom, as the King and the Messiah."[9] Jesus demanded loyalty because he was the embodiment of all that God was, is, and will be (Heb. 13:8). The God about whom he taught his disciples was his Father. Therefore, loyalty to Jesus meant loyalty to God the Father also. And that loyalty was not to be achieved merely through human wisdom or effort (John 13:36-38), but only with the coming of the Holy Spirit who takes charge in Christian teaching (John 14:25) and empowers Jesus' disciples (Acts 1:8) to enable them to live the life of the kingdom of God. For anyone to begin living the life of the kingdom to which Jesus of Nazareth invited his hearers meant a life of experiencing God's love, mercy, forgiveness, peace, and righteousness, all through God's grace, of course, No wonder Paul wrote to the saints in Ephesus about the immeasurable nature of the grace of God as "the unsearchable riches of Christ" (Eph. 3:8).

Second, Jesus preached the good news of the kingdom of God in such a manner that his hearers understood him clearly and gladly. Matthew understood Jesus of Nazareth as one who came not to destroy, but to fulfill the law and prophecy (5:17). Jesus

37

was not enslaved by the rabbinical ways of presenting truth to the Jews; rather, he was always fresh in his presentation. He used parables, stories, and other narrative forms that made people listen to what he had to say. No wonder the evangelists wrote, "he taught them as one who had authority, not as the teachers of the law" (Mark 1:22; see also Luke 4:32).

Third, Jesus was not limited by rabbinical rules regarding where he could preach the good news of the kingdom of God. He preached wherever he found the people or whenever he had the opportunity to do so. However, the evangelists recorded that Jesus often preached at the following places: in synagogues (Luke 4:16; Matt. 12:9); in the houses of the people he visited (Mark 3:20; John 11:20); by the lakeside (Mark 4:1; Luke 5:1); by the roadside (Mark 10:1; John 4:30); in the temple courts (Mark 11:27–12:44); and on a mountainside (Matt. 5:1). Of course we have learned that different evangelists had specific reasons to situate Jesus in particular places when he preached. At the same time, the evangelists are telling their readers that Jesus was free to proclaim the gospel of the kingdom of God wherever he found people and the opportunity.

Apostolic Preaching

It is generally accepted that the apostolic age stretches from the time that Jesus entrusted the preaching of the gospel and the establishment of the church to his disciples, to the time when the last of the twelve disciples died.[10] The date for the outpouring of the Holy Spirit at Pentecost is placed on May 28, A.D. 30.[11] Although we are not certain about the dates of the death of all the twelve, James, the brother of John, is reported to have been the first to be martyred by orders of King Herod (Acts 12:2) in A.D. 44.[12] John, the brother of James, is believed to have been the last of the twelve to die; he might have actually died a natural death at Ephesus. The date of his death is placed at A.D. 98.[13] Therefore, we shall treat the apostolic era as stretching from A.D. 30 to 100. The significance of that era is that the apostles were in control; and their witness to Jesus Christ is an outstanding record of the expansion and development of the church in any generation, as reported by Luke in the Acts of the Apostles and some of the New Testament writings, especially the Pauline Letters.

The Apostolic Preaching Message

The focus of the apostolic preaching was Jesus of Nazareth, whom God had made both Lord and the Messiah. If we look at some of the preaching materials presented by Luke in the book of Acts and some of the writings by Paul as representative proclamation of the apostolic era, we will be able to come close to understanding apostolic preaching as it was then understood. The following would seem to have been the emphasis that the apostolic era gave to preaching Jesus Christ.

First, Jesus of Nazareth (Acts 2:22) whom the Jews had crucified (Acts 2:23) was the same Jesus that God had made "both Lord and Christ" (Acts 2:36). It appears the preachers of the apostolic era labored to make their hearers understand that they were not talking about another Jesus. For example, Peter took pains to explain this by pointing out that this Jesus of Nazareth had a clear proof that he had been sent by God through the evidence of his ministry "to you by miracles, wonders and signs, which God did among you through him, as you yourselves know" (Acts 2:22).

Second, the blame of the crucifixion of Jesus was laid upon the Jews: "Men of Israel . . . with the help of wicked men, put him to death by nailing him to the cross" (Acts 2:22-23; see also 2:36; 7:52; 10:39).

Third, Jesus of Nazareth died on the cross and was buried (1 Cor. 15:4), and "God raised him from the dead" (Acts 2:24, 10:40; see also 1 Cor. 6:14, 15:15). The resurrection of Jesus Christ from the dead was the pivotal saving act of God (in Christ) in the history of humankind; for without it, "our preaching is useless and so is your faith," wrote Paul (1 Cor. 15:14). But because "Christ has indeed been raised from the dead" (1 Cor. 15:20), God had also vindicated Jesus of Nazareth of all his claims, especially the claim that God was his Father (John 8:16-20). Because of that vindication, Jesus had been "exalted to the right hand of God" (Acts 2:33; see also Phil. 2:9); and God had made the same Jesus "both Lord and Christ" (Acts 2:36). No wonder Paul asked, "Who are you, Lord?" (Acts 9:5).

Fourth, the apostolic preaching was based upon the Hebrew Scriptures. With the resurrection of Jesus Christ from the dead, the Christian community understood and interpreted the Hebrew

Scriptures differently from the past. In fact, the early Christians came to understand the Hebrew Scriptures as bearing witness to Jesus of Nazareth as the Messiah of the prophecies. Thus, according to Luke, the Pentecost outpouring experience of the Holy Spirit was to be understood in the light of the prophecy of Joel 2:28-32; and so are all the Old Testament scriptures that are quoted. No wonder the tradition that Paul shares with the church in Corinth repeats the phrase, "according to the Scriptures" (1 Cor. 15:3-10), and again, Paul refers to the Hebrew Scriptures as "the very words of God" (Rom. 3:2).

Fifth, the apostolic preaching emphasized that Jesus was to come back again, soon. "This same Jesus, who has been taken away from you into heaven, will come back in the same way you have seen him go into heaven," said the two men who were dressed in white (Acts 1:10-11). Paul, in his letter to the Thessalonians, consoled Christians by saying, "We believe Jesus died and rose again and so we believe that God will bring with Jesus those who have fallen asleep in him" (1 Thess. 4:14). The early Christian communities were modeled on the basis of that expectation (Acts 2:42-47; 4:32-37).

Sixth, the apostolic preaching was effective because those preachers had been filled with the Holy Spirit. It all started on the day of Pentecost, when, as Luke recorded, "All of them were filled with the Holy Spirit" (Acts 2:4). And in commissioning Paul to preach the good news to the Gentiles, we hear Ananias, as he placed his hands on Saul, saying, "Brother, Saul, the Lord—Jesus, who appeared to you on the road as you were coming here—has sent me so that you may see again and be filled with the Holy Spirit" (Acts 9:17). Possession not so much of as by the Holy Spirit was a prominent characteristic of preachers of the apostolic age.

To the Ends of the Earth

Another factor we need to take note of concerning apostolic preaching was the rapid geographical expansion of Christianity in the Roman Empire in the years between A.D. 30 and 100. Although the Festival of Pentecost was capable of drawing many Jews from several nations to Jerusalem,[14] one could still say that it must have been, at the same time, providential that many

Jews in the Diaspora from as many countries as are mentioned in Acts 2:9-11 were there. They all witnessed the event of the outpouring of the Holy Spirit, and the birth of the church of Christ on earth, in Jerusalem, at the day of Pentecost, May 28, A.D. 30. Bruce Metzger goes on to say that the list of the countries of the origin of those Jews "corresponds exactly with what was considered by ancient geographers to be the sum total of all known nations."[15]

First, it was God's plan to have the gospel preached to all the nations of the earth. Indeed, the rabbinical tradition that held that "the Mosaic law had been proclaimed on Sinai in the seventy languages of mankind, although only Israel hearkened and obeyed,"[16] could have been in Luke's mind as he wrote the book of Acts. Luke shares with his readers what seems to have been the strategy of apostolic-age preachers in presenting the good news to the rest of their known world. This strategy came from the mouth of Jesus himself when he promised his disciples, "you will receive power when the Holy Spirit comes on you; and you will be my witnesses in Jerusalem, and in all Judea and Samaria, and to the ends of the earth" (Acts 1:8). In terms of apostolic preaching, to become witnesses of Jesus Christ "to the ends of the earth" meant preaching Christ in Ephesus, Antioch, Alexandria, Rome, and in the rest of all the known urban centers of civilization of their time.

Both the scriptures and tradition tell us that all the apostles left Jerusalem. Paul's missionary journeys from A.D. 49–58 were undertaken with that conviction of the appointment that he had received the gospel that he preached "by revelation from Jesus Christ" (Gal. 1:12); and equally, like the twelve apostles, received empowerment by the Holy Spirit (Acts 9:17); and was a special chosen instrument of Jesus Christ to carry his name "before the Gentiles and their kings" (Acts 9:15). No wonder tradition tells us of Peter in Rome, John in Ephesus, Thomas in India, Mark in Alexandria; and Luke informs us of Paul and Barnabas in Antioch, and Paul alone in Rome, in chains and under guard (Acts 28:11-20). By the end of the first century, if not long before that, the preaching of the gospel of Christ had reached to the ends of the known world. The church had been planted in almost every urban center. What a strategy of the twelve, and by the twelve—with other leaders of course, like the apostle Paul—

to conquer their known world with the good news of Jesus Christ within the period of a century!

Second, even at this initial stage of the church's development, African representation features strongly. For example, Egypt, with its city of Alexandria that commanded a second position in importance in the Roman Empire, a city that was highly populated by Jews and from which came the Septuagint, the "Bible" of the early church in the Hellenistic world, together with Libya is listed along with the countries of the known world (Acts 2:8-11). Luke informs us about Apollos, a learned man and a native of Alexandria, who preached in Ephesus (Acts 18:24). Further, during those early days of the expansion of the early church, a prominent government official, the eunuch treasurer of Queen Candace of Ethiopia, was baptized by Philip (Acts 8:26-40). Though "Ethiopia" tended to refer to lands south of Egypt, with its people referred to by the Greeks as those with "burned faces,"[17] the man who was baptized by Philip was likely to have come from the kingdom of Makuria or Makura,[18] on the upper Nile River.

Third, it is important that we take note of some of the events that were taking place in the life of the Roman Empire, events that had great impact on the life of the church and its ministry of preaching the Word by this time. For example, we have already noted that, even as early as the year A.D. 44, Herod was persecuting the church. That was followed by a great fire in Rome, which was blamed on the Christians. Hence, the Neronian persecution in A.D. 64, which took the lives of the two great church leaders Peter and Paul in about A.D. 68, and of course many other Christians; the first Jewish War, A.D. 66–74;[19] and the persecution by Domitian in A.D. 95. The hostile atmosphere of war and persecution of people, either as citizens, ethnic groups, or because of their faith, is an experience the church in Africa has gone through many times. African pastors or priests know what it means to preach the Word of God faithfully under such hostile circumstances. We should not, therefore, have difficulties appreciating and following the language used by a book like Revelation, which was written during the period of the persecution of Christians by Domitian.

Therefore, we can confidently say that the strategy to proclaim the gospel of Jesus Christ on the continent of Africa was in the master plan of Jesus' mission to reach every continent (Acts 1:8) and also, as it became revealed at the Festival of Pentecost in A.D. 30, when two African nations were represented; and that the gospel of Christ was preached on the continent of Africa at a fairly early period during the establishment of the church.

Preaching of the Apostolic Fathers

This period stretches from A.D. 30 to 430, a period that yielded some organizational structures important to preaching.

First, a number of developments concerning organizational structures in the life of the church had already begun by the middle of the first century. For example, the apostles created the position of deacons in the life of the Christian community (Acts 6:1-7; 1 Tim. 3:8). Later, Luke reported, "In the church at Antioch there were prophets and teachers" (Acts 13:1). Paul listed the different positions that could be found in churches by the middle of the first century when he wrote, "And in the church God has appointed first of all apostles, second prophets, third teachers, then workers of miracles, also those having gifts of healing, those able to help others, those with gifts of administration, and those speaking in different kinds of tongues" (1 Cor. 12:28; see also Eph. 4:11). The different functions of prophets and teachers were that "the prophets were wandering preachers who had given their whole lives to listening for the word of God and then taking that word to their fellow men. The teachers were the men in the local churches whose duty it was to instruct converts in the faith."[20]

Later, Paul wrote about the development of the position of presbyters or elders, or overseers (NIV) or bishops (RSV) (Phil. 1:1; 1 Tim. 3:1; 5:17)—terms that were used, or translated, interchangeably in the early church. The idea and practice of eldership came from Jewish tradition (Exod. 4:29; Num. 11:16), and was very much part of the synagogue structure. The elders "presided over the worship of the synagogue; administered, rebuked and disciplined where these were necessary; they settled the disputes which other nations would have taken to the law-courts."[21] Thus, as the church expanded and developed, elders were appointed and instructed in the doctrines of the Christian faith (1 Tim. 3:1-7; 5:17-20; Titus 1:5).

By the second and third centuries the position of bishops had been instituted. Those who held this office are recorded in the writings of this period not merely because of their positions, but because of their dedication to Christ and his church. Their commitment to Christ compelled them to live a life of dedication to their faith and ministry to the people, causing most of them to die as martyrs or witnesses of Christ. The list of bishops includes Clement of Rome, 93–97; Ignatius of Antioch, 100–117; Polycarp of Smyrna, 110–155; Papias of Hierapolis, 130; Justin of Ephesus, who died in 165; Melito of Sardis, 169–180; Irenaeus of Lyons, 177–200; Cyprian of Carthage, 248–258; and many others. It is interesting to observe that it was the group that was appointed as elders of the church who eventually claimed apostolic succession in the leadership of the church. This is what Papias had to say:

> I shall not hesitate to set down for you, along with my interpretations, all things which I learnt from the elders with care and recorded with care, being well assured of their truth. For, unlike most men, I took pleasure not in those that had much to say but in those that teach the truth; not in those who record strange precepts, but in those who relate such precepts as were given to the Faith from the Lord and are derived from the Truth itself. Besides, if ever any man came who had been a follower of the elders, I would inquire about the sayings of the elders; what Andrew said, or Peter, or Philip, or Thomas, or James, or John or Matthew, or any other of the Lord's disciples; and what Aristion says, and John the Elder, who are disciples of the Lord. For I did not consider that I got so much profit from the contents of books as from the utterances of a living and abiding voice.[22]

As the church was already in crisis with gnostic teachings during the second century, we begin to see the need by the orthodox church to strengthen its connection with Jesus Christ, who first sent the apostles to preach. Thus, according to Tertullian, A.D. 160–240:

> All doctrine which accords with those apostolic churches, the sources and originals of the Faith, must be reckoned as the truth, since it preserves without doubt what the churches received from the Apostles, the Apostles from Christ, and Christ from God. . . .

44

We are in communion with the apostolic church. . . . This is how the apostolic churches report their origins; thus the church of Smyrnaeans relates that Polycarp was appointed by John, the church of Rome that Clement was ordained by Peter.[23]

Irenaeus wrote exhaustively about the succession of the Roman bishopric, stating that "the church known to all men, which was founded and set up at Rome by two most glorious Apostles, Peter and Paul,"[24] already had a tradition of bishopric succession as follows: after the two blessed apostles, Linus, who is mentioned in Paul's letter to Timothy (2 Tim. 4:21), Anacletus, Clement, Euarestus, Alexander, Sixtus, Telesphorus, who is said to have had "a glorious martyrdom," Hyginus, Pius, Anicetus, and Soter; "and now in the twelfth place from the Apostles, Eleutherus occupies the see."[25]

Among the interesting observations about preaching in the life of the apostolic church I would like to highlight three. First, the most crucial theological issue was to relate what was being preached to men during the apostolic fathers' period to "the apostolic tradition and the faith."[26] In writing about Clement of Rome, Irenaeus made this point: "He not only saw the blessed Apostles but also conferred with them, and had their preaching ringing in his ears and their tradition before his eyes."[27] Papias likewise emphasized that what really mattered and what was to be preached was, first, what the apostles had heard from the Lord and next, what the church had learned from the apostles. It meant that the theology for preaching was carefully examined, and if one was not within the apostolic tradition and the faith, one was not part of the apostolic church.

Second, that martyrdom was considered an effective way of proclaiming and witnessing for Jesus Christ to those who were privileged to suffer it; and even to those who were present as observers of such a glorious event. We are informed that at the festival of Caesar a number of Christians were set to fight or sacrificed to wild beasts.[28] One impressive event of martyrdom and witness was that of Polycarp, a dedicated, respected bishop of Smyrna. Having entered the stadium where he was to be sacrificed to the wild beasts, a voice came to him, "Be strong, Polycarp, and play the man." Though the proconsul repeated an offer to release him if only he would "curse the Christ,"

Polycarp's response was classic: "Eighty and six years have I served him, and he hath done me no wrong; how then can I blaspheme my king who saves me?" Further persuasion by the proconsul led Polycarp to say, "If thou doest vainly imagine that I would swear by the genius of Caesar, as thou sayest, pretending to know what I am, hear plainly that I am a Christian. And if thou art willing to learn the doctrine of Christianity, grant me a day and hearken to me."[29]

Third, the first century saw the development of Christian worship and the place of preaching in the life of the church. Eusebius seemed to have quoted Hegesippus, A.D. 175, bishop of Corinth, who made the statement, "In every succession and in every City things are ordered according to the preaching of the Law, the prophets and the Lord."[30] Therefore, preaching had maintained a central place in the life of the church by the second century and was highly regarded as an effective instrument of the church with which to propagate the apostolic tradition and the faith, guiding the church as the apostolic fathers fought against heresies. Justin Martyr, a native of Samara who rose to the bishopric of Ephesus, gave an explanation of the Christian faith and the practice of worship, written in his first Apology. It is likely he wrote it in Rome, where he suffered martyrdom about A.D. 153:

> And on the day which is called the Sun's Day, there is an assembly of all who live in the towns or country; and the memoirs of the Apostles or the writings of the prophets are read, as much as time permits. When the reader has finished, the president gives a discourse, admonishing us and exhorting us to imitate these excellent examples. Then we all rise together and offer prayers: and, as I said above, on the concluding of our prayer, bread is brought, and wine and water, and the president similarly offers up prayers, and thanksgiving to the best of his power, and the people assent with Amen.[31]

Hans Leitzmann has suggested a more elaborate order of worship that I believe would help us understand and appreciate the importance that the early church placed on preaching within the worship context. Briefly, Lietzmann suggested the order of worship went something like this:

1) *The Old Testament lessons.* Two Old Testament lessons were

read at the very beginning of the worship service. One lesson was from the historical books, and one lesson from the prophets.

2) *Hymn singing.* Hymn singing was based on the text of the Psalms, although other forms of singing were also used. Often a leader or singer rose to lead singing, with the rest of the congregation responding by singing alternative verses.

3) *The memoirs of the apostles.* A lesson from the Pauline letters or from the Acts was read. As soon as that was done, the congregation rose to their feet, as a deacon or presbyter went to the reading desk to read a lesson from the Gospels.

4) *The sermon.* Justin indicated that it was the president or bishop who preached, administering and exhorting the congregation. Leitzmann adds that at times there were a number of sermons preached in one service, starting with presbyters, although not necessarily all of them, with the bishop coming last.

5) *Prayer.* The last element in this first part of worship service was prayer to God. The whole congregation was asked to rise, and together offered prayer to God (Acts 4:24). A deacon invited the unbaptized, those who were about to be baptized, the sick, and the penitents who had been waiting near the door for the bishop's blessing. All these groups would leave, and with the door closed, the second part of the worship service commenced.

6) *Prayer.* Remaining for the second part of the worship service was the congregation of the baptized, the "believers." The deacon recited the general prayers of the church, and the congregation responded with the Kyrie Eleison:

> Lord, have mercy upon us.
> Christ, have mercy upon us.

Following the general prayers of the church, the bishop prayed for the congregation, "to the best of his ability" as Justin would say. He would give his blessing of peace and the people would assent with "Amen."

7) *The Holy kiss.* According to Lietzmann, the above ceremony was followed by a cry from the deacon, "Greet one another with a holy kiss" (Rom. 16:16; 1 Cor. 16:20; 2 Cor. 13:12; cf. 1 Thess. 5:26; 1 Pet. 5:14). The clergy went on to kiss the bishop, and the congregation followed the example. Men kissed men and similarly women kissed one another.

8) *The Eucharist.* This part of worship started with a deacon crying a warning:

> No catechumens!
> No unbaptized!
> No unbelievers!
> No heretics!
> No one who hates another!
> No hypocrites!
> Let us stand uprightly before the
> Lord with fear and trembling!

At that point, a bowl of water would be handed to the bishop and presbyters who performed the ceremony of the symbolic washing of hands. The sacrificial gifts, the bread and wine, would be brought by the deacons to the altar and would be received by the bishop as his presbyters gathered around him. While the congregation observed in silence, the bishop would don an ornate robe in preparation for administering the Eucharist.

9) *A special collection.* According to Justin, at the end of the Eucharist ceremony a special collection by well-to-do members was deposited with the bishop, who used the offering to assist the orphans, widows, prisoners, and other needy persons.

There are two observations about the development of Christian worship in relation to preaching during the period of the apostolic fathers. First, the reading of the Old Testament lessons and the memoirs of the apostles were given prominence as part of proclamation of the Word in public worship service. Obviously, Christians then did not have access to possession of personal copies of the scriptures, so a deacon or an elder had to read as much as he could for the people to hear for themselves what the Law of Moses, the prophets, and the apostles were saying about Jesus. It must have been incredibly spiritually rewarding for those believers to read the apostles' memories about Jesus Christ, the people who had actually walked and talked with Jesus during his earthly life, like Peter, John, and Paul to whom Jesus revealed himself at a later time. No wonder John the Elder, regarding the revelation of Jesus to him on the island of Patmos, wrote, "Blessed is the one who reads the words of this prophecy, and blessed are those who hear it and take to heart what is written in it, because the time is near" (Rev. 1:3).

A few of those believers might have had the privilege of hearing one or more apostles, holding especially dear the memory that they had of some who had died a glorious martyrdom for Christ's name. Hearing the written word was almost as good as listening to the spoken word, for, as Paul wrote, "faith comes from hearing the message, and the message is heard through the word of Christ" (Rom. 10:17). Perhaps that is one reason why in the life of the early church the reading of the scriptures came fairly early in the order of worship. Such reading set the tone of the whole worship experience for the day.

Second, during this period of the life of the church, preaching remained one of the main tasks of the bishop's office. It was the apostles who, in the first century, had said to the church of Jerusalem, "It would not be right for us to neglect the ministry of the word of God in order to wait on tables" (Acts 6:2). Preaching provided an opportunity for the apostles to evangelize and establish the leadership of the church as they moved from one urban center to another. Later, we find that the bishops as the apostles' successors not only did evangelism, but drew people from more rural areas as they established the bishoprics in the urban centers. Because the unbaptized, those about to be baptized, the sick, and the penitents all waited outside at the entrance of the church building for the bishop's blessing, the bishops were accorded an easy opportunity to meet prospective members.

The preaching of bishops helped the early church to follow the correct teachings—the apostolic tradition and the faith as passed on to them by the apostles—and to fight against heresies. It was also time to exhort and strengthen the church, especially during the times of persecution. That was one reason the memoirs of the apostles meant so much to the life of the early church; for the apostles who died as martyrs had set an example for them.

Schools of Biblical Interpretation

By the second century, two schools of biblical interpretation had developed. One was the school of Alexandria, and the other was the school of Antioch.

The School of Alexandria

The school of Alexandria was known for its allegorical interpretation of the scriptures. The school started as a catechetical school, and the first leader of the school who is known to us was Pantaenus.[32] He was succeeded by Clement (c. 160–220), who was probably born in Athens and was highly trained in Greek philosophy. In spite of his knowledge in Greek philosophy, Clement was seeking light, so he went to Alexandria. It is very likely that he was brought to Christianity by Pantaenus. Clement believed that Greek philosophy served "as a 'school master' to bring the Greek mind to Christ, as the Law brought the Hebrews. Thus philosophy was a preparation, paving the way towards perfection in Christ."[33] In his teaching and preaching, Clement applied allegorical interpretation;[34] he was also a rhetorician. Therefore, Clement must have played an important role in laying down the foundation of the tradition of interpreting the scriptures allegorically in Alexandria.

Clement's disciple, Origen (185–254), born in Alexandria, succeeded his master as head of the catechetical school. Origen was born of Christian parents. When his father suffered martyrdom in 202, "Origen exhorted him to courage and himself desired that martyr's crown."[35] Origen was a theologian, scholar, and dedicated Christian. As much as Origen was a careful student of the scriptures, his method of interpretation was allegorical. He taught that those who were educated in the church were the ones who should be able to assimilate "the philosophical traditions of the ancient world," and through applying allegorical interpretation of the scriptures, Origen was "able to incorporate the best of Judaism and Hellenism in the Christian synthesis."[36]

Origen moved to Caesarea where he was ordained presbyter by bishops there in A.D. 230, an act that Demetrius, bishop of Alexandria, opposed vehemently. Until he was expelled from Alexandria and deprived of his priesthood, Origen preached more often, especially with catechism classes after his ordination. As already mentioned, whenever literal meaning failed to give edifying meditation, allegorical interpretation took over, like Paul in his Letter to the Galatians (4:25).[37] Origen moved to Palestine soon after his ordination, where for the weekday morning services he selected "only a lection from the Hebrew Bible . . . ;

a book was read straight through, two or three chapters at a time. It was at these services that most of the two hundred surviving sermons of Origen were delivered. At the Sunday liturgy, short homilies were preached on each of the three readings—Old Testament, Epistle, and Gospel—and it is for these occasions that Origen preached his homilies on Luke, the only New Testament series that has been preserved."[38]

The School of Antioch

The second important school in terms of the interpretation of the scriptures in preaching was the school of Antioch. Antioch was the third most important city in the Roman Empire at that time, after Rome and Alexandria, and the city where the disciples were first called Christians (Acts 11:26). The conversion of Constantine to Christianity in A.D. 312 led to an overwhelming change in the status of Christianity as a religion in the Roman Empire, and to the total life of the church. As Constantine took control of the entire empire, as the sole ruler by A.D. 324,[39] a number of changes came to the life of the church, including recognition of Sunday as the official day of worship, erection of church buildings throughout the empire, more people who started accepting and identifying themselves with Christianity without fear of persecution and, even more noticeably, the appointment of bishops from the ranks of government administrators who had been trained rhetoricians.

It is in this new political and religious context that we need to understand the preaching and interpretation of the scriptures by those who associated themselves with the school of Antioch. The school emphasized the interpretation of the Bible according to its literal or natural meaning, unlike that of the school of Alexandria, which was allegorical. Generally speaking, preaching during the fourth century was a daily task, and Brilioth says, "The sermon had become the act of an office, primarily that of the bishop, who most often spoke sitting on his throne in the apse."[40] The bishop could also delegate the responsibility to preach to the presbyters, "who customarily used the ambos from which the texts were read."[41]

There were two groups of preachers related to the school of Antioch—the Greek and the Latin. Among the Greek, three preachers who distinguished themselves were the Cappadocian fathers: *Gregory of Nazianzus* (c. 390) was a son of a bishop. After studying in Alexandria, Gregory went to Athens, where he studied rhetoric and philosophy.[42] Although Gregory was impressed by Origen, he followed the literal and historical interpretation of the Bible of the school of Antioch. He served as bishop of Constantinople and was known for his eloquence. *Basil the Great* (c. 370–79), a friend of Gregory's, also studied at Athens. Though he was influenced by Origen's writings, Basil likewise followed the tradition of Antioch. He lived as a monk for a while, became known as an eloquent preacher, and later became bishop of Caesarea. *Gregory of Nyssa* (c. 372–95) was more of a theologian than a preacher and administrator.[43] He followed in the same tradition of Antioch regarding the interpretation of the scriptures.

Probably the most prominent of all the Greek preachers was *John Chrysostom*—"the Golden Mouth" (A.D. 347–407) of Antioch, as he came to be known. His Christian mother, who gave Christian instruction at home and also sent her son to good schools for education, raised Chrysostom alone after the death of her husband. Chrysostom studied under the famous rhetorician, Libanius, who had also taught Basil the Great. Libanius had hoped that Chrysostom would be his successor. Chrysostom had trained to become a lawyer, and had actually started his career as a lawyer. His mother opposed his wish to enter a monastery, but he did so after her death. It was in the monastery that he was introduced to the study of the scriptures by Diodorus.

Chrysostom was ordained a deacon in 381 and a presbyter in 386. He became chief preacher in a leading church in Antioch, and his skill as a preacher soon led to fame. Because of his training in law, Chrysostom became a great rhetorician in the pulpit. Above all, he followed in the tradition of the school of Antioch, which interpreted the Scriptures according to their literal and historical meaning. Chrysostom often started his preaching with the words, "Blessed be God. Peace be unto you."[44] Chrysostom's preaching was not only eloquent, but also timely and effective, as Edwin Dargan notes:

> The preacher bore down upon the vices and sins, which marred the city; he complained that the people feared the wrath of the

emperor more than the wrath of God, and dreaded death more than sin.[45]

At the height of his career, as a chief presbyter in a church of his native city, Antioch, Chrysostom moved to the archbishopric of Constantinople, a move that proved disastrous and brought to an early end the most glorious career of preaching that the church had witnessed in the fourth century. His enemies succeeded in deposing and banishing him from that great church of the apostles. He ended up in exile. Being the kind of dedicated disciple that he was, Chrysostom was likely to have thought, "Glory to God in all things."[46]

The Latin preachers from the West followed more closely the tradition of Antioch than that of Alexandria. One notable Latin preacher was *Cyprian* (c. 200–258), son of a Roman officer, who was born and educated in Carthage to be a teacher of rhetoric. He was converted to Christianity, and eventually became a powerful bishop in North Africa. He always felt indebted to Tertullian (160–200), who later joined Montanism.[47] Cyprian became known as a "Christian rhetorician," and his gifts as an orator were praised by Lactantius. In his use of the Bible, Cyprian "applied allegorical method only to a meager extent."[48]

Zeno (d. 380), another Latin preacher who was born in North Africa, became bishop of Verona in Italy.[49] His homiletical productions are merely brief notes that could have been used and expanded in the delivery "or exhortations given by the bishop after the presbyter had preached."[50] He is said to have had rhetorical skills, and to have been a little bit fancy. Though some imitation of the Greek preachers is traced in his homiletical productions, mostly his method of interpretating the scriptures was allegorical.

Ambrose (339–397), bishop of Milan, was another distinguished Latin preacher. Ambrose was born of Christian parents in 339, when his father was Prefect of Gaul. Educated in Rome, he was appointed governor in north Italy in 370–372. His appointment as bishop in 373 directly from his position as governor was prompted by a child shouting, "Ambrose for bishop!"[51] Within a short time he was not only baptized and ordained successively to all the grades of ministry, but also consecrated as bishop.[52] Ambrose was a man of talents, integrity, and likable-

53

ness.[53] He accepted the Milan bishopric with humility, and studied the Bible diligently as well as the writings of the Greek theologians, particularly Origen and Basil the Great.[54] He gained fame as a powerful orator in the pulpit. Ambrose's "homiletical legacy was the exposition of Psalms and the Gospel of Luke."[55]

The greatest of the Latin fathers was Augustine (334–430) bishop of Hippo, who became a theologian. He was a great preacher. He grew up under the care of a devout Christian mother, Monica, and later studied and taught rhetoric in Carthage. In his efforts to seek truth, Augustine turned to Manichaeism, but began doubting its intellectual and moral adequacy. That truth-seeking led him to a rhetoric teaching post in Milan, where Augustine became impressed by Ambrose's powerful preaching, through his eloquence rather than his message.[56]

After Pontitianus, a traveled African, told Augustine of the monastic life in Egypt, Augustine was ashamed of himself, "that ignorant men like these monks could put away temptations which he, a man of learning, felt powerless" to control.[57] He was particularly troubled with his failure to control his sexual feelings, and eventually he was overwhelmed by self-condemnation. While pondering in a friend's garden during the summer of 386, he heard the voice of a child from a neighbor's house saying, "Take up and read." Next to him was a copy of Paul's Letter to the Romans, which he had been reading. This time his eyes fell on chapter 13, verses 13-14. Augustine experienced "the peace of mind and a sense of divine power to overcome his sins which he had thus far sought in vain."[58]

After Ambrose baptized both Augustine and his son Adeodatus, Augustine returned to Africa, where he settled into ascetic life. It was from his retirement to ascetic life that he accepted the call to become a presbyter in Hippo in 391. During the Easter season of his first year at Hippo, Augustine expounded his ascetic ideals, and at the same time displayed his rhetorical skills in his preaching.[59]

Augustine was a very innovative preacher who preached from both the Old Testament and New Testament, according to the seasons of the Christian year. Since preaching was a daily task, although at times he preached twice in a day, he preached a series of sermons that extended from three days to a week.[60]

Augustine's *On Christian Doctrine* was the first attempt by anyone to write on the subject of homiletics. In that book, Augustine shows the relationship between rhetoric and preaching. Some of the main points in his edification to preachers were as follows: (1) "Seek God's guidance in prayer so that he receives his message from above"; (2) "always make the quality of the content and the welfare of the hearers more important than the outward form"; (3) "the wise speaker is greater than the orator; his greatest desire is to be understood."[61] Augustine also applied classical rhetorical ideas to the sermon; he insisted that the task of the speaker was to teach, delight, influence, and to be able to appeal to the intellect, feeling, and will.[62]

Augustine believed that "the sermon was basically exposition of the text."[63] He was a scriptural expositor in the tradition of his Greek predecessors and contemporaries of the school of Antioch. He wrote commentaries on John and Psalms, and his method of biblical interpretation often searched for literal and essential meanings of the text. However, he did occasionally turn to allegorical interpretations.[64] As Augustine prepared the catechumens for the great baptismal festival of Easter, the emphasis of the message in his preaching was the cross, repentance, fasting and self-denial, and good works.[65]

In the preaching of both Chrysostom and Augustine, the preaching of the church was considered to have reached "the highest point of its ancient development."[66] Whereas Augustine as preacher came through to his hearers more as a theologian, Chrysostom came through more as an orator. They were both great men of God who used both the talents and skills that they had been endowed with by God, and those acquired through education for the sake of preaching the gospel of Jesus Christ.

Chapter 3

Preaching of the Middle Ages
and Reformation

Until about the middle of the twentieth century, people writing about Africa referred to it as the "Dark Continent." Though that kind of attitude about Africa is fast disappearing, one still occasionally encounters those who conceive of Africa as a country rather than a continent. Similarly the concept of the Dark Ages, referring to Europe, is now being discarded by historians of the Middle Ages,[1] an idea that should enable scholars to perceive issues related to the Middle Ages more objectively and positively.

In this chapter we are thinking of a period that extends from A.D. 430, the death date of Augustine, bishop of Hippo, to the year 1517, the year when Martin Luther posted his theses. The early Middle Ages represented the time when the Roman Empire and the Greco-Roman cultures were in decline. The Goths and Vandals, Huns and Lombards invaded the ancient Roman Empire to the extent that the emperor surrendered his crown to Adoacer the Ostrogoth in A.D. 476.[2] By A.D. 651 the Arabs had conquered Palestine, Syria, Mesopotamia, Persia, and Egypt.[3] They took Carthage in A.D. 697, and overran most of Spain by A.D. 715.[4]

The decline of the Roman Empire inevitably affected the life of the church.[5] Consequently, it was not only the empire that had become sick, for even those who bore the name of Christian had compromised; and the hierarchy of the church had increasingly become like that of the Roman Empire itself.[6] This chapter will discuss: (1) general observations about preaching, (2) monastic preaching, (3) eleventh- through fourteenth-century preaching,

(4) fifteenth- through sixteenth-century preaching, (5) Luther and preaching, (6) Calvin and preaching, and, (7) the preaching of Catholic reform.

Paul Tillich gives us a hint on how we might understand and benefit most from the writings and studies of the Middle Ages:

> The basic problem of the Middle Ages, one which we find in all its periods, is that of a transcendent reality, manifest and embodied in a special institution, in a special sacred society, leading the culture and interpreting the nature. If you keep this in mind, you can understand everything going on in the Middle Ages. Without it, you cannot understand anything, because then you would measure the Middle Ages by your own standards of today.[7]

General Observations About Preaching

What was the role of preaching in the life of the church of the Middle Ages? First let us note that in the West, the church developed three "theological attitudes" or theological trends that became the context that tended to determine both the worship and theological reflection throughout the Middle Ages: *scholasticism, mysticism,* and *biblicism.*[8]

Scholasticism was a system of the schoolmen or scholars of the day to give "the theological interpretation of all problems of life,"[9] by using philosophy and theology. In other words, scholasticism was not only the theology of the day, it was the only way that the church explained problems of life and their context, such as the existence of God.

Mysticism was "the experience of the scholastic message."[10] In short, a believer applied personal devotion to prayer, study, contemplation, and meeting the demands of ascetic life.

Biblicism "was an attempt to use the Bible as the basis for a practical Christianity, especially a lay Christianity."[11]

It is important to note that the preaching and homiletical pursuits of the church during this time were influenced and guided by one or more of these theological attitudes. It is also important to know that while those theological attitudes could stand in tension with each other (for example, scholasticism and mysticism in Abelard and Bernard of Clairvaux respectively), the three theological attitudes could also be united in the same person.

58

Second, to this day, one of the remarkable things about the church in the East is "a deep sense of continuity with the past."[12] As already noted, when the Roman Empire collapsed under the pressure of the barbarian invasions in A.D. 476, it was only the West that collapsed; the Eastern empire with Constantinople as its capital, was later captured by the Turks in A.D. 1453. Essentially, the Eastern Orthodox church claims that even when Constantinople was captured by the Turks, there was no drastic breakdown in terms of continuity with traditions from the early fathers, as was the case with the Western church; and that their approach to theological reflection remained patristic. Therefore, the theological trend of scholasticism, which was a result of the synthesis of philosophy and theology, should be understood only as a development of the Western church.[13] Thus, the Eastern Orthodox church to this day considers itself in continuity with the "Age of the Fathers" despite their borrowing ideas from both the Roman Catholic and Protestant churches in the West.[14] That historical distinction and attachment to the early fathers claimed by the Eastern Orthodox is important for our understanding of the church and its preaching during the Middle Ages, as well as in Christendom.

Third, preaching was shaped by the diocesan and parish structures: the church flourished after Constantine became the sole ruler in A.D. 324, and it is not surprising that it consequently inherited the ecclesiastical structure of the Roman Empire, manifested in its dioceses and parishes. By the sixth century, Western emperors determined bishopric appointments and even controlled the election proceedings of bishops.[15] The bishops of the major cities of the empire like Rome, Alexandria, Antioch, Constantinople, and Jerusalem were given the title "Patriarch" and authority to exercise greater and wider responsibility over their areas.[16] Because the emperor had other considerations in the election of those bishops, some of them were indeed quite secular. Nonetheless, there remained some upright bishops, "godly and true preachers,"[17] who took their appointments seriously.

The parish became the unit around which all pastoral activities took place, such as mass, which was said daily, baptisms, marriages, and burials. Each parish had a resident priest or priests, who originally were called *presbyters.* The priest also came to be known as *rector, curatus,* the French term for "care of

59

souls"; *parson,* from the Latin word *persona;* and *vicar* the term used in England.[18] The resident priest received his training in the cathedral church of his diocese, and he was supposed to be celibate. Increasingly, instruction that was given to the parishioners was through the preaching of the priest. Therefore, the emphasis of preaching in the Middle Ages was on instruction, for many people came to church because they lived within the parish perimeters, not necessarily because they were members of the church. The content of the sermons was often drawn from the sermons of the early fathers, such as Augustine, and priests were often vigorously engaged in reproduction work, mainly by simply translating or copying sermons of the fathers and reading them to the congregation.[19]

We noted that in the early church, though bishops shared the pulpit with their presbyters, preaching was primarily the function of bishops. In the Middle Ages, the church had spread to small towns and villages, where the presbyters or deacons had to take charge of preaching. Nevertheless, the bishops "were still regarded as the normative preachers."[20] The rise of the mendicant orders was timely in the promotion of preaching in the parishes, because the level of preaching in the parishes had deteriorated significantly under the auspices of the secular clergy. However, some bishops laid down requirements for preaching and even requested the priests to write their sermons. In 1281, John Peckham, a Franciscan and Archbishop of Canterbury, commanded his priests "to preach each quarter, instructing their parishioners in the articles of the faith, the Ten Commandments, the seven deadly sins, the seven principal virtues, and the seven sacraments."[21] In some countries, books on preaching were circulated to assist the priests with their task of preaching.

Finally, the structure and life of the parish affected the image of the presbyter. The priest was originally known as a presbyter or an elder who shared the function of preaching the gospel with the bishop. By the fifth century, liturgy, which was developed around the Eucharist and other forms of worship, was already flourishing. As mass became central to worship and was said daily, although still with a homily included, the image of the presbyter began to change from that of a preacher or prophet to that of a priest. Thus, the theory of the sacrifice of the mass was understood in a mechanistic way, where "the priest stands as the representative of humanity in the repeated sacrifice of the mass. Through the cultic rite he represents an achievement to God which is intended to benefit men. The minister thereby becomes a mediator between God and men."[22] Dargan says that the change of the image of the presbyter to priest in the Middle Ages was "changing him [presbyter] from a messenger of God into a petty mediator and dispenser of God's mercies and punishment!"[23] He goes on to say that it "led to the preaching of discipline rather than Christian morals, of penance rather than repentance."[24] In other words, both the practice and the content of preaching declined in the Middle Ages.

Monastic Preaching

The roots of monasticism can be traced back to a period before Constantine. It flourished as Christianity acquired the status of a state religion. As more people joined the church without fear of persecution, the way was opened to more secular influence in the life of the church as a whole. Concomitantly, there was an increase in entry into monastic life, a life of self-denial, where one chose to leave worldly life and follow Christ in the company of the like-minded. As the institution of monasticism developed, so did the position of abbot, who led the monastery and saw to it that a program for training and discipline was in place. Most of the monks' time was spent in private and corporate prayer, meditation on the Bible and some writings of the fathers, and work, which included copying manuscripts.

The monasteries became the powerhouse of the life of the church to the extent that they put to shame the so-called *secular clergy*—those who did not belong to any monastic bodies, who tended to be too relaxed in their ministry—or those "in the world."[25] Eventually bishops began to look to the monasteries to supply priests for their parishes; and indeed, bishops and leaders of great distinction, like Gregory of Nazianzus, Basil the Great, Gregory of Nyssa, Chrysostom, and Augustine, all had monastic backgrounds.

The abbot, as the chief authority of the monastery, was responsible for the training program and spiritual formation of the monks. His method of communication was primarily through preaching, and he would preach twice a day.[26] "These sermons generally took the form of homilies in which biblical passages were interpreted anagogically to apply to the spiritual life."[27] Persons from outside the monastery would also be invited to preach; and in the case of convents, outsiders meant the bishop under whose jurisdiction that institution was located.[28] Often, monks went to preach in the churches, and some of them were sent out as missionaries.[29] According to Dargan, preaching in the seventh and eighth centuries would be rated lower than at any previous time. "The bishops preached but little, the common parochial clergy [secular clergy] even less; what preaching there was came mostly from monks and missionaries."[30]

In looking at the form of sermons preached during the seventh and eighth centuries, Dargan comes up with the following points: (1) That in content, the Latin sermons were not better than the Greek sermons. They were all short, and the tone of the sermon was primarily to exhort, urge, or encourage the hearer. Exposition was forced and allegorical. (2) Stories about "saints, . . . extravagant laudation of the Virgin and of relics are largely evident." (3) There was no style to speak of, "no strength, life, or beauty, or eloquence." (4) Most of the sermons are preserved in Latin, since Latin was the prevalent language of preaching. (5) As early as the seventh and eighth centuries, however, some of the popular sermons were preached in the vernacular languages, as in Switzerland. In some countries, like England, some of the preachers used interpreters to translate the message from Latin to the vernacular language.[31]

Eleventh- Through Fourteenth-Century Preaching

By the time of Charlemagne's death in 814, the empire in the West had been united once more. Charlemagne had understood that the task of the church was to nurture the people. Even the laws of the land supported the priests in carrying out their duties, especially in preaching to the people every Sunday.[32] There seemed to be a renewal in the desire for preaching. Bishop Theodulf of Orleans in 797 exhorted his preachers:

He who knows the Scripture must proclaim the Scripture, but he who does not know it must at least impart the most well-known parts to the people, in order that they escape the evil and do that which is good, seek peace and pursue it.[33]

With such encouragement, the priests continued translating the sermons of the fathers, especially those of Augustine and Caesarius of Arles. These sermons were used from the pulpit. However, the Frankish bishoprics became concerned that those sermons were not reaching the people.[34] That was indeed a good sign of the need for renewal in preaching.

The centuries from 800 to 1100 are roughly the period of the Middle Ages often considered the Dark Ages. The reasons for that are as follows: (1) It was the time of a serious conflict between the church and state. (2) It was the time when the Danes sacked Hamburg, Paris, and the eastern coast of England, ransacking the monasteries. (3) With the Carolingian empire in shambles, the empire of Louis the Pious (grandson of Charlemagne) was divided among his three sons by A.D. 843.[35]

In spite of these difficulties, positive developments took place in preaching in the eleventh through the fifteenth centuries.

First, there was a new desire and high regard for preaching in the life of the church during this period of the Middle Ages. As Dargan points out, people of all classes showed some respect and interest in the message of the preachers. For example, there was great appreciation for the message of a preacher like Bernard of Clairvaux (1090–1153). He became a monk and was known all over Europe as a mystic, a man of dedication, and, at the same time, a man of action. Bernard was especially known for his love for Christ, and was an eloquent and persuasive preacher.[36]

Second, the Crusades presented a good cause for preaching in the life of the church. Like the christological controversies in the third and fourth centuries, the Crusades stimulated preaching in the life of the church. The conception of relics and the possibility of going on a pilgrimage to the Holy Land had tremendous appeal for the believers of the time. "What more precious relic could there be, or what nobler pilgrimage shrine, than the land hallowed by the life, death and resurrection of Christ?"[37] Even more appealing was the fact that preaching promised the forgiveness of sins to all who went on a crusade.

Third, scholastic theology was beginning to develop in the universities. As universities began to emerge, with theology as the queen of all the sciences, "the logic of Aristotle became a factor in preaching and fostered a newness of the need for coherence and clarity."[38] However, scholarly sermons that were delivered at universities like Oxford and Paris were in Latin.

Fourth, probably one of the greatest events of this time in the Middle Ages related to preaching was the coming of the mendicant friars: Franciscans, Dominicans, Carmelites, and Augustinians. The emergence of the mendicant friars came during a time of rapid growth of the cities and towns of Europe. Earlier monasteries had chosen to hide away from the society they thought would contaminate them; but the mendicant friars went to the growing urban areas and preached the gospel to the people. The mendicant friars "combined the monastic life and its ideals of poverty, chastity, obedience and community living with preaching to those outside their fellowship."[39] Some of the mendicant friars became known as traveling mendicant friars who "often delivered their sermons outside of the context of the liturgical service."[40] The Dominicans, for example, preached to their fellow clergy, urban audiences of merchants and bankers, and university congregations. Often, they preached against doctrinal errors that were made by some heretics. Some of the mendicant friars became missionaries who were sent to preach among the nominal Christians of Europe, as well as propagating the gospel to other countries outside Europe.

During the last centuries of the Middle Ages, the secular priesthood became increasingly negligent. They "lived a life of luxury and pomp that seemed to the laity to be far removed from the original purity of Christ and the apostles."[41] The tendency to borrow from the ancient church in their preaching continued, and the Bible tended to remain a closed book to the parishioners. In general, it became obvious that "the liturgical context of the mass constricted and impoverished the sermon and in return contributed very few life giving impulses to it."[42]

Finally, it is only proper to mention just a few of the influential personalities in preaching during this period that immediately precedes the Reformation period. In addition to the already mentioned Bernard of Clairvaux (1090–1153), a mystic and man of action, are the German Grey Friar, Berthold of Ratisbon (1272), who drew crowds as he preached in the open field; Brother Peregrinus of Poland, who was known for his vulgar oratory that drew people to his preaching sites; Peter Dacia, who was associated with the convents; and Meister Eckhart (1260–1328) another mystic at the University of Paris.[43]

Fifteenth- and Sixteenth-Century Preaching

We have already established that during the Middle Ages, "scholasticism was the theology of that time; mysticism was the personal experiential piety, and biblicism was the continuous critical reaction coming from the biblical tradition and entering the two other attitudes, finally overcoming both of them in the Reformation."[44] We plan to look at the preaching of only two outstanding reformers, Martin Luther (1483–1546) and John Calvin (1509–1564), and the preaching of Catholic Reform. However, let us also acknowledge the presence of many other notable preachers, again by simply mentioning a few representatives.

Starting with France, an eminent humanist scholar called Jacques Le Fevre became well known and loved, and was an influential teacher of preachers. Francis Lambert (1486–1530) of Avignon, was a Franciscan who distinguished himself by his study of the scriptures and his eloquence as a traveling preacher. Having read the early writings of Luther, he decided to go to Germany to study theology under Luther and Melanchthon.

Switzerland became a country fertile for Reformation ideas; reformers came from all over Europe to test and develop their own ideas. Guillaume Farel (1489–1565) of Gap was a very active reformer in Geneva, and was responsible for inviting many young reformers, including John Calvin, to that city. It was through the influence of Le Fevre, under whom Farel studied philosophy, theology, and the Bible, that Farel came to realize "the difference between the Bible and the doctrines and practices of the Catholic church."[45] Ulrich Zwingli (1484–1531) of Zurich was a great reformer in his own right, and a contemporary of Luther. He preached on a series of the books of the Bible. He made reforms in the order of worship by abolishing the mass, replacing it with the simpler celebration of the Lord's Supper, more in line with the New Testament. The Sunday worship service was again given a new form with the sermon as the central point.

Southern Europe discovered it had a number of preachers who preached Reformation ideas, in spite of the heavy suppressive measures in countries like Spain. Juan de Avila, a wealthy man, decided to study the scriptures and became convinced of the evangelical doctrines, which he then preached. Dr. Egidio, who died in 1556, had distinguished himself at the University of Alcala. Having become cardinal of Seville in 1537, Egidio studied the Bible and became known as an eloquent preacher.

There were also reformers in eastern Europe. John Mathesius (1504–1565) was a student and friend of Luther. He spent his whole lifetime working in the pastorate, and was a very much loved pastor. He studied the Bible seriously and was known as a good preacher and promoter of reform in the life of the church. There was Paul Spretter (1484–1551), who was educated in Italy and Paris, and early in his life had embraced Protestant doctrines. He preached at various places in southern Germany with great effect. In 1521, he was in Vienna, where in reply to a monk who had defended celibacy, Spretter delivered a powerful sermon, "in which he not only showed that the Catholic practice was contrary to Scripture, but also took the occasion to attack the whole system of vows as held in the Roman church."[46]

There were preachers who promoted reformation in Northern Europe. Indeed, reformation ideas had spread there like wildfire, both from German and Swiss reformers. The following were some of the preachers: Jan Arends, Peter Gabriel, Nicholas Scheltius, and Peter Datheen. Several preachers who proclaimed reformation ideas suffered persecution and trial, especially in the Netherlands. The martyrs were the best preachers. Before he was burned to death, John of Backer, a preacher who was also married, had responded to the Roman church that "he did not recognize any other rule of faith than Holy Scripture, and that it was not necessary to use other language than that of Scripture itself in order to interpret it; that a man should not rashly violate the decrees and canons, but should observe them when they were in accord with the Word of God; that violence should not be used in religion, but rather gentleness and force of arguments."[47]

England had its reformers as well, starting with Thomas Cranmer (1489–1556), who supported the right of Henry VIII to divorce, and subsequently became Archbishop of Canterbury. There was William Tyndale, who died in 1536, a translator of the Bible. He preached with great courage. Another of the English reformers was John Rogers, who died in 1555, and who had been to Wittenberg where he had met with the reformers. There was also Hugh Latimer, a preacher of great zeal in advancing reform views. Latimer died in 1555.

Scotland had its own reformers, like John Knox (1505–1572), who started his reformation activities in 1542. He was in large measure responsible for the establishment of Protestantism in his country.

In turning to the two leading reformers, Luther and Calvin, this background has at least informed us that there were other leaders in the church who already shared and listened to their views, especially in their search for renewal in the proclamation of the gospel.

Martin Luther and Preaching

It is important to understand Luther's theological thought if we are going to appreciate his approach to preaching. Luther would talk about "particular" or "proper" knowledge of God. He had no problem with the view that God would be known outside the knowledge of Christ, or that God would reveal himself through nature and other forms in such a way that people would rightly know of his existence. Indeed, Luther would say that God is working throughout this whole creation. Luther would not have had any problem with African religion in its claim of God's existence as a Supreme Being. But he would have called that kind of knowledge general knowledge. For Luther, one may have that general knowledge of God and still remain "ignorant of His essential character, His inmost purpose and will, which alone determines the meaning of the things they do know about Him. This ignorance Luther finds dispelled in Christ and Christ alone."[48] Therefore, the "particular" or "proper" knowledge of God "is that given in and through Christ."[49]

Thus, Luther fought against some aspects of the medieval religion, a merely human attempt to have dealings with God at the exclusion of God's revelation in Christ. Hence, Anders Nygren, in describing Luther's attack on them as a "campaign against the *Heavenly Ladders*," says:

The Medieval interpretation of Christianity is marked throughout by the *upward tendency*. This tendency asserts itself no less in the moralistic piety of popular Catholicism than in the rational theology of Scholasticism and the ecstatic religiosity of Mysticism. . . . They all know a Way by which a man can work his way up to God, whether it is the Way of merit known to practical piety, the *anagoge* of mysticism, or the Way of speculative thought according to the "analogy of being." Man must mount up to God by means of one of the three heavenly ladders. Against this upward tendency or ascent Luther makes his protest. He will have nothing to do with this "climbing up into the majesty of God."[50]

Therefore, we can say that Luther attacked the rationalism (scholasticism), mysticism, and moralism in Catholicism—all as "means by which man is presumed to make his way to God, whereas Christ, although in a certain sense He may be described as man's way to God, is primarily and essentially *God's way to man*."[51] Thus, the prophecy of Isaiah was fulfilled when, as Matthew wrote, "The virgin will be with child and will give birth to a son, and they will call him Immanuel—which means, 'God with us,'" (1:23). Or through Christ, God has made God's way to humanity. And that is the good news of preaching Christ. Humankind does not need to climb up to God in heaven, anyway. Instead, God has "made his dwelling among us" (John 1:14); or God has pitched his tent among us; or God has built God's house in our village—God is now our neighbor. With that theological insight of Luther that we have attempted to Africanize at the same time, we shall now turn to Luther's theological understanding of the Word of God and his homiletical practices.

First, for Luther, Christ is the Word of God. In fact, Luther believed the terms *Christ* and *the Word* are virtually interchangeable. However, he would also talk of the Word in relation to the written word—the scripture; and the Word as the spoken word—the word proclaimed by the preacher. In terms of the relationship of Christ and the scripture, for Luther the whole scripture is about Christ; and that was true of both the Old Testament and the New Testament. The purpose of the Bible was to reveal Christ as the Word of God, no matter how obscure some passages of scripture may seem.[52] For Luther, the Old Testament would have to be interpreted in the light of the New Testament "before we can see how 'the entire Old Testament refers to Christ and agrees with Him' and this is what ought to be done, for the law and the prophets are not rightly preached and understood, unless we find Christ wrapped in them."[53]

Luther emphasized two points in preaching Christ: (1) God's moral requirements for human beings (law); and (2) the good news that Christ justifies sinners unable to meet those requirements who turn to him on faith (gospel). Sinners are justified (regarded as righteous) when they hear the gospel of God's good-will toward them and accept it by trusting entirely in Christ, claiming no merit of their own.[54] The centrality of hearing the Word of God or Christ in the written word and through the word proclaimed is an important point to grasp, if one is to understand Luther, and subsequently the Lutheran Confessions. In writing about the difference between the Lutheran and Reformed Confessions views regarding the Bible, Donald McKim notes:

> Lutheran Confessions present no doctrine of the inspiration of the Scripture nor do they make any mention of a special activity of the Holy Spirit in how the process of the canonization of biblical books took place. It has been suggested that the reason for these omissions from Lutheran documents may be that "the interest of Lutheran theology was not in a book as such but in the redemptive content" of the Bible. The thrust of Lutheran Confessions is toward hearing the gospel of Jesus Christ. It is the inspiration of the hearer, not primarily of the book (the Bible) that is primary.[55]

Second, we turn to Luther's homiletical practices. Luther was overwhelmed with the idea that he had been entrusted with the task of preaching and interpreting the Bible, particularly reaching people with the message of the gospel. As a preacher, he had a "strong awareness of divine calling."[56] So when it came to the scriptural message, Luther often went for the central message of a passage that he would have chosen, with less emphasis on verse by verse exposition as such, but always getting to the heart of the scriptural passage;[57] because for Luther, biblical exegesis was about the most important focus for a preacher. That approach freed Luther from the allegorical method of preaching as he searched for the literal and historical meaning of scriptures.[58] Though he often wrote out his sermons, he typically preached extemporaneously. Clarity and the ability for his sermons to be understood by children were important factors in his delivery. According to Brilioth, Luther's criticism of the "Roman service was that the word of God was not given its rightful status."[59] Therefore, he included scripture reading and preaching in morning and evening worship services.

John Calvin and Preaching

First, it would be helpful to understand Calvin (1509–64) as a man of action, and as a man who could be "irritable. Often, his anger would be fierce and lasting. But he was conscious and penitent of that and other faults. Pure and austere in morals himself, he was a rigid disciplinarian and lacking in sympathy for the weak and erring."[60] As he struggled for control of the city of Geneva, those who, like him, disobeyed the laws had to face the wrath of the law and often ended up expelled, excommunicated, or even losing their lives at the hands of the authorities. He was a talented writer, "clear and precise in his expression, a systematic if not a creative thinker, and an excellent organizer."[61] These two qualities—passion for truth and the ability to communicate forcefully—undergirded Calvin's strong drive to fight unrighteousness, and his struggle for the independence of the church from the state in order to achieve those goals. He "had an ethic— a powerful, dominant, driving ethic—and it rested on his bedrock conviction of the absolute and final authority of the Will and Word of God."[62]

It is important to understand Calvin's conception of God if one is going to appreciate what he believed had to be done in fighting all the unrighteousness in the city of Geneva. According to Calvin:

> True and substantial wisdom principally consists of two parts, the knowledge of God, and the knowledge of ourselves. But, while these two branches of knowledge are so intimately connected, which of them precedes and produces the other, is not easy to discover. For, in the first place, no man can take a survey of himself but he must immediately turn to the contemplation of God, in whom he "lives and moves" (Acts 17:28); since it is evident that the talents which we possess are not from ourselves, and that our very existence is nothing but a subsistence in God alone. These bounties, distilling to us by drops from heaven, form, as it were, so many streams conducting us to the fountain-head. Our poverty conduces to a clearer display of the infinite fullness of God.[63]

70

For Calvin, because the human mind was weak to fathom and comprehend God and God's relationship to humankind, the only solution to that problem was for humankind to turn to God and be taught by God.[64] "This is what happens in Holy Scripture, which alone discloses to us the nature of God and ourselves. 'We must go to the Word, in which God is clearly and vividly mirrored for us in His works, and where the works of God are appraised not by our perverse judgments but by the criterion of eternal truth.' "[65]

Second, Calvin considered the Old Testament and the New Testament as a single testimony to Christ. He held strong views about the Ten Commandments to the extent that he would write about the Old Testament in the following manner, "Let us lay down this, then, as an undoubted axiom, that nothing ought to be admitted in the Church as the word of God, but what is contained first in the law and the prophets, and secondly in the writings of the apostles."[66] No wonder Calvin has been criticized for blurring the boundaries between the Old and New Testaments, and that in his moral zeal, Calvin "closes his eyes to all the new values which Jesus brought into the world, and degrades Him to the position of an interpreter of the ancient lawgiver, Moses."[67]

Third, Calvin is said to have understood his ministry in light of Ephesians 4:11-13. Whether that was the case or not, at least Calvin is said to have held a view "that the church is composed of God's elect and that (as the New Testament was taken to indicate) there are properly four classes of ecclesiastical officers, namely, pastors, teachers, elders (or presbyters), and deacons."[68] The churches in Geneva were organized with that kind of ministerial leadership, where pastors were responsible for the proclamation of the Word of God; teachers for the instruction of believers in wholesome doctrine; elders for taking care of the life of each person, "admonishing them lovingly when they see them at fault or leading a disorderly life"; and deacons, for the care of the poor and the sick. Calvin himself was the leading pastor.[69] He viewed his primary responsibility in Geneva as "proclaiming the Word of God and instructing believers in wholesome doctrine."[70]

Calvin conducted two main services on Sunday, one in the morning and another in the afternoon. At midday he would meet with the children for catechism. He also preached on Monday, Tuesday, and Friday mornings. While he preached from the New

Testament on Sundays, during the week he preached from the Old Testament. He "preached steadily through book after book and expounded it passage by passage, clause by clause, day after day, until he came to the end."[71] By handling a number of passages in one sermon, he would preach on a number of ideas at the same time. He is known to have been a faithful and honest interpreter of the Bible, and was horrified with preachers who preached their own ideas "instead of the gospel of the Bible."

> When we enter the pulpit, it is not so that we may bring our own dreams and fancies with us. But on the other hand, the preacher's task is not simply to repeat Bible ideas in Bible language. He must explain what the Bible means and apply its teaching to the congregation before him.[72]

Finally, although Calvin stands with Luther in rejecting that humans receive salvation by good works, Calvin would not go along with the idea that faith is a free act on the part of humanity; "it is rather the free gift of God to those to whom he elects to give it."[73] Indeed, this was Calvin's central dogma of predestination. It is understood that when Calvin talked of predestination, he meant "an eternal decree of God made before time and before the foundation of the world."[74] The secrets of that decree can only be disclosed to humanity in God's Word, and cannot be understood by reason.

> Hence it must be said that God has not chosen those whom He has accepted as his children because of their intrinsic worth, but because He sees them in Christ (Ephesians 1:4); because only in him does He love them, nor could He reward them with the inheritance of His kingdom until he had made them joint-heirs with Christ.[75]

The Preaching of Catholic Reform

There were preachers besides Luther and Calvin who sought change within the Roman church. And not everyone who wanted to see change necessarily left the Roman church; some remained and eventually were able to forge change from within. Therefore, a number of things happened within the Roman church that brought a similar spirit of renewal to the Catholic community.

Paul III convened a council to meet in Trent in 1545. Though the main agenda of that council was curbing Reformation abuses, the importance of preaching and propagating the gospel were also emphasized at that council.

First, the Council of Trent considered preaching to be "the principal duty of bishops,"[76] which was how the Twelve had understood their role amidst the pressure of many things clamoring for their attention in the early church (Acts 6:4). Second, provision "was also made to train clergy in preaching and to establish seminaries."[77] Third, probably even more important than the resolutions from the Council of Trent, was the missionary thrust by the Roman church around the world—making new conquests for Christ both in Europe and beyond—in the Americas, Japan, and China.[78] Spain and Portugal had already begun their exploration of the New World in the fifteenth century, and after the Council of Trent the effort to send out missionaries was intensified. Though the Roman Catholic Church had established missions in West Africa during the sixteenth and seventeenth centuries, the efforts had been sacrificed for the slave trade. Therefore, it was not until "the refoundation in 1848 of the Congregation of the Holy Ghost, whose members worked in West Africa,"[79] that the Catholic church resumed its missionary activities in Africa. By that time, Protestant church missionary societies or boards that had been established either prior to the partitioning of Africa in the eighteenth century or with the colonial settlers in the early nineteenth century, were also beginning to enter the continent to establish missions. Thus, the church in Africa was planted through the preaching that had its roots and foundation in both the reformed churches of Europe as well as the Roman church following the Council of Trent.

From the beginning of Christianity, preaching has been central to public worship. This is a heritage that we owe to the early church and the reformers. We noted the apostles' practice of placing the ministry of the word at the center of Christian worship (Acts 6:1-7; 1 Cor. 1:17). Similarly, throughout the Middle Ages, the mass had been placed at the center of Christian worship until the sixteenth and seventeenth centuries, when reformers such as Luther and Calvin appeared on the scene and likewise recognized the centrality of the ministry of the Word in public Christian worship.

Chapter 4

Defining Preaching
in the African Context

The most common Greek verb that is used in the New Testament for "to preach" is *kerussein*. It is used about sixty times in the New Testament,[1] including in the following texts: Mark 1:14; Acts 10:42; 1 Cor. 1:23. The chief synonyms of the verb *kerussein* or "to preach" are: "to evangelize" (as found in Acts 5:42), "to declare" (Acts 20:27), "to announce" (Acts 17:30), "to proclaim" (Acts 9:20; 17:23). *Kerussein* used in the sense of "to proclaim" probably occurs much more often than the other synonyms (Matt. 3:1; Mark 1:45; Luke 4:18). Thus, one is likely to find the two terms, "to preach" and "to proclaim" used interchangeably. The two terms are synonymous.[2]

Homiletics is often mistakenly substituted for the term *preaching;* the two words are not necessarily synonymous. Preaching refers to the actual act of proclaiming the good news. The word *homiletics* is derived from the word *homily,* which originally came from the Greek word *homilia,* meaning a discourse or sermon. The word *homiletics,* therefore, refers more to the art than to the act of preaching. It refers to the science and skills of proclamation. Homiletics is actually more of what happens in the classroom than from the pulpit. Thus, the difference between preaching and homiletics is that, while the former refers to the act of proclamation, the latter refers to the science and the art of doing effective proclamation of the Word.[3] They represent two sides of the same coin.

Preaching is such a vast subject that every church under heaven and in Christendom is involved in it one way or another.

Therefore, as one begins to think about defining preaching, one cannot help recalling the analogy of the blind people who encountered an elephant—an overused analogy, perhaps, but one which illustrates the immensity of the subject of preaching well. As the blind people touched and felt the elephant, each one of them gave a different description based on the part of the elephant he had touched. Preaching is similarly defined in many and various ways.

Communication contracts theory, for example, suggests that in the process of communication there are four factors, namely, the speaker, the speech, the audience, and the occasion. One could also think in terms of the sender, the message, the receiver, and the contextual situation, or, in typical preaching terms, the preacher, the message, the congregation, and the preaching situation.[4]

In applying this theory of communication to preaching in the African situation, I have had to make adjustments. So, because in this context "the occasion or contextual situation" is rarely different from "the audience or congregation," I have combined the categories of congregation and contextual situation. This leaves us with the following: preacher-centered, message-centered, and congregation and contextual situation-centered definitions. (Some definitions will transcend categories.)

Preacher-Centered Definitions

The Shona people of Zimbabwe have special persons who emerge from among their own people as *svikiro* or *mhondoro*—commonly known as the mediums. Such a medium appears on the scene as a possessed agent of the ancestors who is sent to the people with a message. Whether a man or a woman, a *svikiro's* main qualification is credibility among the people to whom he or she delivers the message. The credibility can be established by fulfilling the following categories: (1) Since a *svikiro* claims possession by ancestral spirit, one under such possession should be able to name the ancestor who is possessing him or her. The ancestor who is named must be known by the elders to fall under the category or function of possessing the living as their medium. It has to be an ancestor who had and still has the respect of the living. (2) A *svikiro* is supposed to know the history of a people

76

to whom he or she is sent. This is important because whatever message one delivers is measured against the history of the people. (3) Finally, a *svikiro* is supposed to understand the culture of the people to whom he or she is sent with the message. If one fails to meet the above standards for credibility, one is rejected as a *svikiro,* or one simply becomes a false *svikiro.*

How then does one claim to be a *svikiro* in the Shona culture? Often, one claims possession by the ancestral spirit and that one has a message for the people. This typically happens when people are already gathered at a special ritual event, or any other social gathering. Such a possessed person is not allowed to deliver the message until the elders or the chief is brought to the scene to listen to the message. The message is meant to be for the whole ethnic group, and not simply for individuals or individual families. When the elders have been gathered, then the *svikiro* is first asked who sent him or her to deliver that message. That is often the most critical question. The elders must also determine whether the individual has the right to claim the title *svikiro,* because normally only one *svikiro* is recognized at a time. After listening to the message, the elders often question the *svikiro,* and test the facts or message to make sure they have relevance to their own history and culture. Therefore, the message of the *svikiro* is accepted or rejected on the basis of his or her authority regarding the ancestor who is named, the accuracy of the historical account, and the understanding of the customs and practices of people. If the *svikiro's* message is accepted, the elders demand a clear statement of what the people are asked to do. If the medium fails to fulfill the above standards, he or she is immediately rejected as a false medium. The people often show their disapproval of a medium by dispersing while he or she is still making the announcement or while he or she is being questioned. If the person claims to be possessed at some other time, the elders simply do not pay attention, and that person becomes known as a false medium.

Like in the Shona tradition of the *svikiro,* the credibility of the preacher is critical. And there are definitions of preaching that focus the importance of preaching upon the preacher. Such *preacher-centered definitions* ask of the preacher: Who is he or she? Who sent him or her? African Christians would resonate with Moses' question, "Suppose I go to the Israelites and say to

77

them, 'The God of your fathers has sent me to you,' and they ask me, 'What is his name?' Then what shall I tell them?" (Exod. 3:13). A preacher who knows the name of the one who has sent him or her has his or her job half done already. Likewise, effective preaching can be done only by a preacher who knows the history—the suffering, the struggles, the fears, and the anxieties—of the people. A preacher needs to understand the customs and traditions of his or her own people in order to communicate the good news. We should never forget that culture is communication.

In this chapter we are not yet talking about the calling of a preacher; rather, we are talking about definitions that explain preaching from the preacher's point of view. In other words, there are people who measure the success or failure of preaching by the credibility of the preacher. Did he or she really receive a calling to the ministry? Can he or she name his God in his or her life, ministry, and especially in the pulpit? What theological education did the preacher acquire? What theological stance does this preacher represent? What school did she attend? Does he respect the culture of the people among whom he is serving?

Preacher-centered definitions deal with such issues in order to establish the role and importance of preaching. Of the many possible aspects for discussion, I have chosen three:

1) The most powerful instrument in God's hand is a personality confronting men and women. A life picked up, lost in its message, a personality incandescent (glowing with intense heat) with the love and power of God, is the most powerful communication force in the world.[5]

2) There is no substitute for the inspired witness, standing in the presence of people, speaking the Word of God. . . . The inspired man, aglow with a warm experience of God with an informed mind is indispensable to the success of the Christian enterprise.[6]

3) Preaching is what God does, not with His Word, but with a man who accepts the Word.[7]

The centrality of the preacher in the whole act of proclamation is common to these three definitions. The preacher as understood above is "the most powerful instrument in God's hand." "There is no substitute for an inspired witness" who stands in the pulpit. And "preaching is what God does . . . with a man who accepts the Word." The biblical theology of these definitions is that the preacher is indeed a possession of God, an instrument of God (2 Tim. 2:21), or God's chosen instrument (Acts 9:15). Ideally, the preacher is one whose face is radiant with the love and experience of God when in the pulpit proclaiming the Word. The preacher may not be aware of it, but the congregation will know that the preacher has been speaking to the Lord (Exod. 34:29).

One local preacher preached what turned out to be his last sermon, for he died on the following Tuesday. Describing the appearance of that preacher in the pulpit to another parishioner who was unable to attend the worship service, a congregant said, "I had never seen his face as radiant as it was that morning! And little did we know that it was a farewell message."

Probably there is no greater motivating force to a preacher in his or her whole ministry than knowing that he or she has been called by God. That is clearly demonstrated in the life of the prophets and the apostles. For example, one of the Old Testament prophets, Amos, was able to withstand the challenge from Amaziah, the priest of Bethel, when he said, "I was neither a prophet nor a prophet's son, but I was a shepherd, and I also took care of sycamore-fig trees. But the LORD took me from tending the flock and said to me, 'Go, prophesy to my people Israel' " (Amos 7:14-15). It would be interesting if one were to find out how many preachers in Africa came up the same way that Amos did—starting from tending their father's cattle, through high school, which they were never sure they would finish, some of them who either had to do their schooling by correspondence studies or had to go to night school in order to qualify for a theological seminary or college. Indeed, many were not even teachers' or preachers' sons, and yet God chose them to become his instruments. And thank God, they can stand before their own congregations and name the God who called them into the ministry of Jesus Christ. They know they are God's true *svikiro* to God's people.

As a preacher, it is important to have that deeply grounded sense of calling, that compelling motivation all the time. That is the reason Kyle Haselden believed that the remedy to the ineffectiveness of preaching could only come about by recovery of confidence in the preacher. That recovery of confidence can be achieved only if preachers are able to name who has sent them, and if they are steeped in knowledge of their people's history and culture.

Message-Centered Definitions

In traditional Africa the message was transmitted in various ways, including by means of the drum. Among the Shona people, the drum summoned people to dancing if there were festivities for celebration. The drum also announced death in the village. During times of ethnic wars, the drum sounded a warning that an enemy had been sighted; the sound alerted all the men of the village to prepare to fight and warned women and children to go to their hiding places. This context made Paul's message to the Corinthians easy to understand: "Again, if the trumpet does not sound a clear call, who will get ready for battle?" (1 Cor. 14:8).

Communicating a message quickly and clearly is a critical task in everyday life. It is equally critical in communicating the gospel through preaching. Thus, there are homileticians who would define preaching from the message perspective. While there are many possible definitions of preaching whose emphasis was primarily the Word of God, the message, for the purposes of this study I have selected four:

1) Preaching, in Bernard Meaning's phrase, is the manifestation of the incarnate Word, from the written word, by the spoken word.[8]

2) Preaching is communication of truth by one person to others. It has two essential elements, truth and personality. . . . Preaching is the bringing of truth through personality.[9]

3) Preaching is the communication of the good news of God's reconciling arts culminating in Jesus Christ as recorded in the Bible, by means of the spoken words of a convinced witness, to a group of listeners, seeking to present God's past acts to contemporary life so that they may become present realities to both the preacher and listeners, calling forth appropriate response.[10]

4) Preaching is thus speech by God rather than speech about God. Certainly, the aim of preaching is also to reveal God, to present

God to persons; but when we preach, our role is not that of the impressario presenting a star to the crowd. We are not here to explain to others that God is eternal, that God knows all things, that God loves us and wants us to love God in return. We are here in order that, through our preaching, God may communicate these things. In other words, revelation is not something within our personal power, it is the concern of God.[11]

We have already indicated that some of the definitions could easily fall under more than one category. However, two points stand out particularly in these message-centered definitions of preaching. First, of course, the Word of God here assumes the central position in preaching. In other words, preaching is defined from the point of view of the Word or message to be preached. Thus, in the definitions before us we read that preaching is, "the manifestation of the incarnate Word, from the written word, by the spoken word"; it is "the communication of truth"; it is the "communication of the good news of God's reconciling acts culminating in Jesus Christ, as recorded in the Bible, by means of spoken words"; and "preaching also has as its aim to reveal God, to present God to persons. . . . We are there in order that, through our preaching, God may communicate these things." The emphasis in all the four definitions is the Word— Jesus Christ as testified to both the Old and New Testaments.

There is an African folktale that goes like this. Once upon a time, *Musikavanhu* (He who created the people) had a message to be delivered to the people. Out of the unlimited sources of messengers at his disposal, and for reasons known only to him, *Musikavanhu* sent a chameleon. The chameleon had to pass through thick forests and mountains and had to cross several big rivers in order to get to the place where the people were located. The chameleon had a problem: he had to change his attire each time he came to a new place. All the beautiful surroundings that he came across attracted his attention. Meanwhile, *Musikavanhu* got tired of waiting for the feedback from the chameleon. Therefore, he sent another messenger, and this time it was a lizard. And at this time also, *Musikavanhu* decided to change his message; for at that time, death was final, and there was no second chance. The lizard moved as swiftly as he knew how. He went through the same thick forests and mountains, crossed

81

several rivers, and was able to deliver the message to the people before the chameleon did. Eventually, when the chameleon appeared on the scene, people did not receive his message, for they had already received *Musikavanhu's* message from the lizard. No wonder, as young boys growing up and tending our fathers' cattle, each time we saw a chameleon we would kill it, because it did not deliver the message of having a second chance after death.

At times one wonders how many people in our churches and communities have been waiting for that message of a second chance. That was clearly Paul's message to the saints in the church of God in Corinth when he said, "For as in Adam all die, so in Christ all will be made alive" (1 Cor. 15:22). That was indeed the message of a second chance that the world has been waiting for. The chameleon failed to deliver that important word.

It is important and entirely appropriate to treat the Word of God and its communication as central in defining our understanding of preaching, because hearing the Word makes the difference between life and death. That is the whole point of this African folktale. As messengers bearing God's message that can make the difference between life and death, preachers of the Word need to feel compelled by a sense of urgency about proclamation. Thus, King Zedekiah clearly realized the importance of God's word when, under difficult circumstances he sent for Jeremiah, even after he had been thrown into a dungeon, only to ask him, "Is there any word from the LORD?" (Jer. 37:17).

The second point in considering the Word of God and its communication central to our understanding of the preaching is noted by Allmen: "Preaching is thus speech by God rather than speech about God. . . . We are there in order that, through our preaching, He may say these things Himself."[12] The miracle of preaching is that in spite of human frailty, it pleased God to save those who believed through the foolishness of what was preached (1 Cor. 1:21). Through the preaching of the Word, God manifests himself once more. As Bishop Gerald Kennedy said, "Not only is it [preaching] a means of spreading information about our faith, but it is in some sense the revelation of the faith itself. . . . The very act of preaching is a part of the Christian revelation."[13]

As one who participates in God's plan to reveal himself to

humankind through the preaching of his Word, the preacher bears tremendous responsibility. Yes, "We are there in order that, through our preaching, He may say these things Himself."[14] Through our preaching, God wants to have the opportunity to tell people, "I love you so much that I gave my one and only Son to die on the cross for you; I forgive every one who entrusts their life to Jesus Christ; I am with those going through all kinds of hardship in life." God wants to encounter people. Our understanding of preaching of the Word brings God close to humankind. People do not have to go to God anymore, for he has already come to us in his Son, and dwelt among us (John 1:14).

The issue of the incarnate Word, the written word, and the spoken word will be dealt with in the following chapter. For now, suffice it to say that making distinctions between these three helps to clarify the task and message of the preacher.

Congregation- and Situation-Centered Definitions

Congregation-centered and situation-centered categories of preaching will be treated as one category, since the definitions seem to apply to both very appropriately. Thus, preaching can also be understood and defined from the congregation's point of view. Ruth Lukanitsch, a Roman Catholic, in writing about participating in a preachers' workshop had this to say about congregation-centered preaching: "In our sessions, we stressed the fact that both the content and the presentation of the homily must be audience-centered; they must convey this idea, at this moment, to this group of individual persons."[15] Beyond the preacher's and the message's point of view, one also needs to look at preaching from the perspective of the people to whom the Word is preached. Therefore, there are some definitions that understand preaching from the congregational or preaching situation point of view. They are as follows:

1) In the New Testament sense of the term, to preach is to confront persons with the "kerygma" and the "didache" of the gospel, to tell them what God did in the days of Jesus, to pass on to them the historical facts recorded in those ancient documents, and to try to persuade them to accept those facts and live by them.[16]

2) Preaching is the communication of the good news of God's reconciling acts culminating in Jesus Christ as recorded in the Bible by means of the spoken words of convinced witnesses, to a group of listeners, seeking to present God's past acts to contemporary life that they become present realities to both the preacher and listeners, calling forth appropriate response.

Here, two factors stand out about preaching that is congregation-centered and situation-centered. First, preaching should indeed be understood and defined from the congregation's point of view. In the two definitions, preaching is defined as "to confront persons with the 'kerygma' and 'didache' of the gospel"; and "the communication of the good news of God's reconciliation acts . . . to a group of listeners . . . seeking to present God's past acts to contemporary life." Again, the critical issue with such definitions of preaching is the question, To what extent does the preacher know the people to whom he or she is going to deliver a message? Or how much does the pastor really know about his or her own congregation? I have always felt that the greatest gift to any ordained preacher is to have a congregation to serve and tend. And what a joy it should be to a pastor to know that he or she has a message for such a congregation every Sunday. The more the pastor gets to know his or her congregation, the more his or her preaching becomes relevant and meaningful to the congregation. One has heard of preachers who enjoy preaching better in other preachers' pulpits than they do in their own. How unfortunate! As a pastor, I would be careful about inviting such preachers to my pulpit.

When it comes to knowing one's congregation intimately one is reminded of the prophet Ezekiel who, knowing how important it was for him to communicate the word of the Lord that had come to him, went to dwell with the Hebrew exiles at Tel Abib near the Kebar River. Ezekiel said, "And there, where they were living, I sat among them for seven days—overwhelmed" (Ezek. 3:15). There are numerous unspeakable blessings to both the congregation and the pastor when preaching is carried out from an intimate relation between the two. As one pastor claims, "Intimate knowledge of his or her congregation, of their concerns, their joys, sorrows, temptations, and sins . . . parish calls, counseling sessions, and the hearing of confessions should equip

84

the preacher" for the kind of preaching that has the tone of understanding and compassion for the congregation.[17] That was exactly the message Jesus sounded when he said, "I am the good shepherd; I know my sheep and my sheep know me" (John 10:14).

The second factor about preaching that is congregation-centered and situation-centered is that people are expected to respond because every message from God to his people is for a purpose. In the two definitions under consideration we read, "and to persuade them to accept those facts and live by them";[18] and, "calling forth appropriate response."[19] Paul Tillich, a leading theologian of this century, is quoted as saying that the task of preaching is to communicate the gospel, "making possible a decision for or against it."[20] One cannot preach the gospel without expecting a change in the lives of people. People have to make a decision one way or another. The funny thing is that the people who listen to the preaching of the gospel know very well that they have to make a decision. The question is: Does the preacher present the gospel in such a manner that helps people to make that decision? Does the preacher always have the courage to extend an invitation in his or her preaching? There is a common misconception among preachers that the only decision that a person has to make is that of repentance leading to conversion. Indeed, there are preachers whose understanding of preaching is nothing beyond calling people to repentance and conversion. There is nothing wrong with that as long as conversions are taking place. That was the main thrust of John the Baptist's message to his people. But even John the Baptist's preaching went farther than repentance, for as he said, "Produce fruit in keeping with repentance" (Matt. 3:8). Happily, it is God who genuinely converts his people, and not the preacher.

There are also preachers who are scared to death of extending any kind of invitation for a decision by their listeners, either as individuals or as a congregation. They are more comfortable with preaching that soothes or appeases their congregation. Nevertheless, Christian discipleship is a pilgrimage. After one has been born again, or born from above, or born of the Spirit, one embarks on the path to Christian maturity. In order for Christians to grow or move toward that goal, there are several decisions to be made as one responds to the gospel in relationship to one's life, family life, stewardship, leadership in the church and community, and many other issues. Preaching must never neglect asking people to make decisions at each stage of their growth in Christian discipleship. The church in Africa will have to keep guard against making preaching another talk show. The purpose of preaching the Word to people is not entertainment; rather, it is delivering God's message in such a manner that people go home knowing and feeling that, indeed, they have been challenged by the Word for action sooner or later.

If a preacher is expecting people to make a decision on an issue that he or she is going to present in his or her message, the message will have to be clear, certainly to the congregation, but first to the preacher. He or she must answer the question: What is God's message? What is God saying to me as the preacher of that Word? Is the message to me alone, as the shepherd, or is it, indeed, God's message also to the people that I am burdened to convey? If it is God's message to God's people, what does God want the people to do? The worst thing a preacher could do is to rush to extending an invitation to the people before he or she has stated the case fully and persuasively and before he or she has given God the chance to speak to the people. Some of us preachers speak so much that, in the process of delivery of the message, we never give God the chance to speak to the people for Godself.

Obviously, we never know exactly at what point in our sermon God will speak to particular persons. At times God even speaks to God's people long before the preacher opens his or her mouth. God may have spoken to his people long before the preacher came into the picture, like Saul who met the Lord on the road to Damascus before Ananias was sent to see Saul (Acts 9:5), or Cornelius, before Peter was even sent to his house (Acts 10:3). In short, hearers of the gospel should not be put in a situation where they have to ask themselves: What are we being asked to do? What am I supposed to decide? If a preacher is going to challenge the congregation to make a decision on any issue, the preacher will have to present his or her case persuasively, then leave the rest to God.

Finally, before a preacher asks other people to make a decision on a matter of crucial importance to the lives of the members of his or her congregation, it helps if the pastor has already made a decision in that regard. It is difficult to persuade other people to travel a road that you have not traveled yourself (Josh. 24:15-16).

Preaching that is congregation-centered calls for both the intellectual and the emotional involvement of the preacher. A shepherd who knows and calls his parishioners by name (John 10:3), will begin asking himself or herself: How is *Mbuya* (grandmother) Gudza going to receive this message? How about *Sekuru* (uncle) Mbofana? Or, how are the young people going to receive this message? Can they all make the same decision from this one sermon? The beauty of preaching is that, even after wrestling with all these questions faithfully and prayerfully, God's voice will be speaking louder than that of the preacher. Yet the blessing to the preacher is that he or she wrestles with those questions anyway.

In conclusion, in this chapter we have attempted to define preaching from three points of view: the point of view of the preacher, the point of view of the message we preach, and the point of view of the congregation and the preaching situation. And we have done so by looking at a few representative definitions for each of the three categories. What this simply means to us is that preaching, like an elephant, is too immense a subject for one person to define conclusively. There is no one point of view that is more correct than all the others. In fact, there certainly can be more categories than I have suggested, just as there are still many other definitions. Blessed is the preacher who takes all these views seriously in studying preaching. The three categories discussed are very much interdependent when it comes to preaching and understanding homiletics.

Chapter 5

Using the Bible
in Preaching

Apastor told the story of his district superintendent coming to preach at his church. He had not sent advance word of the biblical text on which he was going to preach. With the two of them already in the chancel, and the congregation singing the hymn just before the Bible reading, the district superintendent whispered to the pastor to read for him Habakkuk 2:1-5. The pastor frantically searched for the book of the prophet Habakkuk. He was sure it was somewhere in the Old Testament. When the congregation reached the last stanza of the hymn, the pastor went to the district superintendent in quiet desperation and whispered to him that it would be better if the district superintendent read the scripture he wanted to use for his sermon just before he preached. Of course, the pastor did not mention that he could not find the book of Habakkuk in the Bible.

Familiarity with the Bible, the whole Bible, is essential for every preacher, and everyone who aspires to become one. The preacher should never forget that the Bible consists of sixty-six books—thirty-nine in the Old Testament and twenty-seven in the New Testament. The best way to gain familiarity with the whole Bible is to read through the entire Bible at least once every three years. A preacher who takes the reading and studying of the Bible seriously is a blessing to her own soul and also to her parishioners.

Parishioners will often ask the pastor questions on particular biblical texts they have been reading alone or discussing with fellow parishioners. Because most of the preachers in Africa serve more than one congregation, it is not possible for a pastor to be available to each congregation every Sunday, so parishioners tend to save up their questions until the pastor is available. There are also believers whose style of Bible learning is through argumentation. These kinds of communities are as old as Christianity itself, for even Paul warned Timothy about them (2 Tim. 2:14, 24). Rather than simply suggesting church members not indulge in arguments with such believers, the church in Africa can be more proactive. It can provide church members with Christian education that shares the Christian experience of God, as well as the doctrines of the church, by using the pulpit to help believers understand the Bible as the Word of God.

Defining Biblical Preaching

Preaching in Africa has been primarily biblical in approach. But what precisely does this mean? The other two principal types of preaching—doctrinal and topical preaching—are seen by many as biblical, too, and have also served the church well.

Doctrinal preaching concerns itself with the beliefs or teaching of the church. In fact, doctrinal preaching is another way of saying "teaching preaching." Its primary responsibility is to teach members church doctrines from the pulpit. People came to Jesus because they saw him as a great teacher. " 'Teacher,' he asked, 'what must I do to inherit eternal life?' " (Luke 10:25). He taught his disciples and the people concerning their faith or relationship with God in the synagogues, in their villages, by the roadside, by the seaside, and wherever he found them. In addition, he taught "as one who had authority, not as the teachers of the law" (Mark 1:22). Topics of doctrinal preaching include Christian beliefs about God, Jesus Christ, the Holy Spirit, the church, humankind, evil, temptation, sin, suffering, salvation, grace, atonement, forgiveness, the life to come. Doctrinal preaching also touches on several human and social problems, such as human rights, racism, discrimination of any nature, and poverty.

Doctrinal preaching avails opportunities for evangelistic appeal, challenging some of the deadly sins of our generation, and offering Christ at the same time. The Zimbabwe Annual Conference, probably like other African annual conferences, still holds big revival meetings during the months of August or September. At one such meeting, a preacher preached on the theme of forgiveness. In his sermon, the preacher had observed the difficulties in relationships between mothers-in-law and their daughters-in-law, as well as fathers-in-law and their sons-in-law. It was one of the most profitable and fruitful sermons of such a gathering, for many people returned home to be reconciled with their in-laws.

It is important that every preacher engage himself or herself in doctrinal preaching from time to time. If doctrinal preaching is done biblically, it will help parishioners in two ways: (1) it will help the parishioner to understand the Christian faith, and (2) it will help the parishioner to understand what the Bible teaches.

Of equal importance is *life-situation* preaching or *topical preaching* as some people call it. Again, Jesus' use of parables is a good example of how life-situation preaching can be effective. When the Pharisees and the teachers of the law muttered that Jesus welcomed and ate with the tax collectors and "sinners," Jesus told them the parables of the lost sheep, the lost coin, and the lost son (Luke 15:1-31). Jesus did not have to start with a scriptural text in order to tell those parables. Life-situation preaching can also lift up biblical themes, such as the parenthood of God, the brotherhood or sisterhood of humankind, peace and justice, reconciliation, and many other similar themes. African preachers will recall how this type of preaching was used to fight against colonialism, especially on issues of injustice, oppression, and discrimination. One only hopes and prays that the same pulpits that fearlessly waged a war against colonialism and imperialism in the 1950s and 1960s will continue fighting against today's corruption, incompetence, nepotism, tribalism, and all other social evils and hindrances to the establishment and development of just societies for the sons and daughters of Mother Africa.

One can always recognize topical preaching. As James Cox said, "A topical sermon may begin at a great distance from the Bible and be led ultimately, almost inevitably, to the scriptures."[1] That shows us that, for life-situation or topical preaching to be effective, especially in Africa, it has to relate to the message of the scripture, or witness to the Word of God as testified to in the scriptures.

91

While they often do not, doctrinal and topical preaching should use the Bible either explicitly or implicitly. For example, with a doctrinal sermon a preacher could easily use a credal statement as the basis of preaching. With a topical sermon, a preacher may announce a biblical text that he or she may never refer to again in the sermon. Nevertheless, a preacher might not fully realize his or her potential in preaching until he or she has tried the different types of preaching available. And yet, like Paul writing to the church of God in Corinth, I would wish to imitate him in saying, "And I will show you a still more excellent way" (1 Cor. 12:31 RSV) of preaching, and I mean biblical preaching.

I have been involved in the life of the church in Africa for many years now, and have attended many denominational and interdenominational meetings as well as national and international meetings. Whatever the occasion, I have listened to the preaching of the Word with great interest. My observation is that, indeed, the African church regards the Bible as central in its life, and this belief is very much reflected in its preaching, which is overwhelmingly biblical. I have also followed the preaching of some of the independent and charismatic churches in Zimbabwe, and have been equally impressed by their recognition of the centrality of the Bible in the life of their communities.

Yet how biblical is biblical preaching in our churches? The African church is indisputably a church of the Bible in terms of recognizing the Bible as having religious authority to guide and direct life, particularly on religious issues. The problem is with the African church's interpretation of the Bible, and of course one's understanding and interpretation of the Bible having a bearing on one's preaching from it.

That being the case, I would venture to offer a definition of what I believe biblical preaching is: *Biblical preaching is the proclamation of the gospel to people in relation to their contemporary life, through faithful exposition of the scriptures, as one is empowered by the Holy Spirit. Such proclamation often concludes with an invitation for a decision or action.*

There are five components to this definition. First, *biblical preaching is the proclamation of the gospel;* the good news is the message regardless of whether one is preaching from the Old Testament or from the New Testament. The good news in the

92

Bible is found in the saving acts of God that culminate in Jesus Christ. The Old Testament communities were very much aware of the tradition of good news (Isa. 52:7). The prophets always appealed to those ancient saving acts of God in the history of Israel: the call of the patriarchs (Isa. 51:1-2), the deliverance of Israel from slavery in Egypt (Hos. 11:1), both the old and the new covenants (Jer. 31:31-37), and so many other saving acts. In the New Testament, the Christ event is the saving act—the final saving act of God (Heb. 1:1-2) in whom all other saving events find their fulfillment, as the apostle Paul wrote to the brothers and sisters in Christ at Colosse:

> He is before all things, and in him all things hold together. . . . For God was pleased to have all his fullness dwell in him, and through him to reconcile to himself all things, whether things on earth or things in heaven, by making peace through his blood, shed on the cross. (Col. 1:17-20)

Second, *biblical preaching is done in relation to people in their contemporary life.* Biblical preaching recognizes that the message to be proclaimed is from God, and is directed to people, not just for the sake of proclaiming, but for a particular reason. To proclaim means to announce or declare something—a message. And that message has to be delivered to somebody. So the preacher delivers a message to a certain people, for a particular reason. Thus, biblical proclamation assumes that the preacher knows not only the message, but also the contemporary life of the hearers in order for the message to be good news.

This can present a challenge to pastors when it comes to understanding the people of today. For example, one of the problems churches in urban areas face today in Africa occurs when there is an important soccer match and the city erupts in soccer fever. People allege that a true Christian would not have a problem choosing to attend church over a Sunday soccer match. And yet perhaps there would be some justification for a church scheduling its Sunday services and activities so as not to coincide with the soccer games as a tactic to be able to continue attracting and ministering to soccer fans.

Third, *biblical preaching occurs through faithful exposition of the scriptures.* Whether the text is short or long, by "faithful

93

exposition of the scriptures" I mean searching and understanding the original message or historical meaning of the text, the theological reflection that prevailed with the author and the historical circumstances in which the text was written. A preacher would be wise to ask himself or herself the question: What was the original message in the selected text? To whom was it proclaimed? Is there any hint of how the message was received? Why did the people receive the message the way they did? The two most crucial questions for the preacher to ask are: What is the facet of the gospel that is being lifted in the selected text? What is God's message that needs to be proclaimed to the people? The preacher may do an exposition of the text, but he or she must proclaim the message that God wants proclaimed.

Fourth, *biblical preaching occurs as one is empowered by the Holy Spirit.* While it is of course important that a preacher is well prepared for the task of proclamation, mastering contemporary rhetorical skills, exegetical skills in dealing with biblical texts, as well as understanding the latest learnings in theology, there is more to preaching than acquiring skills. After Jesus had been with the Twelve during the period of his earthly ministry, he promised them, "But you will receive power when the Holy Spirit comes on you; and you will be my witnesses in Jerusalem, and in all Judea and Samaria, and to the ends of the earth" (Acts 1:8). Preaching, at its best, is God speaking to his people by the Holy Spirit, at each person's point of need and level, through a preacher who proclaims and witnesses to all that Jesus has done and continues to do for the salvation of all (Acts 5:32).

Fifth, *biblical preaching is often concluded with an invitation for a decision or action.* If God sends a messenger to proclaim his word for him, it is only proper that he expects a response. As a preacher prepares to proclaim God's message, he or she must be clear about the demands of that message so that people respond or decide accordingly. Preachers should never hesitate to extend that invitation, or to challenge or ask people or the congregation to do something, because according to Isaiah 55:10-11, God expects it.

> As the rain and the snow
> come down from heaven,
> and do not return to it

without watering the earth
and making it bud and flourish,
so that it yields seed for the sower and bread for the eater,
so is my word that goes out from my mouth:
It will not return to me empty,
but will accomplish what I desire
and achieve the purpose for which I sent it.

The Making of the Bible

It is always fascinating to review how the Bible came into existence. The entire sixty-six books of the Bible were written over a period of one thousand years, and by authors who did not know one another. Just imagine! Those authors did not even know that what they were writing would one day become sacred scriptures. It is generally understood that before the eighth century B.C., just as in Africa, Hebrew oral traditions were handed down from one generation to another by word of mouth; but, unlike Africa, various other documentary records and compositions were also available that were used by the writers who came at a later time. The Old Testament books, as they have been passed on to us, were composed during the period starting with the great prophets including Amos, Hosea, Micah, and First Isaiah, whose prophetic ministry is dated between 750 to 700 B.C. The canonization process of the Hebrew Bible, which began with the discovery of the Book of the Law in the year 621 B.C., when Josiah was king of Judah (640–609 B.C.) (2 Kings 22:8-13), eventually witnessed the authorization of the Pentateuch as sacred scriptures for the Jews around the year 400 B.C. That was followed by authorization of the Former and Later Prophets in about 200 B.C. The writings were authorized at a later period. The official closure of the Jewish Bible canonization took place in the small Palestinian town of Jamnia when the rabbinic assembly was held in A.D. 90. That must have been the scripture that Jesus of Nazareth was familiar with, as he was quoted by Luke saying, "Everything must be fulfilled that is written about me in the Law of Moses, the Prophets and the Psalms" (Luke 24:44).

It was not until toward the end of the second century that the Christian writings received general acceptance as the scriptures of the early church. For the early Christians, God had broken into the history of humankind and, unlike Yahweh with Israel in the desert, in Jesus God had taken "the very nature of a servant, being made in human likeness" (Phil. 2:7) and pitched his tent in the midst of his people (John 1:14). The apostles were eyewitnesses of the Christ event beginning with Jesus' baptism by John to the time when Jesus was taken up from them (Acts 1:22). The early Christians understood the Christ event as in accordance with the scriptures—the Hebrew Bible (1 Cor. 15:3-8). Thus they regarded the Jewish Bible as "the very words of God" (Rom. 3:2). No wonder that in the canonization process of the Christian scriptures, what we now consider the Old Testament came at the top of the list.

It was around A.D. 180 that Irenaeus, bishop of Lyons (France), wrote about the four Gospels as officially acceptable in the Christian communities. Paul's Letters, the first Christian writings to circulate among the Christian communities, were also accepted by the end of the third century. About A.D. 140, Marcion's canon, which rejected the Old Testament completely and selected only ten letters of Paul and the Gospel according to Luke as the only authentic scriptures, helped to hasten the New Testament canonization process. The Muratorian Canon, which was compiled in Rome about A.D. 170, gives the first list of the New Testament books that the church ever issued.[2] By the time the Synod of Laodicea was held in A.D. 363, all the New Testament books as we have them today, with the exception of the book of Revelation, were generally accepted. However, in the Eastern church the book of Revelation had already been accepted by that time.

It is so thrilling to note that the African church played a significant role in the canonization process of the New Testament. That is something that the church in Africa should be reminded of from time to time. We should celebrate the initiative that was taken by the African church leadership to bring about the canon of the New Testament. For example, Athanasius (A.D. 295–373), bishop of Alexandria, in his Easter pastoral letter of A.D. 367 first listed the twenty-seven books of the New Testament as we know them today. That was followed by the second church council, held at Carthage under the leadership of Augustine, bishop of Hippo, in A.D. 397, when the council officially accepted as canonical the Old Testament and the twenty-seven books of the New Testament, and sought for Rome's approval, which was eventually granted in the year A.D. 419.[3] The significance of the second church council at Carthage was that, again, it was the African church that took the initiative to bring a lasting solution to the canon of the New Testament books. Equally important was the fact that the first time the African church spoke as one church, it was on the important issue of the Bible.

The Authority of the Bible

Having observed how the Bible came into existence, a preacher would need to be clear about the authority of the Bible. In other words, where does the authority of the Bible lie? In our study about the writing and canonization of the Bible, we discovered many people belonging to different faith communities at different times over a period of more than one thousand years were involved in writing and selecting what came to be known as the canon of the Bible. The writing of the Old Testament came out of several Jewish communities, and the writing of the New Testament came out of several Jewish and Gentile Christian communities. These communities of faith decided on the books to accept as the canon of the Bible. In order to find out where the authority of the Bible lies, we shall discuss the Bible as the book of the church and the Bible as the divinely inspired word.

Who would deny that the Bible is the book of the church? It is still the only book that many of our Christian people in Africa possess, which alone is an indication of its importance. Indeed, it was the church that authorized the criteria to determine the canonicity of the Bible, namely, "orthodoxy [meaning conformity to what was called the rule of faith], apostolicity and consensus [meaning continuous acceptance and usage by the church at large] among the churches."[4]

In addition, it was the church that called forth councils to decide on the canon of the Bible. Therefore, a view that was advanced by some people was that, because it was the communities of faith that wrote and also decided on the books to accept in the Bible, it follows that the authority of the Bible lies in the church. Though this argument sounds very logical and plausible, British theologian Alan Richardson counters, "In authorizing a canon of scripture, the church recognized an authority which it did not create,"[5] namely, the saving acts of God in history.

This is a very important principle to remember if one is going to understand the Bible at all. In Shona we have a saying: *Kuzi pikata sandikuti ridza.* Literally it means if you are asked to carry a drum, it does not mean you should play the drum. You may not even know the occasion for which the drum is going to be used. Neither does a midwife who helps a woman in childbirth claim the child as hers because she was the first to hold it. That is what Richardson is saying; although the church worked vigorously to establish the canon of the Bible, that did not give the church authority over the Bible. The church did not have control over the content of the Bible. Thus the authority still lay elsewhere.

A second view is that the source and authority of the Bible is divine inspiration. This view states that the authority of the Bible lies in the fact that the Bible was inspired by God. Who would want to dispute that the Bible is all about divine inspiration? It is certainly a view commonly held throughout the world, including the African churches. It is one reinforced by Paul's letter to Timothy: "All scripture is inspired by God and profitable for teaching, for reproof, for correction, and for training in righteousness, that the man of God may be complete, equipped for every good work" (2 Tim. 3:16-17 RSV). There is no doubt that what Paul is saying to Timothy is that biblical inspiration came from God, or it originated with God himself.

Many Christians or churches would have no problem with that interpretation. The problem comes when we try to interpret how that divine inspiration was communicated to those who wrote the Bible, or how human channels were used by God to convey that divine inspiration. Often this is where the differences among churches or Christians show.

Some Christians would advocate "verbal inspiration of the Bible." This view holds that the Holy Spirit literally dictated the words of the Bible as we have it, that the human authors did nothing but record what was being dictated to them by the Holy Spirit. This interpretation would hold that the Old Testament prophets were simply mouthpieces of God, as God spoke through them, while their own intellectual faculties remained passive. It means that every word that was written in the Bible was inspired. The logical conclusion of such an interpretation of the divine inspiration of the Bible is that, because God dictated the

98

words of the Bible, therefore, there are no errors in the Bible. Others talk of this divine inspiration as "plenary inspiration," meaning "full" or "complete." This term ensures that "no part of the Bible would be omitted" with regard to inspiration and counters a view that "the inspiration of Scripture can rightly be affirmed of the whole without the parts, or of some parts without but the whole."[6] Underlying this is a theological belief that the very words of scripture were revealed and inspired by God.

It needs to be emphasized that the church has always believed in the inspiration of the Bible. Both Jews and early Christians believed that the Old Testament was "written under the special influence of the Spirit of God and that it passed, therefore, a peculiar authority for faith and patience."[7] Bruce Metzger makes a very interesting point in reminding us of the silence of the fathers on the subject of inspiration in their decision concerning the criteria that was used by the early Christians in discerning the limits of the canon. Metzger states that "nothing was said concerning inspiration."[8] He went on to say that "while the Fathers certainly agreed that the Scriptures of the Old and New Testaments were inspired, they did not seem to have regarded inspiration as the ground of the Bible's uniqueness."[9]

So, I suppose the question now is: What was that "peculiar authority" that is claimed by the Bible? Harold DeWolf suggests that

> before each part of the Bible was written there were such events in the experience of the writers as to induce the writing. Inspiration is to be attributed primarily to these experiences and only secondarily to the passages in which they found expression.[10]

In an earlier chapter we came across a quotation that supports this view. It states, "The thrust of Lutheran Confessions is toward hearing the gospel of Jesus Christ. It is the inspiration of the hearer, not primarily of the book [the Bible] that is primary."[11] In other words, divine inspiration initially comes with human encounter with God—the experience of finding oneself in the presence of God, like Moses (Exod. 3:4-6), Isaiah (Isa. 6:1-8), Paul (Acts 9:4-6), and many other biblical characters. Imagine you are Amos, looking after your father's cattle in the open fields of Africa, when suddenly, God says to you, "Go and preach to my people" (Amos 7:15). Or imagine you are the Samaritan woman, with nothing on your mind but fetching some water from a well and returning home as quickly as possible. Suddenly you become engaged in conversation with somebody of whom you begin to ask yourself, "Could this be the Christ?" (John 4:29). I would suggest it is such encounters of biblical characters with God that constituted the "peculiar authority" claimed by the Bible.

That encounter of humanity with God culminated when God, through his Son, Jesus Christ, broke into the stream of human history (John 1:14). For that reason, the "apostles who had been called to become the witnesses of Christ"[12] "constituted the earliest Christian 'canon' or measuring rod, the standard by which the authenticity of the Church's message was to be gauged, for the duration of their life time."[13] The point we are making here is that it was the events—the saving acts of God in the experiences of the biblical characters—that constituted the source or bedrock of divine inspiration. It is those acts of salvation that become the "peculiar authority" that is claimed by the Bible, because the Bible witnesses to those events—the saving events in the experiences of God's people, culminating in Jesus Christ as the final saving event.

The Bible as the Word of God

While all Christians refer to the Bible as the word of God, it is particularly important for preachers to understand exactly what they mean by that. As Dwight Stevenson says, "Before you can preach from the Bible you should settle the question of the relation of scripture and the Word of God. To be fuzzy at this point is to confuse the preaching ministry from start to finish."[14]

First, *Christ is the Word of God.* In traditional Africa the chief's word was a living word. It was active and could accomplish things without his being there. By his word, his subjects would evacuate their villages and the area under his rule to another chief's area; and again, by his word of reconciliation with the other chief, the people would return to their land and villages knowing and trusting they would be safe. The term for the word was known as *soko ramambo* (a word of the king or chief). William Barclay points out that to "the Jew a word was far more than a mere sound; it was something which had an independent existence and which actually did things."[15] He quoted Professor John Paterson, who wrote, "The spoken word to the Hebrew was fearfully alive. . . . It was a unit of energy charged with power. It flies like a bullet to its billet."[16] Stanley Schneider wrote, "The Greek term which is translated 'Word' is the term *logos*. Fundamental to the meaning of the Greek term is this—it means 'that which reveals the inmost thoughts or feelings of a being,' or the 'outward form by which inward thought is expressed.' "[17]

In the community of faith, instead of talking of the word of the king or chief, we now talk of the Word of God. The term "Word of God" has had different meanings in the communities of faith, but all refer to the various ways in which God has manifested himself to his people. While God has revealed himself in various ways, primarily the Word of God is a person, and all other forms of God's manifestation are secondary.[18] Writing his Gospel, John searched for ways in which the gospel of Jesus Christ would commend itself among the Greeks. He used the term *Logos* in referring to Christ—the Word of God—the "Word [that] became flesh" (John 1:14). It was indeed the doctrine of the Word of God that brought about the Reformation in the sixteenth century. Martin Luther held the view, "In the whole Scripture, . . . there is nothing else but Christ, either in plain words or involved words."[19] "Christ and the Word are virtually interchangeable terms for Luther."[20]

There are many African Christians, including some intellectuals who feel very strongly that African religion claimed sufficient knowledge of God for Africans not to have to approach God through Jesus, because Jesus is foreign. I suppose one would have to be in a position where one first declares or confesses that one is a traditionalist, and not necessarily a Christian. That way, one would be in a better position to compare notes with a Christian about their knowledge of God. However, the position of an African Christian is, indeed, to claim whatever knowledge African religion may claim for itself about God; but one must go beyond that now. One who confesses Christ has no choice but to look at and understand God through Christ, for in these last days, that same God that our ancestors informed us about, has also spoken to us by his Son (Heb. 1:2). As African Christians, we believe that God's revelation, starting even with our own ancestors, culminated in Jesus Christ, and that Christ has also become for us the Word of God.

Second, *the Bible is the word of God.* There are Christians who use the Bible as a fetish. They believe that the Bible is indeed the word of God, and they use it to protect themselves from physical harm. A good example is the person who suffers from bad dreams and now sleeps with a Bible under her pillow, or a soldier who keeps a Bible in his pocket for protection rather than reading. It may offer psychological reassurance, but it does not foster spiritual maturity. Traditionally, that is how people use a fetish in Africa, and it gives one false protection. I have attended and participated in worship services where exorcism of evil spirits or demons has occurred. During the service, a Bible is placed on the head of the one possessed as a way of fighting or exorcising the demon. Again, I think this is a way of using the Bible as a fetish.

Third is *the relation of* Christ and the Bible. Having established that the Word of God in the strictest theological sense refers to Christ, we must establish the relation of Christ and the Bible. Alan Richardson is helpful on this issue:

> The Bible is the authoritative historical witness to Christ. It is the testimony of those who actually saw and witnessed to the saving acts of God in history (Exod. 1:2; 12:26-27; 13:8, 14-15; Deut. 4:34-35; 6:20-23; Judg. 6:13; Ps. 44:1; 1 John 1:1-3). This is the significance both of the OT and of the NT. Both testaments witness to Christ: the OT contains the testimony of the prophets to the Christ who should come; the NT contains the witness of the apostles to the fact that Jesus of Nazareth is he.[21]

It is, therefore, important to a preacher to know that the Bible is a living testimony by communities of past generations who witnessed the saving events of God in history. The Old Testament communities witnessed to him who was yet to come; the New Testament communities witnessed to the fact that he had already come—the Christ, the Word of God. Dwight Stevenson reminds us again when he says:

> As a record, however, the Bible is not a mere court record—it is a literary record, which participates in the power of the events that it records. It has the capacity to elicit in the reader and the hearer

the kind of response that Christ first drew forth from those who knew him in the flesh. Far from being a dead letter—that is, when read in faith by the light of God's present Spirit—the Bible is living and life-giving. It surges with contemporaneity. It makes Christ contemporary. It confronts us with the living God.[22]

Having established that Christ is primarily the Word of God, and because both the Old Testament and New Testament testify to the same Christ, we could now conclude that the Bible is therefore the word of God—and yet only secondarily, or in a derivative sense. In other words, the Bible is the word of God because it is a living testimony of those who witnessed to the saving acts of Christ. When we preach, like Paul, "we preach Christ crucified" (1 Cor. 23), the Word of God. If we are faithful to biblical exposition that brings out the historical meaning of the text, then the Bible as a life-giving literary record through the participation of the power of the Holy Spirit in our preaching and the preacher together testify to Jesus Christ. We are reminded here of John quoting Jesus: "You diligently study the Scriptures because you think that by them you possess eternal life. These are the Scriptures that testify about me, yet you refuse to come to me to have life" (John 5:39-40). So just as both the Old Testament and the New Testament testify to Jesus Christ as the Word of God, faithfulness to scriptural exposition should also help us to preach Jesus Christ as the Word of God.

Various Methods of Biblical Preaching

There are several methods of approaching biblical preaching, and since it is entirely fitting that preachers choose particular ways of preaching that fit the text and situation as well as their own style, it is helpful to familiarize oneself with as many of them as possible.

Preachers will want to remind themselves that originally, the Bible was not divided into chapters and verses as we have them today. It was Stephen Langton, the archbishop of Canterbury, who first divided the books of the Bible into chapters in the thirteenth century. Thereafter, in 1560, a French printer named Robert Etienne divided the Greek New Testament into 7,959 verses. The Geneva Bible of 1560 did the same for the Old

Testament and Apocrypha. This was done in order to make it easier to study the Bible.[23]

Regardless of the method of biblical preaching that one chooses, it is important to take heed of Thomas Long's advice: "Preaching is biblical whenever the preacher allows a text from the Bible to serve as the leading force in shaping the content and purpose of the sermon."[24] We will look at four ways of approaching biblical preaching: (1) preaching on a short text, (2) preaching on a longer text, (3) preaching on biblical characters, and (4) preaching on a major biblical theme.

Preaching on a Short Text

Preaching on a short text of the Bible is probably the most common method of biblical preaching. In creating the sermon, the pastor will

1) select a text that is central to the biblical revelation,[25] or to the story or narrative, or to a larger passage of the text. This would be true with many of the Old Testament stories, stories about Jesus, encounter stories between Jesus and people, and many others. A good number of texts from the Psalms, Proverbs, and the sayings of Jesus would fall into this category very easily;

2) study the context of the chosen text in order to be faithful to the exposition of the text;

3) ask himself or herself: What is the gospel in this text that I am supposed to bring to the hearers' attention?

For example, suppose one has decided to preach on the short text, "Lord teach us to pray, just as John taught his disciples" (Luke 11:1). This verse is selected because it seems to be the central text that prompted all that surrounds it. It was a request presented to Jesus about prayer.

The surrounding longer text that seems to form a reasonably coherent unit is Luke 11:1-13. The whole text seems to be dealing with the issue of prayer.

The longer text is loaded with facets of the gospel. It begins with the Lord's Prayer itself; then the midnight friend; and finally how readily the Father is willing to give the Holy Spirit to those who ask him.

The following sermon outline suggests itself as one possibility:

"TEACH US TO PRAY"

I. John taught his disciples to pray.
II. Jesus teaches his disciples to pray.
   A. The Lord's Prayer.
   B. The midnight friend.
   C. Father willing to give the Holy Spirit.

It is important to make the following points about this sermon outline:

1) The preacher selects the central text (Luke 11:1) from the longer text (Luke 11:1-13).

2) The preacher will want to bear in mind that the Lord's Prayer is also found in Matthew 6:9-13. The preacher must answer some questions that he or she thinks members of the congregation may be raising in their minds. The two evangelists put the Lord's Prayer into two different situational contexts, but fortunately, thematically the context is prayer in both instances.

3) The sermon outline very naturally comes from the shorter text itself. While the supporting points for the second main point, "Jesus teaches his disciples," come from the rest of the larger text, the first main point, "John taught his disciples," does not have support from the text. The preacher will have to dig that information from elsewhere.

4) The preacher may want to ask himself or herself some questions: Can the longer text be dealt with adequately in one sermon? The Lord's Prayer alone is very rich. Or would the alternative approach be a sequence of sermons, possibly two to six sermons under the theme, "Teach Us to Pray"?

Preaching on a Longer Text

Longer text means a paragraph, a chapter, the whole narrative, or the whole book of the Bible. Most of the passages of the Bible would fall into this category: Old Testament stories, the parables of Jesus, healing stories, miracle stories, Pauline pastoral issues, and many others. This approach to biblical preaching would likely call for more study hours on the part of the pastor.

When preaching from a longer text, the preacher:

105

1) selects main points from the main parts or themes of the text;

2) studies the context of the text; and,

3) asks, What facets of the gospel are being lifted in the whole long text?

Let us look at another example. Suppose one wanted to preach on the topic "God Calls Moses." Already, a number of considerations begin to work in one's mind:

1) The story about the call of Moses is confined to two chapters of the book of Exodus, chapters 3 and 4. One would have to read those chapters carefully.

2) The context of those two chapters would include chapters 1 and 2; as well as the book of Genesis.

3) The text is pregnant with ideas for preaching, particularly that in Moses, the preacher is confronted by the first Hebrew prophet and liberator of his own people who were slaves, and who became a nation.

An outline of the sermon might look like this:

"GOD CALLS MOSES"

I. God is in a burning bush.
  A. God protects Moses.
    1. Moses is born (2:1-10).
    2. Moses flees to Midian (2:11-22).
  B. God has a mission for Moses (3:7-10).
    1. God remembered his covenant with Abraham (2:23-25).
    2. God calls Moses from a burning bush (3:1-4).
    3. God tells Moses who God is (3:6, 14).

II. Moses is overwhelmed.
  A. He tries to give excuses.
    1. Who was he to go to Pharaoh? (3:11).
    2. The Israelites may demand to know God's name (3:13).
    3. "I am slow of speech and tongue" (4:10).
    4. "O Lord, please send someone else to do it" (4:13).

106

    B. God provides signs for Moses.
       1. "What is that in your hand?" (4:2).
       2. "Put your hand inside your cloak" (4:6).

III. Moses accepts God's call.
    A. God gives to Moses Aaron, his brother, to help (4:14).
    B. God assures Moses of his security in Egypt (4:19).
    C. "Moses took the staff of God in his hand" (4:20).
    D. The elders of the Israelites believed the message of Moses and "they bowed down and worshiped" (4:31).

The sermon outline comes from the whole scriptural text of Exodus, chapters 3 and 4. If the preacher studies the two chapters, as well as Exodus chapters 1 and 2, in addition to being enriched by his or her knowledge of Genesis, this outline could provide a beautiful biblical sermon. And it should be a sermon with a great message, because there are so many people in our congregations who feel exactly the way Moses initially felt about the call to lead the children of Israel out of slavery. The central message is that God does great things in history through people who use what they already possess. No wonder Moses never left his staff behind anymore—in fact, it was then "the staff of God." This is simply an example of how one could handle a longer text in preparing a sermon.

One might also preach on an entire biblical book. Instead of preaching a summarizing sermon, why not do a sermon series? For example, the book of Revelation suggests itself. I have always believed that some historical circumstances in a number of African countries, like countries of other continents, provide opportunities to preach from books like Revelation. This is a book that was written when Christians were entering a period of persecution. I found Revelation speaking our language during the time when our country, Zimbabwe, was going through the war of liberation in the 1970s. That was a time when one had to be careful about with whom one talked, and even with whom one worshiped. And so people talked and prayed for "bushes," "trees that grew without attention in the mountains," and "stones exposed to all kinds of weather." That was symbolic language that parents and worshipers in church used to refer to their sons and daughters who waged the guerrilla warfare for the liberation of the country. One had to be an insider to understand what people were talking about.

That is the language of the book of Revelation, but with a profound message to the seven churches in the province of Asia, and the rest of Christendom. Preaching from the book of Revelation today in Africa could still be a blessing to the church, not only from the point of view of understanding the book, but especially for its message for many of our people who have suffered at the hands of corrupt, inefficient, selfish, and undemocratic governments. The message, "I am making everything new!" (Rev. 21:5), has remained the message of hope for many of our African people. We must continue proclaiming the gospel for a new Africa.

Preaching on Biblical Characters

Preaching on biblical characters is probably one of the favorite approaches to biblical preaching in Africa. That could be the reason why it has often been said that African preachers use the Old Testament more than the New Testament. Indeed, African preachers love to preach about Old Testament characters like Abraham, Isaac, Jacob, Moses, and many others. The advantage with those Old Testament characters is that the materials about them are readily available. In the New Testament it is a little different, in that the materials surrounding the biblical characters are more on theological concepts than they are about the characters themselves. For example, I have heard sermons about Nicodemus. Many lay preachers would put more emphasis on the fact that he went to see Jesus at night. For them that is like Christians who go to a traditional healer at night so that they are not seen by anybody. Though some similarities are plausible, the central theme of that text is actually "no one can see the kingdom of God unless he is born again" (John 3:3).

The same difficulty is prone to arise with NT characters like Cornelius. Preachers often become deluded with such characters, emphasizing the aspect of the text that has personal qualities, like "He and all his family were devout and God-fearing; he gave generously to those in need and prayed to God regularly" (Acts

10:2). As important as that aspect of Cornelius's life was, Cornelius, his family, and his neighbors were God's vehicle for a new thing that even surprised the "circumcised believers" who had accompanied Peter to Cornelius's house; and the new thing was that "the Holy Spirit came on all who heard the message" (Acts 10:44) while Peter was still preaching. These were Gentiles, and even Peter wondered if he was doing the right thing to accept the invitation. Possibly the reason why the Holy Spirit came while Peter was still preaching was that Peter, in fear of the circumcised believers, might not have taken the initiative to lay his hands on the Gentiles so that they would receive the Holy Spirit. God, himself, took the initiative to break down the barriers in his new community. Therefore, I suggest that the New Testament characters delude especially our lay preachers, who may not have had the opportunity for theological education to know how to handle them. That could be one of the explanations why some preachers, including the clergy, would more easily go to the Old Testament characters than to those of the New Testament.

There are two important principles to follow when preaching the gospel by using the biblical characters. First, a thorough study will have to be done in order to understand the historical and socioeconomic circumstances of the stories of such characters. It may happen that the materials for the sermon construction can be found in different books of the Bible, which means that one would have to take some time to gather such materials from the various books. One may also want to look at other sources beyond the Bible, such as commentaries and other books written on the biblical character in question. At least in Africa, parishioners will quickly identify with such biblical characters. It is like one is talking about his or her ancestors. In this case, they become ancestors of faith.

Second, one must always remember that even when dealing with a biblical character, the central point to be preached is the gospel—the saving acts of God that constitute the central theme of the Bible, both in the Old and New Testaments—and not simply the life of the biblical character. Therefore, the preacher would be looking at the relationship of the biblical characters with God, rather than merely the characters as individuals.

Preaching on a Great Biblical Theme

The Bible is full of thematic issues that beg to be preached, such as God, Jesus Christ, the Holy Spirit, the church, redemption, reconciliation, repentance, forgiveness, righteousness, humanity, sin, evil, and many others. We benefit greatly by being nourished through sermons that tackle some of these doctrines.

Some guiding principles for this kind of preaching are:

1) A preacher would have to plan a series of sermons from two to six weeks. One of the criticisms against thematic preaching is that a preacher cannot deal with a doctrinal theme sufficiently in one sermon. For a pastor who has concern for his congregation, and who is likely to grow too, both intellectually and spiritually, a series of sermons on thematic preaching is highly recommended.

2) It is always good for a preacher to buy a good book on the theme that he plans to preach on, or simply for the purpose of continuing one's education. The preacher would need to give himself or herself sufficient time to study books and the Bible at the same time as one prepares for such thematic preaching.

3) Such thematic preaching could also be done through expounding a series of biblical passages if properly planned. The preaching could also be approached from the doctrinal point of view, meaning one could use other church creeds, such as the Apostles' Creed.

Regardless of the approach one takes in biblical preaching, one is likely to discover that the Old Testament prophets, no matter where and how they started their preaching, would always relate their preaching to some of the major saving acts of God in the history of Israel, including the patriarchs (Isa. 51:1-2), deliverance from slavery in Egypt (Amos 3:1-2), the covenant (Jer. 31:31), and indeed many others. One would also find that true of the apostles as they preached the gospel of Jesus Christ; regardless of where one started, they often went back to the *kerygma*—the life, teachings, death on the cross, and the resurrection of Jesus Christ, as the saving events of God in the life of his Son for the salvation of humankind. James Stewart, a great preacher and author, shared a story about two people who had a conversation after a long time of separation. Stewart quotes one of the men who said, "Whatever we started off with in our conversations,

110

we soon made it across country, somehow, to Jesus of Nazareth, to His death, and His resurrection, and His indwelling." That is the principle for any preacher who is interested in biblical preaching. No matter where one begins, ultimately, it is Christ to be lifted, as he indeed promised: "But I, when I am lifted up from the earth, will draw all men to myself" (John 12:32).

Chapter 6

African Spirituality
for Preaching

A few years ago, a pastors' school meeting for the Zimbabwe Annual Conference of The United Methodist Church was held at Old Mutare Mission. Since schools were still in session, the pastors were asked to join the schoolchildren in the Sunday worship service. The preacher of that day was not the bishop of the annual conference, nor a district superintendent, nor a pastor from one of the large churches of the conference. Instead, it was a full-time local pastor, Joseph Makuto. My memories of the preaching event that day are as clear as if it happened yesterday. The preacher announced the following text for his message that morning: "In a large house there are articles not only of gold and silver, but also of wood and clay; some are for noble purposes and some for ignoble. If a man cleanses himself from the latter, he will be an instrument for noble purposes, made holy, useful to the Master and prepared to do any good work" (2 Tim. 2:20-21).

As an introduction to his message, the preacher displayed two plates that the students used for their meals in the dining room. One plate was clean and the other was dirty. He asked his listeners which one of the two plates they would prefer to be served from. Obviously, the response was unanimous and thunderous, "From the clean plate." From there on, it took the preacher only about ten minutes, if not less than that, to get his message across to the hearers—the students, teachers, and his fellow pastors—before he sat down. The job had been so well done, that it became the talk of the day. The preaching that morning had been authentic and effective, and it had results.

When we talk of the spirituality of a preacher, we are thinking of a life that has been saved from the wrath of God, a life that has been "reconciled to him through the death of his Son" (Rom. 5:10). We are thinking of a life that is in a saving relation with God, seeking not to conform any longer to the pattern of this world, but to be transformed by the renewing of the mind (Rom. 12:2). Indeed, we are thinking of the total person—the heart, the soul, and the mind—actively "being transformed into his likeness with the ever-increasing glory, which comes from the Lord, who is the Spirit" (2 Cor. 3:18). Because in this chapter we are talking of the spirituality for preaching, we think particularly of gifts of grace that manifest themselves in the life of a preacher as the marks of genuine Christian spirituality. Some of these are: (1) a compelling sense of calling; (2) a burning desire for preaching as a vocation; and (3) glowing compassion for people. We shall look at each.

Compelling Sense of Calling

Preaching that is undergirded by a compelling sense of calling often bears the following characteristics. First, the secret of Joseph Makuto, for those who had come to know him as a preacher, was that *he always preached as a witness* (1 John 1:1-3). He lifted Jesus Christ in his preaching and not himself (John 3:14-15). The listeners went away with the impression that Makuto knew from firsthand experience what he was talking about. Makuto's life and preaching often remind me of the words of Phillips Brooks, the renowned Episcopal bishop, who wrote:

"This is the message which we have heard of Him and declare unto you," says St. John in his first Epistle. "We are His witnesses of these things," says St. Peter before the Council at Jerusalem. In these two words together . . . we have the fundamental conception of the matter of all Christian preaching. It is to be a message given to us for transmission, but yet a message which we cannot transmit until it has entered into our own experience, and we can give our own testimony of its spiritual power. . . . If you and I can always carry this double consciousness, that we are messengers, and that we are witnesses, we shall have our preaching all the authority and independence of assumed truth, and yet all the appeal and convincingness of personal life.[1]

114

As preachers are called to proclaim the gospel obediently, they become the messengers or ambassadors (2 Cor. 5:20) and witnesses of Jesus Christ—witnesses who have firsthand experience of the risen Christ (Acts 1:22). That is essential for any preacher if he or she is going to engage in preaching that is witnessing at the same time. In Africa today, a preacher would find life unbearable if he or she did not believe himself or herself to have been called or appointed by God both "as a servant and a witness" (Acts 26:16) in order "to preach the gospel" (1 Cor. 1:17). People who are in other professions have so much to boast about in terms of material gain as a result of their expertise and labor in their various professions. That would not necessarily be true with the majority of preachers. A United Methodist missionary medical doctor, Samuel Gurney of the Zimbabwe Annual Conference, in giving his report to the conference once said:

> Others come up to the Conference reporting many various sheaves which they have gathered from the fields in which they have labored, but the medical missionary can give no such glowing report. He can only tell of the uprooting of noxious weeds, the blasting of rocks, and the preparation of the soil for seed. The harvest is yet all in the future; and so apparently little has been done.[2]

Dr. Gurney was an ordained minister as well as a medical doctor. His words would hold true for many other preachers. However, that does not mean that preachers work less than their counterparts. As a matter of fact, when we look at the work of the early African preachers and those early missionaries, we find that they were people who did the blasting of rocks, uprooting of noxious weeds, and preparing the soil for both political and economic change in Africa. Like the Old Testament prophets, they preached against the socially unjust systems that have prevailed on the Continent for so many centuries up to now. Consequently, many lost their lives as they sought to witness for Christ amidst hostile forces. But that has not silenced their testimony. Thank God, because the numbers of those who witness for Christ are increasing each day in Africa.

Second, Africans have always acknowledged *a sense of calling* even in their traditional life. For the sake of the church in Africa, one would even dare say that the concept of a call from God was not completely an unknown idea in African traditional religion. Among the Shona people of Zimbabwe are special people known as *svikiro* or *mhondoro,* meaning a medium. These are technical names for these people, because from time to time they become possessed by the family or clan or ethnic ancestral spirit and speak to the people on behalf of the ancestral spirits. When these people become possessed, they cannot speak until the village elders of that family, clan, or ethnic group are gathered to listen. It is the elders who determine whether the individual is the rightful medium or not, and at the same time, whether what the medium says is correct in terms of their history and customs. Therefore, the message of the medium is accepted or rejected accordingly. But such a person, be it a man or woman, who functions as a medium is highly respected in African traditional society. To a large degree, that could be one of the reasons even non-Christian people in Africa have great respect for a preacher. They believe people are called to perform special functions.

Likewise some African people with a vocation of traditional healing also believe they are called. It is not everybody who claims that, but there are some who belong to that category. In 1974, co-laborer in Christ Nhamoinesu Mumbiro and I visited an elderly and reputable *n'anga* (traditional healer, or medicine man, or herbalist) in the Honde Valley area, in the eastern region of Zimbabwe. The name of the *n'anga* was Sadanga. He was quite advanced in age when we visited with him. I would have placed him at not less than ninety years old at the time, for he claimed that when he was a young boy looking after his father's cattle he saw Cecil Rhodes. The purpose of our visit to Honde Valley was primarily to interview Uncle Sadanga (as we shall call him from now on) on the relation between traditional healing, which was his vocation, and African religion. Obviously at such an advanced age, Uncle Sadanga was no longer a practicing *n'anga*. He was already retired.

Uncle Sadanga shared with us quite at length about his life. He told us that his father was also a *n'anga,* and that at times his father took him along on trips when he was called or invited to heal people at villages near and far. Uncle Sadanga would go with his father in the forests, along the banks of rivers, and climb up mountains as they looked for medicinal herbs. He told us that

116

often his father would send him alone to look for particular medicinal herbs with which he was already familiar. As a young boy, if he found some medicinal herbs while looking after his father's cattle, Uncle Sadanga always brought such items to his father's attention. He told us that his father would take time to teach him the true medicinal herbs, and what were not would be thrown away. The impression that Mumbiro and I got from Uncle Sadanga was that he had gone through a thorough, though informal apprenticeship training program under his father.

We asked Uncle Sadanga about the role of God in traditional healing. He explained to us that he knew that there was God, and that none of the ancestors ever questioned the existence of God. He gave us the name *Nyatene*, a local personal name for God. Like all other personal names of God, in the Bantu cultures such names have no meaning. Another personal name of God in the Shona culture in Zimbabwe is *Mwari*, and it has no meaning. However, Uncle Sadanga had become well known in the area as a traditional healer, and we wanted to know how he accounted for that marvelous work. Uncle Sadanga's explanation was very simple: though he knew his herbs, it was God who did the healing. If a patient was not healed he would try again and again or even refer the patient to another traditional healer. If God did not show a way to heal the patient, there was no way a traditional healer could do anything outside God's power. We asked him, "Would you therefore talk or pray to God in order for God to show you the way?"

"No!" the answer came swiftly. He even took some time laughing at us. "How can I talk to someone that I don't know. I have never seen God in my life, and no one has. If people hear me talking to someone that I have never seen before, they would think that I am out of my mind," Uncle Sadanga explained.

We then asked Uncle Sadanga how he had inherited his father's position as a traditional healer.

"As you know very well, in our Shona culture you don't inherit anything from your father as long as he lives," Uncle Sadanga started explaining. "However, before my father died, he had instructed me not to do anything in relation to traditional healing as a vocation until he came back to me. And I did exactly what he had told me to do. After his death, I stayed for fourteen years waiting and living just like any other man with his family in the village. Several people came to be healed, and they knew I had helped some of them as I worked with my father. At that time, I could not do it. It was not until one evening, after fourteen years, that my father came to me in a dream and instructed me to carry on with the vocation of healing. Filled with joy, I picked up my tools and started telling everybody that, at last, my father had come to me and told me that everything was all right now."

Our last question to Uncle Sadanga was, "You really believe in your father, don't you?"

"Yes," he responded with a glowing face. "Look at it this way," he started explaining. "I knew my father when he was still living. Now he is with the other ancestors, and as one of the ancestors is in the realm of our next life where God is. They are the ones who can talk to God on our behalf. Therefore, I talk to my father, who talks to his own father, and I ask for their protection. We know it is because of those prayers by our ancestors that God protects the children who look after the cattle in the forests from wild animals and snakes, the women as they look for firewood in the mountains, and both men and women who travel on long journeys. They also approach God on our behalf to pray for rain and for our fields to be more productive. Everything comes from God. Therefore, I talk to my father, and my father talks to his father, and so the chain of command goes until those that we don't even know, but who know us, approach God on our behalf. If I did not trust my father, I would have broken the link, and even God would not be pleased with me. The fact that my father came to me in a dream and instructed me to carry on with his vocation was also a sign that God was pleased."

Clearly, African religion acknowledges a sense of calling from the realm of the ancestors where God dwells. Maybe it is because of the hierarchical nature of the African religion's belief in the one Supreme Being—*Musikavanhu* (Creator of people)—where a worshiper gains access to God through one's ancestors that African traditional religion has been misinterpreted as a worship of ancestors. Yet the story of Uncle Sadanga suggests that more accurately it is a belief in the dead-living or ancestral spirits who now live in the same realm with God, and that it is God who determines all that happens in human life. The ancestral spirits are not merely a passive hierarchical linkage; rather, they actively serve day and night as the intermediaries or intercessors of the living before God, and vice versa. Hence, Uncle Sadanga's patience in waiting for the word from his ancestors, a word that he believed had *Nyatene's* approval, and a word that he believed was his call to traditional healing. It did not matter that Uncle Sadanga had undergone apprenticeship training under his father while he was still living. The word still had to come from the realm where *Nyatene* resides.

Third, some of the scriptures that are so moving to one's soul are those texts that deal *with the calls and the commissioning of various leaders in the Bible.* There are so many of them, like the call of Abraham (Gen. 12:1-9); Moses (Exod. 3:1-23); Isaiah (6:1-7); Jeremiah (1:4-19); Ezekiel (2:1-10); Amos (7:10-17); Peter, Andrew, John, and James (Mark 1:16-20); Zacchaeus (Luke 19:1-10); the Samaritan woman (John 4:27-38); Paul (Acts 9:1-19); and many others. The tradition of being called for the task of prophesying or preaching has been passed on from one generation of Christians to another, and the powers to approve those who claim a call reside within the churches. It is important that Christian communities exercise such powers, for in Africa we have seen a number of wandering preachers both from within African countries themselves and from abroad who are unattached and unaccountable to a particular Christian community. The early church had a similar problem. Hence, John's letter in which he wrote, "Dear friends, do not believe every spirit, but test the spirits to see whether they are from God, because many false prophets have gone out into the world" (1 John 4:1). Nevertheless, a call to preach the gospel will always remain integral to the biblical and theological teaching of the church.

The fourth factor to remember about a calling is that it is at the same time *God's willingness to protect his servant.* I am always tickled by the story of Jonah, who is alleged to have stayed inside a fish for three days and three nights. I often wonder what really saved him? What gave him hope to see the sun once more when he called, cried, and prayed to the Lord "from the depths of the grave" (Jon. 2:2) while inside the fish that had swallowed him? Jonah must have realized that in spite of all his shortcomings and disobedience, God had called him and commissioned him to go and preach to the city of Nineveh. Jonah knew that God's mission was to be fulfilled. As a matter of fact, Jonah realized afterward that being swallowed by the fish was God's plan to save

119

him from the hostile waters of the sea; and at the same time God was remaining faithful to his covenant to Jonah. So it happened that "the LORD commanded the fish, and it vomited Jonah onto dry land" (Jon. 2:10).

Political uncertainties in several African countries have created and brought about untold suffering to many of its citizens. Some have been jailed or exiled. Others have lost whatever property they had and have become destitute. There are many others who have gone back and forth to neighboring countries as refugees. For a long time, preachers have also suffered this humiliation on the continent of Africa. Because it has frequently been the church that has come forward to provide supporting services under such turbulent situations, a preacher has often been found at the forefront of these hostile events. Several leaders, including preachers, have lost their lives. There are still many preachers of the gospel who could testify like Jonah that he or she was vomited onto dry land because God is not yet finished with Africa. God still has a mission to be fulfilled on the Continent. For those who are called, the answer does not lie in running away from Africa for some other foreign countries. As in the situation of Jonah, no matter how dark it may become or how hostile the situation may be, it is well to remember that there is a covenant of protection until God's promise for Africa is fulfilled. Let us not forget that we have been called by God.

A Burning Desire for Preaching as a Vocation

One of the issues that has often created tension in the church is about theological education for pastors. For example, who models the preachers? Is it the church from which the ministerial candidate comes? Or is it the theological institution that provides theological education? Currently, the pattern is for denominational churches to determine who becomes a candidate for theological education, with each denomination establishing its own criteria of selecting such candidates. The theological institutions, both those that are church-related and those that are departments of religious studies at universities, set up their own academic standards, which candidates from all churches or individual persons without church sponsorship must meet. At the university level, that means theological students who aspire to ordination, and students who study theology as part of their religious studies for teaching purposes study a good number of theological disciplines together. This pattern of theological education at the university level prevails throughout Africa.

Having said that, there are three points that I need to raise in relation to theological education for our young men and women who aspire to become preachers in the African church of the new millennium:

First, it is up to the church that is sending a student to study theology for ordination to see that the institution to which they send a student is staffed and equipped to provide the kind of theological education and orientation that that church wants its pastors to receive. If the churches choose to support their students in studying theology in university departments of religious studies, that is up to the churches. Regrettably, whether a student is sent to a church-related institution or to a secular university's department of religious studies, the church tends to lose control of the theological education that takes place in those institutions. At times we have seen that even where there are councils to run church-related theological institutions, the church is often not satisfied with what goes on; and the more the church may want to be involved, the more conflicts are likely to arise. This trend is likely to increase in the future.

Second, the time has come for churches that send students to theological institutions for ordination purposes to take a more active role in the theological training of their own students. The churches may not always have the influence to determine the curriculum or all the appointments at the theological institutions where pastors receive their theological education. But the church has the right to a certain kind of theological training for their students. There is no way churches can simply approve a candidate, send him or her to a theological institution (particularly at a university), and expect that student to come back as a trained minister.

The churches in Africa can take an active part in their pastors' education by:

- making sure that such students have adequate financial support;

- making sure that for married students the welfare of both the spouse and the children are taken care of;
- opening doors for such students to be involved in weekend practical ministries and intensive internships during holidays;
- arranging frequent visits from the church officials to meet and talk with their candidates;
- showing interest in their students by discussing with the dean or head of the institution the spiritual and academic development of the students;
- providing needed denominational books and other material resources for students;
- allowing some church pastors to teach courses, especially in practical theology, in such theological institutions;
- arranging for regular reports from the dean's office or the authorized official of the institution to be sent to the appropriate leaders of the churches.

Indeed, there are many other things that could be done to bring ministerial candidates for ordination closer under the auspices of the church, and especially under the wing of experienced pastors. It really does take that much of the church's attention to cultivate and provide theological training to students of theology, and surely it is worth it for the church to receive pastors or preachers with appropriate theological education and training. The churches, together with theological institutions in Africa, can easily turn out first-rate preachers of the gospel that Africa needs in the next century. Thomas Long struggles with the same issue. As he writes:

> Those who preach not only participate in the church's common ministry, they are also shaped by it. Seminaries are sometimes jokingly called "preacher factories," as if it were the task of theological schools to take people and fabricate them into ministers. This is not the case at all. Ministers are not "made" in seminaries. Seminaries train ministers; ministers are made in and through the church. People come to seminary to gain deeper knowledge of the Christian story, but they were first taught that story by the Christian people in the church.[3]

I want to think that Long and I are talking about the same thing; and if there is any difference, it might be simply a matter of semantics. If I were to use Long's own words, I would say: (a) I agree with him completely when he says that people come to seminary to gain deeper knowledge of the Christian story; and (b) I would go on to say that the terms "train" and "made" mean more or less the same thing. Therefore, I would conclude that the training of a minister begins, as Long rightly says, with the church, which first taught him or her the Christian story. Some churches would not allow their candidates to go to seminary or college until they have participated in some leadership role in the life of the church, or have passed a preaching program for lay preachers of that church. Professors and lecturers in theological institutions have already found that several students come with that kind of training anyway, and it is not always easy to change that basic training. That is a good indication that the church will have already started the "training" or "making" of its ministers. I would move on to say that, throughout the years, whether a student is in seminary or college receiving theological education, or gaining deeper knowledge of the Christian story, the church must continue with its training program through other ways as already indicated above.

Anyone who has been involved in ecumenical theological education will have noticed that, while students may come from different churches, they react differently to a number of social, moral, and other issues. They often respond according to the training they have already acquired from their individual churches, and they react according to their church's or denomination's expectations and positions. So while students come to theological seminary or college for theological education or to gain a deeper knowledge of the Christian story, I would contend that, basically, the training and making of ministers is more efficiently carried out through the church itself.

The churches must open doors for such training, just as hospitals open doors for medical students during their training. There is much that the church could learn from the way medical doctors are trained. One of the basic requirements for the training of medical doctors is to make sure a teaching hospital is made available. The churches ought similarly to be made available for the training of future pastors. Otherwise, the church in Africa will end up with pastors whose minds are full of theories and theological ideas but with little practical foundation or formation. The church may also end up with young pastors who are frustrated and hostile to the establishment, situations that in the past have led to breakaway religious movements.

The process of ministerial training and formation rightly begins before the student goes to the theological seminary or college. It should continue through seminary or college until the student graduates and, thereafter, carry on in other forms of continuing education, until the minister retires. The church must take a keen interest in the process of forming its ministers from start to finish. We can never talk meaningfully about ministerial formation and spirituality of our students in theology without their full participation in the life of the church, and vice versa. Spirituality of the students in a theological institution is often understood in the context of the church that has sent those students, which leads me to our third point: Are most of our talented graduates of our theological institutions in Africa aspiring to become pastors?

The African churches have had quite a number of pastors who have gone overseas for further studies in theology. Are most of those young men and women aspiring to return to Africa and serve as pastors? Who really inspires them to become what they should be? Or who is their model? Henry Mitchell, an African American preacher and scholar who has authored numerous books on preaching, wrote with great profoundity when he said,

> I'm the director of a center out in Los Angeles, called the Ecumenical Center for Black Church Studies. Perhaps the most important difference between us and any other institution for theological training is not so much what we study in terms of a particular group of people, but the fact that we want at every point to have professors who are also pastors. We do not want to train people who all the rest of their lives are identifying with professors and aspire to professorship, rather than identifying with pastors, aspiring to be shepherds of the flock—aspiring above all to serve laity. You can't sit where they sit if you've always got your eye off somewhere on a professorship. All too many people have been misfitted because that's really what they've been programmed for.[4]

At times, one wonders if the churches in Africa are not facing the same situation in the programs of training our pastors today? How many of our young people who are going overseas for graduate studies aspire to become better and more efficient pastors in some of our most challenging urban and mission centers? What is the image of a pastor in our African churches today? What can we do so that our pastors become the kinds of models that will attract the young pastors who come out of our theological institutions every year?

Part of resolving that problem is for the churches in Africa to take a very active role in the theological training of our men and women as discussed above. Some of our prominent and effective pastors who serve churches that can give support should provide opportunities for our theological students to work closely with them. The image of a good professor or lecturer who may have touched one's life during one's theological education is not bad; maybe the influence was because such a professor was a man or woman of the church. Therefore, he or she was able to give both theological education and training at the same time. That is commendable, and those are the people Mitchell is saying should be entrusted with theological education in our institutions. The only unfortunate thing about such good professors and lecturers is that, after a few years, all they may be able to offer with certainty will be theological education alone. They do not have a local church to offer the practical aspect of the ministry as he or she would want. It takes a willing pastor and a well-organized program of the church to offer hands-on training.

This idea of combining theological education with theological training is not necessarily a new idea at all. One of the greatest theologians of the early church, Augustine, bishop of the small town of Hippo, was the first church leader to establish a cathedral monastery "in which study and church administration were combined."[5] While other church leaders formed monasteries in the desert or mountains apart from the rest of the world, Augustine discovered the need to train monks within the context of the everyday life of the church. The day-to-day life of the church is the best context for theological training to take place. Universities originated in the cathedrals in the tenth through twelfth centuries. There some of the outstanding preachers received their theological education and training at the same time. When Paul wrote his letter to the church of the Thessalonians, sending his greetings jointly with Silas and Timothy, saying, "You became imitators of us and of the Lord"

(1 Thess. 1:6), he knew that as the leaders of the churches they had established, both he and his coworkers had a responsibility for training, especially the leadership of those churches.

Yes, preachers are born from the churches, through the ministries of those churches. The churches must continue providing theological training while theological seminaries or colleges provide theological education. The pastors of such churches that open their doors to young men and women studying theology, like Paul and his coworkers, are models for our young pastors. We hope and pray that a day will come when, in the church-related theological institutions, the churches in Africa will be able to attract and appoint the kind of personnel that will make our institutions academically and spiritually vibrant. Ideally, one is thinking of professors and lecturers who are ordained, academically and spiritually in tune with the sponsoring churches and registered students, devoted to the life of the church, and who possess substantial and good experience in the pastorate and are mature enough to give guidance and counseling to students. Such personnel need to be able to provide the kind of theological education our aspiring preachers ought to have, and the kind of persons who can work with churches in order for both theological education and training to take place simultaneously. Theological education and theological training can be most effectively carried out when theological institutions and the churches work together.

Pastors who have just started their first appointment in a parish often complain that the theology classroom is not very practical or relevant enough in preparing them for the real world the parish "and they perceive it as remote from the practice of ministry."[6]

I want to talk about the spirituality of a pastor who really inspired me. This pastor is now deceased. In the mid-1970s, I had the opportunity to spend a day with another Makuto at his fine home in the Murewa area. That was Daniel Makuto, an elder and a member of the Zimbabwe Annual Conference of The United Methodist Church, and a man I had admired for quite some time. Daniel, who at that point was a few years before retirement, had found himself a beautiful place to build his home at Nyamutumbu as he prepared for his ensuing retirement. The place had plenty of water, and he had developed a very productive vegetable garden, which included some fish ponds. As he led me around, showing me his accomplishments, Daniel shared with me his philosophy of life in general, and especially his commitment to the ministry.

His circuit was in the communal area, where churches often struggled to raise enough money to pay a pastor. Yet Daniel told me, "I will never stop preaching the gospel just because my people have failed to pay my salary." Then he stretched his hand out, pointing to his beautiful house and all the land that the chief had given to him. He regarded all that property as a gift from God. In addition to what God gave him, he was able to do all the construction with the meager salary that a pastor in a rural church would earn. He went on to make another point, as he lifted and showed me his hands. "John, God gave me these two hands not to sit on them, but to use them. I use these hands in the pulpit when preaching, and I use the same hands in my garden. At times it takes my churches two to three months before I receive a salary. But there has never been a day that passed by without my family having a meal just because my circuit was unable to pay my salary. God called me to preach the gospel, and I am so committed that I would not allow the devil with his tricks to stand in the way. The Lord has been so good to me for all these years. He blessed me and my wife. We have had children, and we have a home so that when retirement comes, at least I can have some rest."

Daniel Makuto was a God-fearing pastor and a good example of a pastor who loved and devoted his life to the task of preaching as a vocation.

When I left Daniel Makuto's place late that afternoon, I was reminded of the apostle Paul's style of ministry recorded in his letter to the church of the Thessalonians: "Surely you remember, brothers, our toil and hardship; we worked night and day in order not to be a burden to anyone while we preached the gospel of God to you" (1 Thess. 2:9). Daniel Makuto taught me a good lesson about making a commitment to preaching the gospel a life's vocation. He was in the ministry of The United Methodist Church because, through Jesus Christ, God had called him. Therefore, his message was, if God has given you brain, feet, and hands that you can use to support your family and yourself, the failure by a circuit to support a pastor should never stand in the way of preaching the gospel. Daniel Makuto proved that his philosophy worked, because he retired to a beautiful house surrounded by a beautiful garden. He retired with dignity.

We shall now look at some of the factors that call for commitment in preaching.

In committing oneself to the task of preaching one must at the same time *commit oneself to the life of prayer.* The gospel that we preach is actually "the power of God for the salvation of everyone who believes" (Rom. 1:16); and it can be preached only by the empowerment of the Holy Spirit (Acts 1:8). In teaching his disciples on perseverance in prayer, Jesus concluded by saying, "If you then, though you are evil, know how to give good gifts to your children, how much more will your Father in heaven give the Holy Spirit to those who ask him!" (Luke 11:13). The joy of the life of prayer is that when we submit our life to God, and in prayer pour out our soul to him (1 Sam. 1:15), "the Spirit himself intercedes for us with groans that words cannot express" (Rom. 8:26). That means the life of prayer can be a blessed life and great experience for any preacher. The life of prayer does not come easily to us. The best we can do, often, is to recognize the importance of prayer in the life of the Christian community as well as in our own life, and learn by doing. Oscar Cullmann, a renowned New Testament scholar, had this to say about prayer: "Praying is at the same time both the greatest gift of grace vouchsafed to us and a difficult task which has to be learned."[7] Having realized that praying is a gift, preachers need to exercise the gift continually (1 Thess. 5:17).

Every preacher will have to find time, possibly a regular time, to be in prayer. It is true we do take time for prayer at the table before we eat, or we do have family prayers; and so often a preacher may be involved in group prayers at the church, and obviously during worship services. That is all good and should be emulated, but still a preacher of the Word needs time to be alone with God in prayer. I am always intrigued by the story of Jacob when he realized it was critical to be reconciled with his brother, Esau, whom he had cheated twice in his lifetime. Jacob had taken Esau's birthright over a bowl of stew (Gen. 25:32), and had received his father's blessing by pretending to be the older son, Esau (Gen. 27:1-29). Knowing he had to settle this matter once and for all with the Lord before meeting Esau, Jacob sent ahead of him all that he possessed, including his servants, his children, and his two wives, and he remained alone while he wrestled with God (Gen. 32:22-32).

A preacher will have to find that time to be alone. The place could be at the church office, or it could be at home after everybody has gone to bed. Then he or she can "close the door and pray to your Father . . . who sees what is done in secret" (Matt. 6:6). We need time as preachers when we can both listen to and pour out our soul before the loving and forgiving God, just as Jesus so often did himself (Mark 1:35; 3:13; 6:46; 9:2; 14:35; Matt. 14:13; 14:23; 17:1; 26:39; Luke 4:42; 5:16; 6:12; 9:18; 9:28; 22:41). Jesus knew the secret of prayer; for him it was talking to his Father all the time. It was like picking up a telephone and engaging in a conversation. It takes a life of prayer to commit oneself to the ministry of preaching God's Word to God's people.

Commitment to preaching calls for *a life of study.* Many pastors are appointed to serve a congregation or congregations after three or four years of study at a theological seminary or college. For most pastors, that marks the end of their formal education. Yet the need for informal education never comes to an end in the life of a leader. It is not within the scope of this chapter to talk about the different types of informal education; rather, I am more interested in how a pastor may organize his or her own time to engage in productive reading and studying. (This subject is covered more thoroughly in chapter 9.)

It is easy for a pastor coming out of seminary or college to feel he or she has a lot to share or preach in his or her first appointment. It is always good to start that way. The task that each pastor battles day and night is to maintain that spirit and feeling of contentment. One has to continue growing. As one begins to gain understanding of pastoral experience through practical involvement, one needs to relate those experiences simultaneously to one's heart and mind. As one prays, one needs to study, too.

One needs time to read and study the Bible. As we go through seminary or college, often we receive shocking experiences one after another about how we should learn to interpret the Bible, and there often seems little time for reflection. Reflection that would enable us to discover the interrelationship of the Bible with the rest of the theological subjects must wait until we are alone in the circuit situation. When a pastor gets into that circuit, that is the time to grow, the time to study the Bible not simply for information, but for the formation of one's spiritual life and growth.[8]

It is not the reading of the Bible only that will make us grow spiritually and intellectually. We need to read and study other books, too, and not just theological ones, but books in any and all disciplines and genres.

Glowing Compassion for People

I am fascinated by African preachers who show immense compassion for their own people. I am thinking of Daniel Cocker of Liberia, Bishop Samuel Ajayi Crowther of Nigeria, and Bernard Mizeki, Johannes Chimene, and Nehemiah Machakaire of Zimbabwe. Let me elaborate on four of these African preachers.

First, Daniel Cocker was a local preacher of the Methodist Episcopal Church, who through the American settlement program of freed slaves, together with many others, settled in Liberia in 1822.[9] Among the first several African American immigrants back to Mother Africa were Methodists, and Cocker quickly organized them into a society. Thus he became the founding leader of the Methodist Episcopal Church, now The United Methodist Church in Liberia. Other sources claim that he organized the society while still on board the ship that brought them back home to Africa. One can easily note the enthusiasm that Cocker must have had as he, together with other members of the new society, brought back to their homeland the new faith in Christ, through the Methodist Episcopal Church. He started preaching, and he organized those who were already Christians and the new converts into Methodist societies. The man had great compassion for his homeland, urging his people to turn to Christ, through whom they would understand God more clearly. By the time the first missionary of the Methodist Episcopal Church, Melville Cox, was sent to Africa by the Mission Board in 1833, Daniel Cocker and his friends had already planted the seed of United Methodism on the continent.

Samuel Ajayi Crowther, bishop of Nigeria from 1864 to 1877, is another African leader who had great compassion for his own people. Crowther also was a former slave. He was fortunate though, because he was released from slavery before traveling across the Atlantic Ocean and was able to be reunited with his family in his home country of Nigeria after years of education, including theological education in Sierra Leone. He became the first African bishop of the Anglican Church on July 23, 1864.[10] He became bishop of the Niger Mission, which was hardly seven years old. His appointment was regarded as a unique experiment which "made Ajayi Crowther a romantic figure, the symbol of the Negro race, its ability to evangelize and its capability to rule."[11] One of the things that comes up again and again as one reads about the ministry of Crowther is his relentless effort to establish missions along the Niger, as well as his desire to push northward of the Niger. He saw these missions as a way of penetrating the country and villages of his people to evangelize and to establish schools. He even negotiated with the Moslem leaders, including "the Sultan of Sokoto to receive Arabic Bibles from the Church Missionary society."[12] He was a bishop and a preacher with great passion for his own people.

The third African preacher, Nehemiah Machakaire, was converted to Christianity in the Methodist Church of Zimbabwe while working in Harare at the turn of the century. Immediately following his conversion, he left Harare and his employment, and went back to his home village, Muziti, which is located in Chief Makoni's area. He started preaching the gospel to his own people. When Eddy Greeley, a missionary of the Methodist Episcopal Church, visited the village in 1907 or 1908 he found a church already in existence. The people had already built for themselves a church building that accommodated 600 to 700 people. Machakaire and his church were invited to join what is now The United Methodist Church, which they did. To this day, Muziti church has remained one of the strongest rural congregations of the Zimbabwe Annual Conference. Again, that is work that came through a person who had a glowing passion for his people.

The fourth African preacher on whom I wish to elaborate is Johannes Chimene, who was converted to Christianity while he was working in the mines of the Transvaal, South Africa. He became a Methodist while in that country. Upon returning home, unlike many other people who would return to South Africa again and again during those years, Chimene, entirely at his own initiative, started preaching among his own people with great passion. It was in June 1906 when the two missionaries of the then Methodist Episcopal Church, Robert Wodehouse and Eddy Greeley, went to what is now Masvingo Province of Zimbabwe. Thinking they were on a pioneering trip to establish a mission station of the Methodist church, they found Chimene already preaching to a large following. Invited to join the Methodist Episcopal Church with his people, Chimene accepted the invitation. Chimene had this to say at the 1908 mission conference: "I have been preaching and praying with my people all the time. They are asking for the way now. The people are calling for the teachers. They say that the darkness is great."[13] Although, by missionary comity agreements the work of the Methodist Episcopal Church was eventually surrendered to the then Dutch Reformed Church, today United Methodism is growing strong in Masvingo Province. It would be good if United Methodists would never forget that they are building on a foundation laid down by Johannes Chimene, a pioneer and compassionate preacher among his own people at the turn of the century.

Apparently, a preacher with glowing compassion for his or her people does not necessarily develop it through prayer, though prayer has something to do with it; neither do they develop it by studying the Bible, although studying the Word has something to do with it. Often, compassion for one's parishioners comes by looking them straight in the face. That often was how compassion moved Jesus—when he saw the crowds (Matt. 9:36; Mark 8:2), he would tell that they were harassed by their leaders, and that they were hungry. When he came across a person who had lost probably the only thing that made life meaningful to him or her, like a widow who had lost her only son, "his heart went out to her" (Luke 7:13), for he was moved by sorrow. As Jesus traveled and came into contact with the people whom his Father had sent him for, he was often moved with compassion, because in them he saw harassment, hunger, poverty, loneliness, emptiness, and meaninglessness of life. This was true because he saw beyond their physical, facial expressions. The *United Methodist Reporter* of August 7, 1998, featured an article entitled, "Altar Rail Supports First Steps on New Legs," with a photograph of Angolan women who had lost their legs because of land mines. Through the cooperation and ministry of The United Methodist Church in Angola, the Board of Global Ministries of The United

Methodist Church, the ministries of health and of women of the government of Angola, the International Committee of the Red Cross, and technicians from India, those women had been provided with artificial limbs. What a ministry! It shows that someone has compassion for these people.

A pastor with a glowing compassion for people is a preacher who is willing to look his or her people right in the face, and yet be able to see what is beyond the faces. It means the pastor would have to be able to perceive what people may be saying beyond their words and behavior. It takes a person who has also received and experienced the love and mercy of God to relate to one's people and parishioners so compassionately. The preaching of such a preacher will always be characterized by a message that comes through with both a ringing pain and a sense of hope through the power of the gospel. There is a great need for preachers with genuine and gracious compassion as messengers and witnesses of Jesus Christ in the pulpit today. Spirituality doesn't mean absence of sin, but devotion to a relationship with God through Christ, and a constant seeking for purification from all unrighteousness (1 John 1:9).

Chapter 7

African Characteristics of Preaching

Norwegian missionary Kare Erickson, who served in the Zimbabwe Annual Conference of The United Methodist Church for a number of years, once said that as the waters of a river flow through various regions of a country or countries, the water picks up the color of soil of a region through which the river flows. That means when Christian preaching came to Africa with missionaries, inevitably it had to pick up the African culture. In 1918, as the flu epidemic raged throughout East, Central, and Southern Africa, leaving thousands of people dead, churches that worked in those countries reported a religious awakening—a revival during which hundreds joined the church, with men and women called to serve ministries of their churches. The United Methodist Church in Zimbabwe was not an exception.

After it ended, two reports about the revival emerged, one from three missionaries who reported on "The State of the Church" to the Rhodesia Mission Conference of The Methodist Episcopal Church, as The United Methodist Church was then called. The report stated:

> Last June there came upon our native teachers a baptism—a Pentecost. We are not impressed with the gymnastics that some went through, but a large number of our men became flaming fires with a heavy burden for their people rolled upon them.[1]

There was an unofficial, independent report about the same revival from African teacher Jonathan Machiwenyika. This is what Machiwenyika wrote about the preaching of James Hatch, a

Congregational missionary from a neighboring mission, Rusitu, at Old Mutare Mission, in June 1918:

> During his preaching, some people became fainting, others crying, and others saying that they were inspired with the Holy Spirit. The church was filled with various noises from various people. That day, our Methodist Church was filled with the Holy Spirit, and it became clear in our minds that Reverend Hatch had really said what he had perceived.[2]

Both reporters acknowledge that something happened in the lives of the people during the revival. The missionaries said it was "a baptism—Pentecost"; the African teacher said, "our Methodist Church was filled with the Holy Spirit." In describing exactly what happened, the missionaries perceived it as "gymnastics." Most Africans would not have understood what was meant by the word *gymnastics.* The African teacher described the event almost the same as that of Pentecost in Acts 2:1-4. Even if Machiwenyika had understood the meaning of the word *gymnastics,* most likely he would not have perceived the event the way the missionaries did. The most important thing about our observation is that both the missionaries and the African teacher, and many living Christians who still testify about the event to this day, agreed that something unusual in the life of their church had happened, and there were tangible results of the event. The difference was only in their cultural understanding of the event.

That is precisely the reason why Christian preaching has to be understood by the nature or color of the culture of a people to whom the gospel is preached. In order to talk about preaching the gospel in Africa in the twenty-first century, we need to look at some of the characteristics of the preaching that has developed in Africa already.

Preaching by Divine Calling

The matter of call was dealt with extensively in chapter 5. We learned that many denominations in addition to independent churches in Africa uphold the idea of divine calling to the ordained ministry of the church of Jesus Christ. To appreciate the practice and impact of calling by Christ to the ministry of the church, it is helpful to study not only the scriptures but also African religion, where calling is by and through the ancestors in order to communicate to God's people. Just as in traditional African life a medium was accepted or rejected on the basis of the compliance of his or her testimony with the history and customs of the people, as judged by the elders, so in the churches divine calling is subjected to the approval of the people of God. People may not always realize it, but as one studies African religion, one cannot help thinking that the African churches are beginning to understand and appreciate their knowledge of God and God's church in the light of the wisdom of their ancestors, in addition to the scriptures, of course.

There are some practices in the church that the Africans have followed precisely, not simply because they were taught these by the missionaries, but because the new practices dovetailed beautifully with African traditional life. Thus, while the practice may ostensibly have been accepted as a new teaching from the missionaries, subconsciously the Africans accepted it because it was already their way of doing things. That might be the reason why, theologically speaking, the traditional thought forms and idioms should be brought to the surface within the life of the church in Africa. We may find that it would be more meaningful for the church to take the route of the ancestors to explain what is going on in the life of the church (for example, the call to ministry), rather than always taking the route the missionaries used. Rather than conceiving of this as replacement, I prefer to think of it as cultural enrichment and complementary theological reflection of the life of the church in Africa.

Preaching as the Central Focus in Worship

African preaching is central to worshiping; preaching brings the whole worship experience together and gives it meaning. In traditional African life in Zimbabwe—and most likely in other African countries—the message of a *svikiro* or *mhondoro* (medium) is what would be comparable to Christian preaching. It is often when there is a disaster, like a drought, an epidemic, or any other disaster of similar nature, that such a medium is consulted for a message from the ancestors. The message is meant to give meaning and direction to people so that life may continue in spite of the disaster.

When one walks into an African church to worship, there are a number of things that one is likely to see happening. It may take about fifteen to forty-five minutes for people to gather in the church, and the church building is likely to fill up to capacity. Most of the people walk to their churches, some walking long distances. Some or all church attendants dress in their church uniform. In the mainline churches, the uniform is often for men's and women's organizations; in some independent churches, all members have uniforms. Not all churches have this practice. Probably it is a practice more common in Southern Africa. Most of them would be carrying their Bibles and hymnbooks as they walk into the church building. As the worship begins, singing is often good and inspiring. Prayer is not something left to the preacher or liturgist alone; rather, there is often spontaneous praying by a number of people. Often the pastor has to limit the number of members who offer prayers. In some worship services, the whole congregation may be involved in an act of prayer, raising their hands as a sign of praising God, which was also a way Christians of the early church prayed.

There are a number of other things that take place in an African worship service—the Lord's Supper, baptism of both infants and adults, exorcism of demons, accounts of conversion experiences, testimonies, healing prayers, and many other experiences. Any number of these experiences may be present in a single worship service. Preaching in the African context must bring coherence to all these happenings. Many believers in Africa do not go to church primarily to hear a dynamic preacher, although such preachers are a blessing, but because they want to worship. An effective preacher in Africa is one who is able to understand all that is going on in the life of the congregation and prepare sermons that will bring meaning to the lives of those who have been bereaved and are mourning, those who have been bruised and hurt, those who seek healing, meaning, and genuine faith for their life. It is often preaching that enables worship to achieve that goal, and for this reason preaching is central in African Christian worship on Sundays.

Preaching as Participatory

Preaching assumes a congregation, and it is shaped by and shapes the congregation. As young children growing up in a village, we always enjoyed telling fables. As one person narrated the fable, others responded after each statement with the word *dzepfunde.* I never came to know exactly the meaning of the word. But everybody responded and it made telling one's story more interesting. If one's playmates did not respond, it meant the fable was not interesting, and no one was actually paying attention. My concern with preaching as we have learned it from Western missionary churches is that it does not emphasize preaching as participatory. My mother often told us about a cynical nonchurched person in our village who stumbled into a church worship service on Sunday afternoon. To the amusement of the cynic, he saw one person standing alone in the pulpit, talking, or as he put it, "scolding men and women" who were so cowardly that they never answered back.

The African independent churches have done a better job in promoting participatory preaching. Not only do they respond by shouting "Amen!" or "Hallelujah!" they have other ways of responding to show that they follow what the preacher is saying and that they are with him or her. Who could share a better demonstration of participatory preaching than our brothers and sisters of the African American churches in the United States. There are some churches in Africa that are moving toward the idea of participatory preaching, and we ought to commend them for that move. Often, this is what it takes to be involved in effective participatory preaching.

Preaching must be approached as a communication or conversation between the pulpit and the congregation. By a conversation, I mean the preacher must present himself or herself in the act of preaching with the understanding that the people in the pew follow every word that he or she says. Whether the preacher communicates by pronouncement or persuasion, the whole act of preaching remains a conversation. In such a conversation, the congregation should provide ongoing feedback to the preacher by saying "Amen" or "Hallelujah," nodding their heads, applauding, or shouting joyfully. To me that would be the meaning of the term *dzepfunde,* which seemed meaningless in the Shona

139

culture other than being a response to the storyteller that "we are with you. Carry on!" Some preachers raise questions from the pulpit to which they expect answers from members of the congregation. By encouraging the congregation to answer back, it gives the preacher a better opportunity to communicate the message with everybody involved.

Another way of expressing participatory preaching is through singing. African Christians love to sing, and there is no better place for them to do so than at church. Very often, as in Zimbabwe, churches have men's and women's organizations, and their members are identified by their uniforms. These organizations are arms of the church—they bring people to Christ through prayer meetings that they hold in homes on their own, without pastors involved. From time to time, they sing in their congregations, and singing is often accompanied by African instruments, including the drums. They are always a source of inspiration to the whole congregation and to the pulpit. A pastor who is able to work with these organizations is always harvesting a new crop on Sunday morning. The people love to sing when they come to church, and they should be given time to do so. Many people love to hear inspiring singing from the church choir. I have witnessed preachers who have asked either the men's or women's group to sing before the preachers delivered the message.

In addition, it is always a blessing to have a preacher in the pulpit who has the gift of singing. He or she should never hide that talent, for that is a light that one should put "on its stand, and it gives light to everyone in the house" (Matt. 5:15). I have often observed that some of the most effective preachers in the pulpit are preachers who have a talent for singing, and who use the talent wisely. In other words, after preaching for a while, especially when coming to the climax of their message, they know exactly when to present their message through a song. That is indeed a blessing to one's ministry.

A singing congregation is likewise a blessing before the Lord, and should adopt the attitude of the psalmist who cried out, "But I will sing of your strength, in the morning I will sing of your love; for you are my fortress, my refuge in times of trouble" (Ps. 59:16; see also Acts 16:25). "I will sing of the LORD's great love forever; with my mouth I will make your faithfulness known through all generations" (Ps. 89:1). We should encourage singing.

It is one way various groups of believers in the church—young and old, men and women—can feel they are participating in the propagation of the gospel of Jesus Christ.

Participatory preaching is at the same time corporate preaching. A preacher is never alone when he walks into the pulpit to preach the Word. Probably one of the most encouraging things about the *Rukwadzano rwe Vadzimai* United Methodist Church (Women's Society of Christian Service) in the Zimbabwe Annual Conference, is that early every Sunday morning these women go to their sanctuaries for prayers. One of the things they often do is pray for the preacher who will be in the pulpit that Sunday. They believe they can contribute to the effectiveness of preaching through their prayers. What a spirit of encouragement that brings to the pastor when he or she walks into that pulpit knowing that there were people in the sanctuary early in the morning praying for the message he or she is to deliver.

The author of the Letter to the Hebrews made a similar point about the collegiality of the Christian life when he wrote, "Therefore, since we are surrounded by such a great cloud of witnesses, let us throw off everything that hinders and the sin that so easily entangles, and let us run with perseverance the race marked out for us" (12:1). Some of the people who constituted "a great cloud of witnesses" that surrounded the readers of the letter were already listed in the eleventh chapter of the same letter—starting with Abel, Enoch, Noah, Abraham, and many others who came after them "who were all commended for their faith" (Heb. 11:39), together of course with the Christian generation. A preacher preaching on this text with imagination would include in the list of "such a great cloud of witnesses" all the preachers who had served that congregation. Yes, it would mean all persons commended as people of faith in the history of the church in Africa, and of that congregation since its origin. And it would be fitting for a preacher to ask how those saints—or even Jesus—would preach on a particular text.

Preaching That Uses the Bible

One of the strong characteristics of the church in Africa is the use of the Bible as the basis of preaching. As this book is devoted to this topic, I shall be brief here. However, it is true that in both the mainline and independent churches the use of the Bible in preaching is heavily emphasized. Often, preachers interpret the scriptures in such a manner that they search for the historical meaning of the scriptures. However, with some of the lay preachers or those pastors who may not have had theological education, both in mainline and independent churches, interpretive approaches are quite diverse, and some preachers would tend to go for allegorical interpretation of the scriptures.

In some of the independent churches, like the apostolic churches, there are special Bible readers in the congregation. The preacher asks one reader to read a verse or more at a time, upon which the preacher then expounds. Then another reader from another side of the congregation would read the next part, and the preacher would continue with his or her exposition of the scripture. This would go on until the intended scripture reading of the day is covered. It is a very creative and participatory way of doing preaching. Although some of the apostolic churches have church buildings now, usually they would meet in the open fields, under a tree. The preachers do not stay in the pulpit, and of course, if they are meeting in an open field, that would leave room for a preacher to get closer to the next reader of the scripture, and as the preacher does the exposition of the scriptures he or she will be moving around in the congregation. This way of preaching brings the preacher closer to the people who will be sitting on the ground, and because of the participatory approach, very few people are likely to sleep during preaching!

This use of the Bible in preaching calls for church members to bring their Bibles with them to church. Each time a new reader announces the next reading, everybody opens his or her Bible. The preacher may plan to preach the sermon from one chapter of a book of the Bible, or he or she may have passages of scripture read from different books. If this method of preaching is done properly, it is one of the best ways of teaching a congregation to understand the Bible. It encourages the congregation to read the Bible at home. The initiative for this comes mainly from the African independent churches, rather than from the mainline churches.

Preaching Without Notes

Preaching without notes has a strong tradition among African preachers. It is similar to extemporaneous preaching, which will be discussed in another chapter of this book. It is not just walking into the pulpit and waiting for the Holy Spirit to give the message. The Holy Spirit does not do what a preacher should do for himself or herself. Preaching without notes is one of the best methods of sermon delivery, because it typically engages the congregation more directly and usually assumes a more conversational style. Yet it requires careful planning, preparation, and a lot of practice.

Telling the Story

African traditional life has a rich heritage of storytelling. In telling stories, one does not need notes. What one does need to know at the outset is the purpose of telling a particular story. That would be true with the use of proverbs. The purpose is the guiding beacon that will make the story deliver the goods. A profound sense of wisdom and imagination is typical of effective storytellers.

One of the things that I enjoy when I go to my village home is to have some of the elderly village people come to our home for conversations and discussions. I often visit families in the village who have lost family members through death during our absence. We sit with them, and talk about life in general. I also like sitting with the men under a tree at funerals and listening to the discussions. As a sign of respect, a pastor is typically invited to sit inside, but in my village I always love to join my community outside as one who was born and grew up in that village. I love to attend family gatherings that are arranged to meet at home, meaning at the village where both those working in the urban areas and those in the village get together. It might be a meeting for a niece or some other relative who is marrying. I like visiting people in our village who may be enjoying their traditional drink, just to greet them and have the opportunity to listen to their discussions and inject some ideas for discussion. These are the people who are still endowed with the riches of African traditional culture. One has to talk to them to know. Most often when I am among them, I raise questions and I listen, for among these people are some great storytellers.

As preachers of the gospel in Africa, we have a great story to tell, the story of Jesus Christ. The more we can tell that story in ways that mirror traditional African ways of telling stories, the more effective we will be in reaching the people with our message. I once listened to a preacher's sermon on "The Sermon on the Mount" (Matt. 5:1). The way the preacher described the disciples climbing up the mount, where finally Jesus sat down and started teaching, sounded like they were climbing up Mount Kilimanjaro. How wonderfully inviting!

There are three areas to emphasize in "storytelling" preaching. First, every preacher knows that there is one, and only one story to tell, and that is the story of Jesus. He is the story of the church and he is the story of the preaching of the church. Second, as one reads the Bible, which is a witness to Christ, it is also telling the same story. Third, the wisdom and imagination of the preacher is, therefore, invited to perceive each passage of scripture as telling the story in its own way; and above all, to uphold preaching the story of Jesus as the story we love to tell to the world. And one can use one's imagination in telling the story without distorting the central message of the text. For example, suppose I wanted to preach on the text, "Jesus Prays in a Solitary Place" (Mark 1:35-39). With a bit of imagination one might begin:

Very early in the morning, after cocks or roosters had crowed the second time, Jesus woke up. He looked around; all his disciples were fast asleep. He knew they were very tired, for they had had a busy schedule on the previous day. In addition, this was still the beginning of their work and ministry with Jesus. However, it was time for Jesus to talk to his Father before moving on to another village. Because Jesus did not want to disturb his disciples, he tiptoed his way out of the house and disappeared into the woods. As much as he needed time to rest, for Jesus, time in a solitary place was valuable because he used such an opportunity for prayer—time to talk with his Father.

To the surprise of the disciples, when they finally got up, it was already after sunrise. They had not realized how tired they had become because of the activities of the previous day.

Even worse, to their embarrassment, there were crowds of people surrounding the house in which they had stayed for the night, who wanted to see and hear Jesus again. Others had brought disabled members of their families and relatives to be healed by Jesus. Fortunately, one of the disciples, maybe the beloved disciple, knew Jesus' favorite place for prayer. After spotting him in deep prayer, they all waited until Jesus was through with his prayer, for they did not want to disturb him. That was when Peter told him about the many people who had already gathered to wait for him in the village. However, Jesus replied, "Let us go somewhere else—to the nearby villages—so I can preach there also. That is why I have come" (Mark 1:38).

If one is going to tell the story of the gospel with imagination, it means one has to be very acquainted with the text of the scriptures from which one is preaching; and one has to be acquainted with the story of Jesus Christ, the Word that one preaches.

The Whole Gospel to the Whole Person

One of the characteristics of African preaching today is the preaching of the whole gospel to the whole person. It is the whole person who needs salvation, not just some parts of the person. We shall now look at how African preachers in the new millennium may want to view (1) the whole person; and (2) the whole gospel.

The Whole Person

First, in traditional Africa one knows another person by his or her social relations. People typically want to know what ethnic group you belong to, your clan, or your family. All this may mean much more than your first name. Only a very strange person would not be free to disclose these connections. The point is that in this society one is somebody because one belongs. Individualism has no place yet. Maybe, because of urbanization, industrialization, and globalization, individualism may gain ground in the future in Africa, just as it is already happening on the other continents. For now, many of our urban working people live two lives—one in the city and another in the village.

During the public holidays, instead of going to holiday resort areas, these urban people still go back to the villages in great numbers. Many of them continue to regard such public holidays as providing the opportunity and time to renew relationships with families and relatives, as well as the time to perform traditional family ceremonies or simply meet as families.

During the initial years of the church in Africa, that was the reason why, if a chief became a Christian, he asked missionaries to establish a church and school in his area. It would not make sense for the chief alone to become something that was different from the people. To this day, one of the reasons the church is growing so fast in Africa is partly that when one person makes the decision to be a Christian, that decision may affect a number of other family members. And the African churches understand that now; we don't need to be awakened to the fact. We are not always just dealing with an individual, or an individual church member. Be reminded once more that in Africa we belong one to another. No one ever stands alone. An individual represents a family, extended family, clan, or ethnic group. Sometimes this fact of identity is announced through the use of totems.

We need to remind ourselves that our success or failure as African nations, communities, and families, whether in the area of politics, church, or general development, depends very much on the way we view our relatedness. This relatedness can be a blessing in the hands of angels; but it can also be a curse in the hands of the devil. Nevertheless, the truth needs to be told. We belong—one to another.

Second, the African understanding of a person is of a unified whole. A person is body and spirit together. One component without the other is no person. Illness of the body is not always found in the body; it could also be because all is not well with the spirit. Often it takes a traditional healer to discover that problems. When a person is dead, his or her body is treated not just as a corpse; it is treated as if the person were still alive. In fact, many Africans believe that the spirit of the dead person attends its own burial ceremony. The spirit is present with the mourners, only at that point of one's life one has become what is known as the living-dead.

In the Shona culture of Zimbabwe, in the eastern region of the country, a special ceremony is performed a year after one's death.

There is a belief that after death, the spirit moves back and forth between the grave and one's former home. The person is still a wandering spirit until the ceremony has been performed. The ceremony is known as *chenura,* meaning purifying or relieving and preparing the deceased from the state of confusion and wandering that was caused by death, to another form and state of life that the deceased must move on to, and to be received by the ancestors in the next community of the living-dead. From that point, the deceased would be referred to as *mudzimu,* meaning corporate spirit. Again, one ceases to be perceived as an individual spirit wandering, living, and acting alone, or as an individual; rather, one becomes part of the family or clan corporate spirit—a well-settled community of the living-dead. The ultimate goal of every individual in the African community is to be accepted in the other community by the ancestral spirits so that one becomes part of the corporate spirit—*mudzimu.* In the ultimate state of life as *mudzimu,* one will have acquired power and influence. While the living can no longer have power over the living-dead, except by means of an appeasement, *mudzimu* has power and influence over the living. Therefore, it is following the ceremony that the deceased, as part of the community of the living-dead or *mudzimu,* assumes the responsibilities of looking after the living members of his or her family. Parental responsibilities do not end with death. One must continue guiding and protecting one's children—the boys as they go to look after the cattle, and the girls as they go in the forests to look for firewood (and of course, nowadays as they go to school every day). The children also need protection from any harm to their bodies, and protection from the evil spirits that seek to destroy the spirit of a child.

I would be the last one to disagree with the statement that culture is dynamic, and that maybe one cannot always look at a people by their traditional culture in an age of technological development. My plea at this stage is simply that, though Africa is a fast-changing continent, unless the gospel addresses some of the issues related to the roots of African cultures, the church remains a foreign transplantation.

This was just a glimpse of the traditional African view of the whole person. We shall now turn to the gospel that is being preached in Africa today and maybe to be preached in the new millennium.

The Whole Gospel

First, when we talk of preaching the whole gospel in Africa, we mean celebrating the good news of Jesus Christ who has visited the homes, villages, farms, mining towns, and the cities of Africa. The gospel has been heard and received as follows:

1) That "God so loved the world that he gave his one and only Son" (John 3:16), Jesus Christ, "who, being in very nature God, did not consider equality with God . . . taking the very nature of a servant, being made in human likeness" (Phil. 2:6-7). John would say that he "became flesh and made his dwelling among us" (John 1:14). But this Jesus died on the cross for our sins (1 Cor. 15:3), which made him cursed under the law (Deut. 21:23); he was buried, "but God raised him from the dead on the third day and caused him to be seen" (Acts 10:40). "Therefore, God exalted him to the highest place" (Phil. 2:9) "to the right hand of God, he has received from the Father the promised Holy Spirit and has poured out what you now see and hear" (Acts 2:33). Briefly, one would say it would be the proclamation of the *kerygma,* meaning the life, teachings, death, and the resurrection of Jesus Christ.[3]

2) As the Christian community increased in numbers, the Twelve acknowledged another important component of the gospel that had been just as important as proclamation to the life, ministry, teachings, and the spirit of Jesus of Nazareth, namely, taking care of the poor, prisoners, blind, oppressed, hungry, thirsty, strangers, naked, sick, and many others (Luke 4:18-19; Matt. 25:41-46). They realized that the Christian community had to look after the widows of the Grecian Jews just as much as they did the widows of the Hebraic Jews (Acts 6:1-7). Even more astonishing to Peter and those of the circumcised believers who had accompanied Peter to Cornelius's house, was when "the Holy Spirit had been poured out even on the Gentiles" (Acts 10:45) while Peter was still preaching. That was a dimension of the gospel that assisted the early church to begin to understand the wholeness of the gospel. They began to realize that Jesus had not preached only to the Jews, but had come into contact with people who were of non-Jewish tradition, like the Canaanite woman (Matt. 15:21-28); he stayed in Samaria for two days (John 4:40); he had healed a servant of the centurion (Matt. 8:13); and, indeed, Jesus was the light of the world (John 8:12).

148

Thus, like their Master, the Christian community had to learn to break down barriers of every kind. It was, indeed, time for the Christian community to realize and acknowledge the richness and wholeness of the gospel. Increasingly, as the church reached out into the Gentile world, especially through the ministry of Paul, Barnabas, Silas, Mark, Timothy, Titus, and many others, additional barriers that had been set up by the circumcised believers, especially on the issue of circumcision, had to be boldly challenged and broken down (Acts 15:1-35; Gal. 2:1-10).

Thus, both the "ministry of the word" and the ministry "to wait on tables" (Acts 6:2) belonged together and complemented each other. The two ministries are both reflected in the ministry, teachings, and the very sacrificial life of Jesus. The two components contribute significantly toward the realization of the unitary nature and wholeness of the gospel of Jesus Christ. At no point should the unity and wholeness of the gospel be viewed as divisible by the "different kinds of gifts" given by the same Spirit, or the "different kinds of service" or ministries to which we are called by the same Lord (1 Cor. 12:4-5). That was the way the early church understood the gospel—the very power of God in its wholeness. That is the way the gospel has been understood on the continent of Africa—the gospel that touches not only a person's spirit, but also his or her own body, including all the social dimensions. That is the whole gospel that Jesus taught and preached; that is the whole gospel that the early church preached.

Second, as African Christians, I find no reason why we should not join in affirming what the author of the Letter to the Hebrews wrote:

In the past God spoke to our forefathers through the prophets [or ancestors and mediums] at many times and in various ways, but in these last days he has spoken to us by his Son, whom he appointed heir of all things, and through whom he made the universe. (Heb. 1:1-2)

We celebrate the preaching of the gospel that has motivated not only the establishment of the numerous Christian communities throughout Africa by proclamation of the gospel, but also the social and economic development of the people of Africa

149

through the establishment of schools, hospitals and clinics, and technical schools in the areas of agriculture, carpentry, and many other areas of human development.

The African people have responded positively to the way the gospel has been proclaimed in Africa. Mistakes were made in the past and, surprisingly, they continue to be made today, though no longer by missionaries. But that happens with every organization; and maybe that is a good sign of our humanness. In spite of all that, there is a general acceptance that the church's demographic center is steadily making a shift "from the north and west to the south and east: Latin America, Africa, and Asia."[4]

In relation to our topic of preaching the whole gospel to the whole person, I would cite three reasons Christianity has gained acceptability in Africa:

1) African religion has paved the way for Christianity. When one looks at the region where Christianity is spreading and growing fast, one discovers that it is in the whole sub-Sarahan area—an area that has been predominantly under African traditional religion. The African people have always believed that there is God, that God could not be manipulated by human beings. Africans have always believed in communal life over individualistic life. They have always believed that death was not the end of life, and that family life and communal life continued in the world of the living-dead. Therefore, what Christianity brought to Africa was Christ, who enabled the African to understand God more clearly than he or she had through the mediums and the ancestors. That is one of the reasons the African has responded to the preaching of Christ so spontaneously.

2) The gospel, presented faithfully and obediently, addresses the person as a total being—body and spirit. Thus, the salvation that African Christians expect from the whole gospel is total salvation, as William Barclay has said: (a) salvation from physical illness (Matt. 9:21; Luke 8:36); (b) salvation from danger (Matt. 8:25; 14:30); (c) salvation from life's infection (Acts 2:40); (d) salvation from lostness (Matt. 18:11; Luke 19:10); (e) salvation from sin (Matt. 1:21); (f) salvation from the wrath of God (Rom. 5:9); (g) salvation which is eschatological (Rom. 13:11; 1 Cor. 5:5; 2 Tim. 4:18; 1 Pet. 1:5).[5] The message and ministry of Christ was directed to the whole person; as he said, "I have come that they may have life, and have it to the full" (John 10:10). The salvation

that people expect through the preaching of Jesus Christ is already present reality (Titus 3:5); but at the same time it is an eschatological event that is yet to come, as mentioned above. Presenting the gospel in this manner to the African who believes in life now and life after death sounds very attractive to most Africans, all the more so when one talks of the communion of saints that lives through Jesus. As he said to Martha, "I am the resurrection and the life. He who believes in me will live, even though he dies; and whoever lives and believes in me will never die" (John 11:25). The African people believe in that message of the resurrection and the life in Jesus Christ both now and here-after.

3) Finally, the African people have always believed that God can intervene where justice is expected to prevail. Because persons live in family and community relations, when injustice is done it is the whole people who grumble and suffer. Under such circumstances, the ancestral spirits and God himself all become unhappy. Thus, the God who sent Nathan to rebuke David after the latter took Uriah's wife and had Uriah killed (2 Sam. 12:1-14) is the kind of God in which the African people have always believed. The God who sent Elijah to meet Ahab about Naboth's property that had also led to Naboth's murder (1 Kings 21:1-22), was the God of justice; and that is the same God in which the African people have always believed. In spite of the hardships Africa has suffered under the partitioning, enslavement, colonization, and the exploitation of the natural resources of Africa, the African will never lose hope. Justice will have to prevail. The African finds consolation in the words of prophets like Amos: "But let justice roll on like a river, righteousness like a never-failing stream!" (5:24). Indeed, the whole gospel must also touch the whole person, including his or her social, political, and economic situation. The gospel has the power to challenge the evil spirit of corruption, greed, nepotism, and regionalism that has destroyed the promise of nationhood and freedom that political independence was expected to deliver to so many of the African countries. Thus many would agree with Paul's words: "For our struggle is not against flesh and blood, but against the rulers, against the authorities, against the powers of this dark world and against the spiritual forces of evil in the heavenly realms" (Eph. 6:12).

In the Shona culture, we have a saying: *chigunwe chimwe hachiurayi inda,* meaning, one finger cannot kill a louse. What it means for us in relation to the preaching of the gospel in Africa is that both the personal gospel and the social gospel, or the ministry "of the word" and ministry "to wait on tables" together are two fingers of the gospel that will bring about salvation to Africa. When we look at some of the men who were chosen "to wait on tables," like Stephen and Philip, we find that they did not end up just as administrators. As men who were "known to be full of the Spirit and wisdom," they equally served as preachers of the Word (Acts 7:1-53; 8:4-8, 26-40). Instead, in Caesarea where Philip resided, he became known as "Philip the evangelist" (Acts 21:8). The African church has never found it difficult to understand that the two arms of the gospel belong together, to be in a worship service on a Sunday morning and attend a political rally in the afternoon. The African preachers will have to keep vigilant against "the hired hand" (John 10:12) type of preachers who discredit the wholeness of the gospel that was preached by Jesus, the early church, and the reformers, the gospel brought by missionaries and proclaimed by the earliest African evangelists upon whose foundation we are now building.

There is a great need to develop the cultural qualities of African preaching as more and more of our young pastors pursue graduate theological studies, especially on the Continent itself. Knowing that preaching does not develop in isolation from other disciplines in the life of the church, it is important to have workshops organized either at the national or international level, inviting African scholars to present papers from their own particular disciplines, pointing out areas of cultural identity. This would include disciplines like biblical studies, African theology, African church history, and the whole field of practical theology. For a workshop of that magnitude to happen would take considerable effort even from experienced organizations like the All-Africa Conference of Churches, and faculties of theology like that of Africa University, to put together a program and find some financial support for it. It is high time for the African church to share with the rest of Christendom her experiences, discoveries, and dreams in a scholarly manner.

Chapter 8

Planning for Preaching

Every pastor will need to plan a preaching program. One of the things every pastor in a charge, circuit, or parish wants to do is to make sure that he or she knows all his or her lay preachers and that a preaching plan is made available to them so that every preaching point of the circuit has somebody assigned to it for preaching every Sunday. The pastor can help his or her lay preachers in order to strengthen the preaching ministry in the circuit or parish. However, in this chapter we are concerned about the preaching program that a pastor may come up with, either for himself as the pastor or for his or her lay preachers as well. Such planning is very important to the life of the circuit or parish.

We are reminded of Jesus soon after his baptism by John: "At once the Spirit sent him out into the desert, and he was in the desert forty days, being tempted by Satan" (Mark 1:9-13). In fact, Jesus did not go into the desert to be tempted by Satan; rather, he was planning, and in the process, Satan brought certain ideas to Jesus' mind. When Jesus left the desert after forty days, he had a plan for his ministry. Later on, we read Paul's testimony, when he wrote to the Galatians, "But when God, who set me apart from birth and called me by his grace, was pleased to reveal his Son in me so that I might preach him among the Gentiles, I did not consult any man, nor did I go up to Jerusalem to see those who were apostles before I was, but I went immediately into Arabia and later returned to Damascus" (Gal. 1:15-17). What Paul is affirming is that the mission revealed to him to preach Christ among the Gentiles was actually God's plan (Gal. 1:12; Acts 9:4-16).

153

The preaching plan that we are talking about is roughly a plan for two months, three months, six months, or even, more preferably, for the whole year. The main point is that it is important for a preacher to plan in blocks of time. One could plan for one month if that is best, considering the circumstances under which one is working. Another thing that would help toward good and effective planning is to take two to six days away from the busy pastoral duties to do nothing else but plan the sermons for a given time—coming up with a blueprint, for example, of what one is going to preach on for the next three months. One does not have to construct the sermons, but one should pick the topics as well as the texts from which the sermons are going to be preached. This would be the time to start "a nursery garden" for sermons. If those sermon seedlings are properly "nourished" they will grow to healthy sermons that will be ready for preaching in due course. We will talk a little more about the idea of "a nursery garden" in the next chapter. At the moment, suffice it to say that every pastor needs time to plan a preaching program.

Realizing that a pastor with a circuit of ten churches depends so much on the help that he or she receives from the lay preachers, one could use such a planning time as a time of retreat with the lay preachers for a day or two—for instance Saturday and a half day on Sunday. That means the pastor will have taken even more time for planning of that kind of retreat. Maybe one would lift the themes that will be important during the time for which the preaching program is being planned. Given the church year context, one could stimulate and steer discussions in such a way that the lay preachers, like their ordained counterparts, will not always fall back to their favorite texts, but venture to go for those texts that need attention, that the lectionary may call for preaching. Again, we are talking about planning for a preaching program for the pastor alone or for the lay preachers of the circuit or parish as well. For such planning to be realistic and effective, a pastor will have to pay attention to the following items: (1) church calendars, (2) important national days, (3) the church year, and (4) preaching the lectionary.

Church Calendars

United Methodists have both a conference calendar and a district calendar. The calendars consist of conference and district events that all the local churches must incorporate into their own programs. While some of the events are so flexible that they do not necessarily have to be done on the date suggested, they all are important for sustaining the life of the conference and district because of the connectional structure of The United Methodist Church. For example, the Zimbabwe Annual Conference observes the Harvest Sunday toward the end of July and throughout August as some of the congregations may so choose. There are various special Sundays that the congregations observe, including raising scholarships for high school students, Africa University Sunday, Men's Sunday, Women's Sunday, United Methodist Youth Fellowship Sunday, and many others. I would like to think that many other denominations have their own special Sundays that they observe for certain ministries and needs of their communities and society.

An effective pastor would want to take advantage of such special Sundays, regardless of what is celebrated to get the message across to his or her congregation. For example, Harvest Sunday has become so important in the life of the United Methodists that they are able to raise millions of dollars (Zimbabwean) today, having raised only $15,000 in 1975 when the program was still beginning. Today, Harvest Sunday is stretching the imagination of every pastor when it comes to planning for it, because every pastor knows what people can do if properly organized. Planning is the key to success.

It is true that the pastor is not always the one to preach when a congregation is observing Sundays of the various groups of the church, but the pastor should see to it that the worship service and the preaching plan are well planned ahead of time. Therefore, pastors should never ignore the events of the church calendar. The worst thing that can happen is for a pastor to be uninformed about a special Sunday and to plan another program on that Sunday. Planning for preaching takes into account all the special Sundays as they have been designated by the church at all the levels.

Important National Days

Every nation has its important days, including Independence days. In Zimbabwe, the days that we grew up celebrating as

155

Rhodes' and Founders' holidays have now been changed to Heroes holidays. There are many other days outside the Christian calendar that Zimbabwe observes as public holidays, including Africa Day, Defense Forces Day, and Workers' Day. In Botswana, outside the Christian calendar they observe Labor Day, Sir Seretse Khama Day, and President's Day. In Zambia, they have Youth Day, Holy Saturday, Labor Day, African Freedom Day, Heroes Day, and Independence Day. In Malawi they observe John Chilembwe Day, Labor Day, Freedom Day, Republic Day, and Mother's Day. In South Africa, they observe Human Rights Day, Family Day, Freedom Day, Workers' Day, Youth Day, National Women's Day, Day of Reconciliation, and Day of Good Will. In Swaziland they observe King's Birthday, National Flag Day, Umhlanga Reed Day, Somhlolo Day, and Incwala Day. The list could go on and on.

These are all important days, and mostly days of great political importance for the Southern African nations. This would be true of the countries in other African regions—East, West, Central, and North. It would be naive of any preacher to think that, because these days mark primarily political public holidays, therefore, Christians do not have to pay as much attention as the politicians do. My challenge to the pastors is that such national public holidays present an opportunity for great preaching. Each one of the public holidays is likely to be close to a Sunday. I would suggest that the Sunday before the public holiday would be the best time to bring a message that has relevance to some of the great national public holidays. Suppose one were to take a holiday like Independence Day or Heroes Day. Many of our African pastors know that several political leaders died through brutal treatment at the hands of the colonial governments. Many died in prison, others in detention, and many more died by drowning when they were thrown into the ocean tied up in bags from which they could not free themselves. There were those who were brutally beaten and tortured to death. Those people included lawyers, medical doctors, ministers of religion, teachers, and other professionals. Many more in the villages were massacred, and their homes, food, and other belongings burned. Some people were buried alive with their hands and feet fettered. Pastors will recall the young freedom fighters who died because their clothes, food, and drinking water had been poisoned with biological and chemical weapons that we did not know about or understand. Some of those people who became victims of such torture and death were leaders in our own communities. They were so many, and most of them were dedicated to the cause of freedom—the political freedom that we enjoy today, and that future generations will enjoy. What an opportunity to bring a message of dedication and to build confidence in the people themselves. It is an opportunity to deliver a message of assurance in our faith and hope that we must always proclaim, "Your God reigns!" (Isa. 52:7).

In 1974, after political leaders were released from prison, the churches of Harare, Zimbabwe, quickly organized a worship service of thanksgiving for the release of these brothers and sisters. Some of them had been in prison or detention for ten years. Many of those politicians attended the worship service.

The day is fresh in my memory, partly because I was asked to deliver the message. My topic was "Waiting for the New Day." The text was Acts 27:29: "Fearing that we might run on the rocks, they let down four anchors from the stern and prayed for day to come" (NRSV). The thrust of the message of the sermon that Sunday afternoon was that, in spite of all the hardships and the subsequent shipwreck that Paul and the people he sailed with suffered on the long journey to Rome, God's angel had appeared, and stood beside Paul telling him, "Do not be afraid, Paul. You must stand trial before Caesar; and God has graciously given you the lives of all who sail with you" (Acts 27:24). After the shipwreck, Paul encouraged those who sailed with him not only to keep their hope alive, but "just before dawn" he also urged them to eat. Paul took some bread and gave thanks to God right in front of them all. "Then he broke it and began to eat. They were all encouraged and ate some food themselves" (Acts 27:35-36). The purpose of the message to our political leaders and all who attended the worship service was to reinforce their courage in the protracted political struggle by pointing out that, just as Paul had been assured to reach Rome in order to stand trial before Caesar's throne—an appeal that Paul had made in Jerusalem during his trial before Festus—so were the political leaders and the congregation assured of God's justice, and that a day was yet to come when political independence and freedom for all the people would inevitably be a reality. The message of that sermon was very clear that afternoon. Just as the captain of the wrecked ship finally "dropped four anchors from the stern and prayed for daylight," so it was going to be with those who had highjacked the political powers of the country. They would come to their senses, and fearing even more bloodshed in the land than there was already, "they dropped four anchors from the stern and prayed for a new day."

At the end of the worship service, the spokesman of the political leaders thanked the preacher for the message of hope and direction. One of them said that he could not quite find positive meaning of their release from detention until he attended the worship service that afternoon. Thank God, they left that worship service with their daunted spirits lifted once more, and some sense of hope in what they aspired to accomplish. Indeed, their release then might have been another attempt to look for possible options of resolving the political impasse that had crippled the country for a long time. Independence for Zimbabwe was still six years away. Sure enough, it happened that, when we eventually celebrated Zimbabwe's Independence on April 18, 1980, some of the political leaders who had worshiped with us on the Sunday we had recognized their political efforts and activities as they had struggled to liberate the country politically, emerged as cabinet ministers of a new government for a new nation, and above all "for the new day" that we all had waited for, for a long time.

A number of the public holidays are days that bring our nations together. While some of them are not worthy of the pastor's attention because they are declared holidays for purely political reasons, the majority of them, if properly observed, can become a blessing to the church. We should never lose sight of the fact that God acts in history, and we know that a number of leaders survived colonial brutality through divine protection. We also know very well that hundreds of thousands of African people have suffered under postindependence leadership, leadership that has caused so much havoc, also causing so many to die and many others to be exiled. However, that should not silence prophetic preaching in Africa. Africa is turning around today, and many people would like to hear the message of hope again. Many politicians and other people in high positions are prepared to listen to the word of truth. The important days that we observe as public holidays can serve as a blessing, not only to the congregations, but to some of our politicians who need encouragement.

In addition to lifting up important national days, the pastor can also lift up for prayer international disasters. At the time of this writing, two massive bombs exploded outside the United States embassies in Kenya and Tanzania (August 7, 1998) claiming the lives of many people, with many more being injured. The pastor can always show solidarity with the victims and the bereaved families by sharing the information as an announcement to the congregation, and lifting up events pertaining to such tragedies and disasters in the pastoral prayer. However, there could also be either communal or national disasters affecting members of the congregation in such a manner that the event begs for guidance from God's Word. It is at such moments that the Spirit of God may need an obedient and flexible servant who would respond by proclaiming the word of comfort and God's peace in the midst of disaster and death.

The Church Year

Every pastor will have to learn sooner or later that one has to plan preaching within the context of the church year. "The Church year is centered upon the reality of salvation history, focused in the Christ-event."[1] Reginald Fuller says that there actually existed only two main celebrations in the earliest church: "the Lord's Day, or Sunday, and the period of the *Pentecoste*."[2] While the observance of the weekly Easter in commemoration of the resurrection of the Lord started in the days of the apostles (Acts 20:7), the special Easter festival was not celebrated until after the New Testament times. We have already made reference to Justinus, commonly known as Justin Martyr, who wrote about the worship of early Christians, saying, "We hold our common assembly on the day of the sun, because it is the first day, on which God put to flight darkness and chaos [lit. matter] and made the world."[3]

Thus, early Christians' observance of the Lord's Day was based on more than one reason: (1) Old Testament scriptures point out, it was on "the first day" of creation (Gen. 1:5) that God caused light to come into existence (Gen. 1:3). (2) The concept of the light as symbolism of Christ found support from the Old

Testament and the emerging New Testament teaching. Malachi 4:2 became a favorite quotation: "But for you who revere my name, the sun of righteousness will rise with healing in its wings." The righteous and devout Simeon, who lived long enough to participate in the presentation of Jesus at the temple, referred to Jesus as "a light for revelation to the Gentiles" (Luke 2:32). One could easily say that the quotation had reference to Isaiah's message about the servant of the Lord: "I will also make you a light for the Gentiles, that you may bring my salvation to the ends of the earth" (Isa. 49:6). (3) Finally, Justinus wrote, "and on the same day [the sun's day or first day] Jesus Christ our savior rose from the dead."[4]

That having been said, we need to take another step in order to make the connection. We need to bring up the important factor of Mithraism—a cult of the sun. Oscar Cullmann points out that the Roman emperors, one after another, built temples for this sun god, who was to be worshiped by all subjects of the Roman Empire. At the same time, the Christians regarded the "light" or "sun" as a symbol of Christ. Ambrose made reference to this fact, when he said, "Christ is our new sun!"[5] Consequently, Constantine, who was seeking peace and harmony in his empire, decided to combine the worship of the sun god with that of Christ. Because the sun was one of the Christian symbols, in A.D. 321 Constantine introduced the Christian Lord's Day, Sunday, as an officially authorized weekly day of rest. At the same time, it coincided with a day dedicated to the sun god of the Roman world. It was that action by Constantine that gave Sunday legal status as the day of rest.

Another important day on the church calendar is Christmas Day. Many of our believers still believe that Jesus of Nazareth was actually born on December 25. In fact, it was not until the fourth century that the celebration of the birth of Christ on December 25 began to spread from Rome to the other churches. It is most probably correct to say that the majority of the early Christians did not know anything about the festival of Christmas. On December 20, 386, John Chrysostom of Antioch, in teaching his congregation about the new Christmas festival, urged them to attend worship on December 25, so that they would celebrate Christ's birth, "that mother of all festivals" he called it. In the most persuasive manner, he appealed to his congregation that every person should "leave his home, that we may behold our Lord lying in the manger, wrapped in swaddling clothes, a wonderful and awe-inspiring sight."[6] It was by that Christmas message that Chrysostom was able to persuade his congregation to accept the Roman custom of celebrating Christ's birth on December 25.[7] With the observance of a number of Christian festivals, emerged the church year or calendar that provided "a kind of a hermeneutical framework in which the liturgical use of Scripture is set."[8] Hence, the following seven seasons that constitute the church year: Advent, Christmastide, Epiphany, Lent, Eastertide, Pentecost, and Kingdomtide.

Preaching the Lectionary

The word *lectionary* may be new to some of the readers of this book, especially some of our lay preachers. We may want to start with the word *lectern,* which is the reading desk or stand in a church from which the Bible is read. It is often placed in the opposite position from the pulpit. The word *lection* means a reading, or a part of scripture that may have been chosen for reading at a public worship service. That means a reader would read a lection from the lectern instead of reading it from the pulpit. Therefore, a dictionary definition of the word *lectionary* is "a sequence or list of lections to be read in church services during the year."[9] The selection of these lections is not done at random; it is arranged in a very orderly manner so that the result is a meaningful lectionary. Each denomination tends to have its own lectionary, although lately we have also seen some ecumenical lectionaries. There are some churches that do not use lectionaries at all, because they believe that the use of a lectionary limits the freedom of the preacher to select his or her text as the Spirit may lead.

It is generally accepted that the origin of the lectionary in Christian worship came from Judaism, where reading of the law and prophets was observed in the synagogue (Luke 4:16-21; Acts 13:13-15).[10] We also noted that in the early church, two Old Testament lessons were read in a worship service, to be followed by memoirs of the apostles—a reading from the Pauline Letters or the Acts of the Apostles. And as a deacon or presbyter moved toward the lectern to read a lesson from the Gospel, the congre-

161

gation rose to its feet. With time, some changes have been made, and in The United Methodist Church today, the lectionary consists of three readings: a reading from the Old Testament, a reading from the Epistles, and a reading from the Gospels. The preacher can choose one of the three, or use all three for the focus of the sermon.

There are a number of advantages to using a lectionary for preachers and churches in general. First, preaching from the lectionary assures a pastor of a preaching program or plan. When a pastor has to decide what he or she is going to preach on a weekly basis without using the lectionary, he or she is bound to encounter a dry spell. Using the lectionary guides the pastor on what to preach on successive Sundays.

Second, preaching from the lectionary is advantageous to pastors in that, while each pastor tends to have favorite biblical books and texts that one is likely to use all time, the lectionary is prepared in such a manner that it covers all the books of the Bible. For a pastor who takes sermon preparation seriously, preaching from the lectionary is bound to help one develop not only intellectually in the study of the Bible, but also spiritually.

Third, as more and more pastors use church lectionaries, some of them are ecumenically prepared. Increasingly, there will be seminars and workshops when pastors from various denominations are likely to use some of these preaching materials together. Again, this will enable development of a pastor's intellectual life as well as appreciation for the spiritual life.

Finally, at times it gives a congregation a sense of belonging when they know the lectionary followed in preaching is actually the same lectionary followed by other member congregations of the same denomination. At the same time, it can also be a blessing in the spirit of cooperation to the churches, when they know that the lectionary followed in their pulpit is an ecumenical one.

The Church Year

We now turn to the seven seasons of the Christian or church year. Here, I shall attempt to recapture and refocus what I have written in *Biblical Proclamation for Africa Today*. As already indicated, the lectionary presents salvation history as clearly focused in the Christ-event: his life, ministry, teaching, death on the cross, burial, resurrection, ascension, exaltation, sending of the Holy Spirit, and second coming—all in seven seasons of the Christian year. It is important that one understand the biblical and theological rationale of each one of the seasons.

Advent Season

The word *advent* means a coming or arrival. For Christians, the season of Advent marks the coming of Jesus. Since the middle of the sixth century, the season of Advent marked the beginning of the church year, and is, therefore, the first season of the Christian calendar. The season of Advent consists of four Sundays immediately preceding Christmas.

The focus of Advent is "last things."[11] This is a very topical subject; there is no way we can push it aside. Whether in the highly industrialized countries or the developing countries, there are always questions about the end of the world, and we have apocalyptic passages that beg for preaching (Matt. 10:23; Mark 9:1; 13:26-31); or those who want to know about the life of believers after death (Luke 23:43; Rom. 8:11; 1 Thess. 5:10); or many who are always asking to know what will happen on that day concerning the general resurrection (1 Cor. 15:12-58; 1 Thess. 4:13–5:24); and several others are curious about what will happen on the last judgment day (Matt. 25:31-46). We have several Old Testament Advent lections as well, Isaiah 2:1-5 and Psalm 122:1-9, to mention two.

The theme concerning the last things is a favorite topic of a number of African churches, especially with some of the independent churches. Several of the mainline churches tend to be silent on this important theme. There is always a feeling that we do not want to drive people away. If we preach the lectionary faithfully, there is no way we can avoid preaching Christ and the end of time.

Christmastide

We have already covered that the feast of Christmas came into the picture at a later date. We understand that it was first testified at Rome in the year A.D. 336.[12] This is a very brief season, consisting of one or two Sundays, but with a message of great impact. Its message is basically that of the Incarnation: after sending all the prophets, God has now sent his one and only Son (John 3:16). His Son has come to dwell among us, and we have beheld his glory (John 1:14); "Who, being in very nature God, did not consider equality with God" (Phil. 2:6); and Immanuel— "God with us" (Matt. 1:23; see also Isa. 7:14).

In the African tradition, especially among the Shona people whom I know fairly well, when a son of your chief visits a village or a community in his father's area, it is just like the visit of the chief himself. The son would be treated just like the father. His visit would be regarded as the visit of the father, the chief. Thus, we can say with Paul "that God was reconciling the world to himself in Christ, not counting men's sins against them" (2 Cor. 5:19). Again, traditionally speaking, it was *Musikavanhu* (the Creator of people) who came among us through his Son. That is the message of the season of Christmastide.

Epiphany

The word *epiphany* means appearance or manifestation. The feast originated in the East[13] and refers to appearances or manifestations of God. The author of the letter to the Hebrews was right when he wrote, "In the past God spoke to our forefathers through the prophets at many times and in various ways, but in these last days he has spoken to us by his Son" (Heb. 1:2). The author of the letter was talking of the various appearances or manifestations of God. Then came other manifestations: the visit of the Magi (Matt. 2:1-12); the baptism of Jesus (Mark 1:11); Jesus' changing water into wine (John 2:9). The Epiphany season usually takes four to nine Sundays, beginning with January 6, which is celebrated as the Day of Epiphany.

I am always fascinated by the African traditional conception of heaven, which is not so much a place "up there"; rather, it is a state of life, or life in another realm where both God and the living-dead reside. The living-dead have many advantages. They have access to *Musikavanhu* (the Creator of people); they see the living, and are always trying to help the living. Thus, when we talk of people's relation with God, it is not so much of God's transcendence (meaning distance), as it is his immanence (meaning presence) with his people. Therefore, it is from that realm of another state of life that God steps into history—our own state of life, to manifest himself. If we listen and look around us carefully as people who are willing to be instruments, we will see that God is always manifesting himself through Christ as he has taught us, and is always talking to us through the Holy Spirit. "This is my Son, whom I love; with him I am well pleased. Listen to him!" (Matt. 17:5). That is the message of Epiphany.

Lenten Season

The season of Lent is a forty-day period that always begins with Ash Wednesday and ends with Easter Sunday. This is a time for fasting and penitence—a time for self-examination (Ps. 51:1-19; Joel 2:12-18; 1 John 1:5-10). It is time to overcome temptations and hardships (Matt. 4:1-11; Mark 1:9-12). It is also a time to understand God's acts in the history of humankind (Exod. 17:3-7; Rom. 5:1-8; John 4:5-42). This is the time when the preaching of the gospel needs to highlight the God who comes face-to-face with his people—the God who gave his own Son to die for the still ungodly (Rom. 5:8). The message of the Lenten season focuses on God's grace to demonstrate God's unmerited and boundless love and mercy for the purpose of justifying humankind, so that they receive the forgiveness of sins, become filled with peace and joy, and eventually become an acceptable offering to God "sanctified by the Holy Spirit" (Rom. 15:16).

The concept of fasting was observed in the Shona traditional life. There is even a saying, which goes like this: *Kuda chimwe kuramba chimwe.* That means, if you want something that is so precious, you may have to give up something. There are times in life when you cannot have all that you want. Thus, in traditional practical life, as the Shona went out hunting for a week or two weeks, or even for a day, all who went on the hunting safari were expected to abstain from sex the night before the expedition. Women joined in those expeditions too, especially if the expeditions were for a longer time. Often, when they went into an area where they wanted to hunt, before they started, the hunters prayed. In the prayer, which was always led by one person, the hunters asked ancestors to take care of them, especially with the young ones. Then, a statement was made that if anyone had been involved in sex the night before the hunting safari, he or she was not supposed to be there. So quietly one would depart, if there was such a case.

The point we are making is that the Lenten season gives the pastor an opportunity to concentrate on that aspect of the gospel where people have to do some self-examination, and even fast for something that they believe is so precious for their own or other people's lives. There is an assurance from Jesus for this single-mindedness of the Christian life. He said to his disciples, "No one who has left home or brothers or sisters or mother or father or children or fields for me and the gospel will fail to receive a hundred times as much in this present age (homes, brothers, sisters, mothers, children and fields—and with them, persecutions) and in the age to come, eternal life" (Mark 10:29-30). So Lent is a time to focus on the life in Christ as we know and experience it now, and eternal life in Christ as we intend living it forever.

Eastertide

"Easter is the Christian festival celebrating the resurrection of Jesus Christ. Eastertide includes Easter Sunday and six other Sundays, with the last being designated Ascension Sunday."[14] The weekly observance of Sunday as the first day of the week, in commemoration of the resurrection of Jesus by his disciples, started during the time of the apostles (Acts 20:7). The special Easter festival was not celebrated until after the New Testament times. The whole story of Christ's passion and resurrection composes what one might call the "heartbeat" of the gospel. In the passion story we are taken to the very depths of love for others: "No one has greater love than this, to lay down one's life for one's friends" (John 15:13 NRSV). In the resurrection story, we are taken to the very heights of victory: "Death has been swallowed up in victory. Where, O death is your victory? Where, O death is your sting?" (1 Cor. 15:54-55). The resurrection of Jesus from the dead meant the end of terrorism of humankind by death: "For as in Adam all die, so in Christ all will be made alive" (1 Cor. 15:22). The doctrine of the resurrection of Jesus Christ from the dead is a unique claim, first by Jesus himself before and after his death, and later by the eyewitnesses to his appearance after death, as Peter said, "by us who ate and drank with him after he rose from the dead" (Acts 10:41); or Paul, who claimed, after asking, "Who are you, Lord?" the Lord's answer came swiftly, "I am Jesus, whom you are persecuting" (Acts 9:5). Paul gives us a record of more eyewitnesses to the appearances of Jesus after his resurrection (1 Cor. 15:3-8).

Although Africans believed in life after death, there is nothing as exciting and sounding as such good news as the resurrection of Jesus Christ, and the hope that it gives to all believers. As Paul said, "He died for us so that, whether we are awake or asleep, we may live together with him" (1 Thess. 5:10). There are many scriptures that deal with the message of the resurrection, both of Jesus and of humankind, including all the Gospels, Paul's Letters, the Pastoral and General Letters.

Pentecost

The season of Pentecost is one of the favorite seasons of preachers in Africa. They love to preach about the coming and the power of the Holy Spirit. The season of Pentecost consists of eleven to sixteen Sundays, beginning with Pentecost Sunday. Originally, Pentecost had been the Jewish harvest festival—the Feast of Weeks. As it lost its meaning, it came to symbolize the giving of the Torah at Mount Sinai. For Christians, Pentecost came to mean the birth of the church (Acts 2:1-4). The promise of power that Jesus had made to his disciples had been fulfilled (Acts 1:8); and the prophecy of Joel, when he talked of the day of the Lord, had also been fulfilled (Joel 2:28-32). The message of Pentecost is that, just as God came into the world by his Son, God continues his work in the world through the Holy Spirit. Again, it was through the promise of Jesus, "I will ask the Father, and he will give you another Counselor to be with you forever—the Spirit of truth" (John 14:16). Jesus went on to say, "But the Counselor, the Holy Spirit, whom the Father will send in my name, will teach you all things and will remind you of everything I have said to you" (John 14:26). Indeed, the message is clear; the ascension and exaltation of Jesus at the right hand of God meant that in no way would his disciples and the ensuing church at any moment have to claim the status of orphans in the world (John 14:18); the Holy Spirit has come to stay. What a message!

As much as the theme of the Holy Spirit is popular in Africa, it is also a theme open to misunderstanding and abuse. The churches in Africa will have to remain open and sensitive to the guidance of the Spirit, to share with one another the accomplishments of the Holy Spirit and, especially, to discern what the Spirit is saying to the African church today. One of the unfortunate things that has always happened is listening to what the Spirit is saying to Africa with the Western ear and with the Western way of interpretation. Among all other themes about the Holy Spirit, every preacher in Africa ought to have time to deal with themes that include the gifts of the spirit or spiritual gifts (1 Cor. 12:1-31; Eph. 4:1-16) and the fruit of the Spirit (Gal. 5:22-26), for the sake of the unity of the African church.

Kingdomtide

"Kingdomtide (known as Ordinary Time in many church traditions) consists of 13 to 14 Sundays. It is one of the longest seasons, running through the months of September, October and November."[15] The message of this season is proclamation and the announcement that "Your God reigns!" (Isa. 52:7). The Synoptic Gospels are goldmines for the theme "the kingdom of God" (Mark 1:15; Luke 10:9) for example, or "the kingdom of heaven" (Matt. 5:3). Again, there are several parables that deal with the kingdom, including the parable of the sower (Matt. 13:1-23), the parable of the weeds (Matt. 13:24-30), and many others. "The Synoptic Gospels viewed the ministry of Jesus as the fulfillment of the kingdom: for example, Jesus and Beelzebub (Matt. 12:22-28; Mark 3:22-27); Jesus and John the Baptist (Matt. 10:1-10; Luke 7:18-28); Jesus in the synagogue at Nazareth (Luke 4:18-21), and many other scriptures."[16] The Old Testament is rich on the theme of the kingdom of God, for example, the prophets Isaiah (49:6) and Amos (5:23-24).

A creative preacher in Africa would look at the earthly kingdoms that exist today in many countries of Africa. There are chiefs or kings who, in spite of the limitation to their powers by government, are very concerned with the welfare of their people. Often, the chiefs want to make sure people have the basic needs of life—a place to build a house, a field to grow food, water for the people, schools for children, hospitals and clinics for their communities, and peace in the area. Indeed, a chief who has his people at heart, even nowadays would approach government in order to talk about some of these things. But as we have already said, the power of the chiefs is limited, and has always been limited. The good news about the message of the Kingdomtide is that, unlike the earthly kings or chiefs whose powers are limited, and who come and go, Jesus Christ who is exalted and now sits at the right hand of God, reigns now (Isa. 52:7); "For he must reign until he has put all his enemies under his feet. The last enemy to be destroyed is death" (1 Cor. 15:25-26). What a message of hope for a people who have suffered death day and night!

This kind of planning for preaching would give the pastor an opportunity to think through the options he or she has, both with the short and long seasons of the Christian year. Some of the possibilities are to plan for a series of sermons based on one subject, such as "the Holy Spirit" or "the Kingdom of God," as well as many other topics that one might want to think about. Such series of sermons could be preached from various books of the Bible. The general focus on such sermons would be for people to understand the Christian doctrine, but each sermon would have its unique purpose. Another option would be to plan for a sequence of sermons that comes from one book of the Bible, touching several topics. The focus on such preaching would be for people to understand the whole book as a unit. There are several options: the parables of Jesus, the healing stories of Jesus, the sayings of Jesus, personalities of the Bible, and many others. However, the point we are making in this chapter is that these things need to be planned. No one can make the congregation understand the importance for the minister to take some days off to plan his or her preaching except the minister himself or herself, especially when the congregation sees the results of such efforts.

Chapter 9

Preparing Sermons
for Preaching

I will never forget my first sermon as a seminary student. I had prepared my sermon for days, if not weeks. My fellow seminarians were people who had served as teachers and local preachers. They had the experience of preaching, which I admired each time one of them was in the pulpit. I came straight from high school, with very little experience of leadership, let alone the experience of standing in front of people and delivering a sermon. I was scared as I realized my turn would soon come. When the day came, I seemed quite prepared, and started my sermon very well. What surprised me was that, after about five minutes into the delivery of my sermon, I was already down to my conclusion. The sermon that I had on paper could have taken me twenty to thirty minutes of preaching; but alas, it was all condensed into five minutes. Needless to say, my classmates were shocked. What they could not understand was that I was more shocked about the experience than they were. I could not understand how my sermon had suddenly evaporated.

That painful experience made me ask myself several questions: What is a sermon? Is it what one prepares on paper? Or is it what one delivers from the pulpit? Or is it what the congregation hears from the pulpit? What about parts of the sermon that remain in your heart, that are never delivered, partly because of pulpit-fright or because one simply forgets? Or is a sermon more than all this?

Defining the Sermon

A sermon, by its nature of being in the category of communication, is dynamic and not easy to define. As much as we may want to come up with a satisfactory definition, maybe it is even more important to be aware of the mammoth task of what it means to work on sermons for Sunday after Sunday.

Martin Luther King Jr. wrote, "A sermon is not an essay to be read, but a discourse [communication by talking] to be heard . . . a sermon is directed toward the listening ear rather than the reading eye."[1] This view is supported by Fred Craddock, who pointed out that, even if some sermons are written and read aloud or published, "none of this alters the fact that preaching is by its nature an acoustical event, having its home in orality not textuality."[2] So we could safely say that a sermon is oral communication of the gospel in the context of worship.

One could also look at the sermon and message as two distinct but inseparable components of preaching. Thus, I would say a sermon is like the packaging of a gift, but not the gift itself. A sermon communicates the message—the message that Jeremiah experienced when he said, "But if I say, 'I will not mention him or speak any more in his name,' his word is in my heart like a fire, a fire shut up in my bones. I am weary of holding it in; indeed, I cannot" (Jer. 20:9). That experience of Jeremiah with the word in his heart, like fire shut up in his bones, was a message for which Jeremiah had to prepare a sermon. Perhaps every preacher has had the experience of Jeremiah—the experience of a burning message within, and at times even the sermon seems to be a hindrance in expressing what one might be going through. However, there has to be a sermon if one is still to speak "in his name."

In Zimbabwe, as in some of the other African countries, women carry babies on their backs. They have a cloth specially designed to carry and protect the baby from the sun. This cloth is a *mbereko*. When a young mother with her baby visits a neighbor's home, often after sitting down she will bring the baby from her back to her lap with its *mbereko*. This is one way young mothers show off their babies. The women in the group want to take turns holding the baby. With Shona women, the baby must always be handed over to the other person with the *mbereko* covering the baby. Naturally, the *mbereko* and other clothes of the baby can always be adjusted depending on weather, that is, if it is a cold or hot day. That way, one would then be able to enjoy holding and playing with the baby.

As I thought about the relationship of the sermon and the message, I could not help thinking that, like *mbereko,* a sermon is a cultural packaging that serves a very special purpose of communicating God's Word through the preacher to the people. Like *mbereko*, the sermon is strained by the cultural context—the length of time that one preaches, the manner in which the sermon is delivered, and in many other ways. And now comes a great horror! One could very easily preach a wonderful sermon, but it could be only packaging. That is like *mbereko* without the baby. If the Word has been correctly heard by the preacher, the Word will give form to the sermon as the preacher wrestles with the Word. Unfortunately, this will not mean less work to the preacher in the preparation of the sermon. It might even mean more time than usual. In the strictest theological sense, the preacher mounts the pulpit to preach neither the Bible nor a sermon; rather, he or she mounts the pulpit to preach the Word.

There are two definitions of the word "sermon" that I need to share with readers. One is given by Ilion Jones, who quotes J. R. P. Sclater's definition: "A sermon is 'truth strained through a human personality.' "[3] What this definition is saying to us is that, just as the sermon and message are distinct but inseparable components of preaching, so are a sermon and a personality. It is always good to work hard on a personality. It is always good to work hard on sermons; however, one wonders if we put just as much time in preparing the preacher's personality, so as to allow truth to flow freely to the parishioners. More often, it is not the sermons that people dislike, it is the personality through whom such sermons come forth.

That leads us to the second definition, given by John Knox, who also supports this view: "The sermon is an offering to God—or rather, it is the preacher offering himself to God—and the preparation is a disciplined act of devotion."[4] Knox goes on to say, "But the aim of preparation is clear; it is a man prepared, not a sermon prepared."[5] A preacher may graduate from the best theological seminary or college in the land; but a preacher will never graduate from preparing himself or herself to remain credible in the pulpit. One must continuously present oneself "to God as one approved, a workman [or workwoman] who does not need to be ashamed and who correctly handles the word of truth" (2 Tim. 2:15). This is just a caution, that as the preacher works hard on sermon preparations, he or she needs just as much if not more preparation as a person before God.

The Sermon Idea

Henry Davis describes a sermon idea as the "central thought" or "central idea" or "generative idea" or "germ idea" of a sermon.[6] The moment one is aware of the fact that one is going to preach, the next question in mind is, What am I going to preach about? You may be lucky and be given a theme for the occasion. But you may be told, "You can choose what to talk about." Whatever topic a preacher selects, one would still want to narrow it down to a size manageable for the occasion and time given. The beginning of every sermon is a sermon idea.

Davis goes on to give five characteristics of a sermon idea as follows: it has an expanding force; it must be true to the gospel; it must be loaded with realities of human interests; it must be one of the many facets of the gospel of Christ; and it must be narrow enough to be sharp.[7] Every preacher should find the above guidelines or characteristics of a sermon idea helpful in sermon preparation.

However, there is another characteristic of a sermon idea that a preacher needs to be aware of: a sermon idea that comes to a preacher already as a message, but in the form of a problem, yet begging to be preached. Often this happens through the pastor's involvement in the lives of the parishioners—for example, a sudden and tragic death that might have occurred in one of the families. The message that may come to the pastor through the tragic event or crisis may not necessarily be the message to be preached at that occasion. But it captures the imagination of the pastor so much that, as he or she ponders the circumstances surrounding it, the pastor may feel a burden to preach a particular message to the congregation. The pressure to do so increases if the experience or circumstance is one common to several people. The pastor may begin to search for a genuine comforting word from the Lord. When that kind of situation arises, the preacher will not be simply looking for one of the many facets of the gospel of Christ; he or she will be waiting for a healing message from the Lord for hurting people with grieving hearts.

Most often, when people are surrounded by the forces of death, they may want to turn to the pastor for answers, more or less like King Zedekiah, demanding of Jeremiah, "Is there any word from the LORD?" (Jer. 37:17). Like the prophet Habakkuk, a preacher occasionally will have to learn his or her task the hard way, "I will stand at my watch and station myself on the ramparts; I will look to see what he will say to me, and what answer I am to give to this complaint" (Hab. 2:1). That is how some of the germ ideas of a sermon come to us—painfully, but demanding us to preach them.

Where do the sermon ideas come from? We may need to say at the outset that many sermon ideas come to a preacher, but most of them do not come ready or mature for preaching. Therefore, every preacher may want to develop what we will call, for lack of a better term, a "preaching garden nursery" for sermon ideas. This nursery would simply require a notebook and a pen with you all the time or within easy access. A preacher who is preaching-minded is "like a tree planted by streams of water" (Ps. 1:3), and because his or her delight is in the law of the Lord, upon which he or she meditates day and night (Ps. 1:2), one is bound to have more sermon germ ideas than one is able to preach. Keeping a notebook and pen handy is helpful, because sermon ideas come in strange ways and at very odd times. It is a practice that I have found helpful for the past thirty-one years, even during the time when I did not have regular preaching appointments in the life of the church. It becomes a treasure that a preacher cherishes and revisits from time to time, even if one may not always choose ideas for preaching from that nursery when one needs a sermon. One's preaching garden nursery can often either yield a sermon idea or enrich one's current thinking. Some of the sermon ideas need more time to ripen or mature through further study and reading of the Bible or other books on the topic. Hence the idea of a "preaching garden nursery."

First, when a preacher is engaged in his or her regular Bible reading and study, or listening to someone else preaching, or doing Bible study with parishioners, a text may jump out, begging to be preached. It is always up to the preacher to judge whether the idea is mature enough for preaching or not. If not, the only way that idea is going to be ready is through meditation and more reading and studying on the subject. But it may also mean that the right occasion for preaching the idea has not yet come. Hence, the preaching garden nursery. Some sermon ideas may demand more than one preaching to the same congregation in order for the purpose of the sermon idea to be realized and appreciated more adequately.

Second, a sermon idea may come to a preacher as a major theme. Thus, a preacher may want to preach a series of sermons on a theme from one book, or one that will touch a number of books of the Bible. For example, one could preach a series of sermons from the book of Acts on the theme of the Holy Spirit: The Promise for Power as Witnesses for Jesus (1:8); The Holy Spirit Comes at Pentecost (2:1-12); The Assurance of God's Presence and Power (4:31); The Holy Spirit and Those Chosen as God's Instrument (9:15-19); The Holy Spirit and Racial Barriers in the Church (10:1-48); The Holy Spirit and Mission (13:1-3); The Holy Spirit—the Promise to All Believers (19:1-7); and many other scriptural passages from the same book. The topics above have been picked off the cuff, but they are topics that could be narrowed and sharpened for preaching; they are topics that would represent roughly the central thoughts of the sermons to be developed.

Third, sermon ideas come from reading good books. A preacher will need to be in the habit of regularly buying good books to read. They could be books on theology, history or another social science subject, or science. Novels and biographies of heads of states and other outstanding political and civic leaders make interesting reading. Suppose one is planning to preach a series of sermons on a biblical theme. One may want to look for a good book on the subject. A pastor cannot grow intellectually by continuously going back to the notes and books he or she used in theological seminary. Everything is changing, and changing fast. In the Shona culture we have a saying: *Matakadya kare haanyararidzi mwana.* That means, if a baby is crying today because of hunger, a parent cannot stop it from crying because it was fed yesterday. Reading good books on the latest issues in theology, biblical interpretation, and international affairs is likely to help create a flourishing preaching garden nursery of sermon ideas.

Fourth, sermon ideas come from the pastoral contacts and relationships that a pastor develops. As a pastor meets the parishioners at the baptism of their children, confirmation classes, weddings, Bible studies, home visitations, hospital visitations, counseling sessions, burials, and other pastoral calls, those experiences may give the pastor some insight about his or her parishioners—their joy, happiness, and peace, and the growth of faith in their own lives and families. He or she would also have some knowledge concerning the struggles, the fear and anxiety, as well as the grief that other families may be suffering. Once in a while mutual conversation between the pastor and members of a family has a way of bringing certain issues of concern to the surface. Again, here lies an opportunity to realize the importance of the preaching garden nursery for sermon ideas.

Fifth, sermon ideas can come from the news media. Reading the newspapers, listening to the radio, even watching television provides fresh information about both national and global issues. The world is always undergoing traumatic experiences: international and regional wars, people displaced from their homeland, natural disasters. Thefts, drug trafficking, bank robberies, and many other activities of yet more serious corruption are reported on the front pages of our national papers and on radio and television. The media provide the preacher with information concerning the state of our national and international affairs, which constitutes the socioeconomic and religious context in which the gospel is to be preached. Reading accounts of the world in which we live inspires the preacher to begin entertaining sermon ideas on the Bible's relevancy to today's problems.

Sixth, sermon ideas could easily come from the parishioners themselves if they are asked what aspects of the gospel or issues would they welcome being addressed from the pulpit? They are the ones who are visited and bombarded with literature from different religious movements, like the Jehovah's Witnesses. They are the ones who are told not to go to traditional healers when illness is in the family. They are the ones who know what unemployment means when both a father and a mother lose their jobs. They are the ones who see the corruption of our social systems—like bribery, which seems to be a growing trend for people to use to get and achieve what they want in life. This is another way to add to our preaching garden nursery.

There are very few pastors in Africa who serve only one congregation. Most pastors serve more than two congregations, and they might insist that the idea of parishioners suggesting ideas for sermons would not work. But I contend that if a pastor were to announce to a congregation in advance that the message he or she was going to deliver on some future Sunday was from one of their own suggestions, it would generate a significant amount of interest and expectation. It would, indeed, give a congregation a feeling of achievement and belonging if they learn of their contribution toward the preaching program of their pastor in their charge or parish. However, we ought to emphasize that the pastor does not prepare to preach a sermon idea from the parishioners simply because they proposed the idea. It is the pastor who should be in a better position than anyone else to know whether to feed his or her people on milk or solid food (1 Cor. 3:2; Heb. 5:12). Granted, at times we do not know for sure until we have tried what some of our parishioners may be saying to us.

Seventh, sermon ideas come from the use of a church lectionary. Since we have already covered this subject in chapter 8, suffice it to say that the use of a church lectionary in preaching can be a blessing to a pastor. It gives the pastor more time to plan his or her sermons, but only if one begins studying the texts on which one is going to preach well in advance so that the message to be delivered begins to take its natural course in the mind and life of the preacher.

The Sermon Outline

The sermon outline often has two functions for the preacher. The first function is to guide the preacher to proceed with the sermon in a logical and systematic way from one point to another. If the outline is properly organized, the movement of the sermon will sound very natural; it will also enable the congregation to follow the movement of the sermon. The second function of the sermon outline is to enable the message of the sermon to flow smoothly and naturally. In quoting Halford Luccock, Thomas Long writes, "The power of a sermon . . . lies in its structure, not in its decoration."[8] Long goes on to say, "Form is as important to the flow and direction of a sermon as are the banks of a river to the movement of its currents."[9]

Preachers often talk about three parts to a sermon, but I would like us to consider five components to a sermon. Each component equally deserves the attention of the preacher in order for the sermon to become what it should be. They are: (1) the subject, or topic, or theme; (2) the introduction; (3) the sermon body; (4) the conclusion; and (5) the use of illustrations. As one collects the materials for sermon construction, one must begin to think in terms of these five components of a sermon and file the materials before one actually sits down to design the sermon.

The Subject

A preacher may find a sermon idea from reading the Bible. He or she may even have a text from the Bible for the sermon. Still, one has to decide on the subject of the sermon. Equally, a preacher may find a sermon idea from a life situation, a pastoral situation, or a counseling session. Again, one still needs to decide what the subject of the sermon is going to be. The point at this stage of preparation is that the sermon idea should be turned into the subject of the sermon. To come up with a subject for preaching means that one has already made the decision, and the subject should not be too broad or too narrow. For example, if a preacher tried to preach a sermon on a topic like "The Love of God," chances are that the subject would be too broad for one sermon. One could preach on the subject, but homiletically one could probably not do justice to the topic in one sermon. On the other hand, a preacher may want to preach a sermon on "Doubting Thomas" only to find that even after reading all passages of scripture where Thomas is mentioned, the supporting materials to the topic are limited. However, such sermon ideas one may want to keep in the preaching garden nursery until the subject is mature enough for preaching.

At the same time, it is important to come up with a topic that is appealing, a topic that captures the imagination of the hearers for a sermon. In the 1940s, Newell Booth, then a United Methodist missionary bishop for Africa, wrote a book, *The Cross Over Africa,* in which he described the Africans as "A Stranger in His Own Land." It was the type of preaching topic that begins to participate in the preaching of the sermon long before the preacher opens his or her mouth. It was a germ idea, or topic

179

packed with truth about the African situation. A reader of such a topic can more or less follow the message of the sermon, long before it is preached. That shows the power of a good sermon topic. Further, hearers of sermon topics like "A Stranger in His Own Land" may forget the details of the sermon long after the sermon has been preached. But for anyone who knows what Africa has gone through since the partitioning of the Continent by outside powers, slave trade, colonialism, and neo-colonialism—where Africans may have political power, but with someone else still in control of the economic power—the topic "A Stranger in His Own Land" captures the imagination.

The Introduction

The purpose of an introduction in preaching is twofold: (1) *To gain the attention of the congregation.* Unlike other audiences who may be preoccupied with talking, and with their minds still on different subjects discussed before the speaker, in a worship situation the problem of gaining the attention of the people may not be a serious one. Often, the problem is to run the risk of losing the interest and high sense of expectation that may have already been there. Nevertheless, the preacher must still plan to capture the attention of the congregation for the moment they might have been waiting for. (2) *To introduce the subject of the sermon.* Once the subject of the sermon has been announced, there is an expectation on the part of the hearers. It is in the introduction that the hearers first learn about what is coming in the rest of the sermon. Often, a good introduction has one or more of the following characteristics: forcefulness, brevity, pertinence, interest, timeliness, and worthiness. Let us look at each characteristic.

First, a forceful beginning in a sermon is important. At times, it happens that a preacher speaks to a church where he is not well known, and people will be wondering what he or she looks like and sounds like.[10] It is often those opening statements of a preacher that makes him or her capture or lose the attention of the congregation. Every preacher ought to remember that, when it comes to preaching, one does not have to be "ashamed of the gospel, because it is the power of God for the salvation of everyone who believes" (Rom. 1:16). Because the gospel by its very nature is power, we do not need to apologize. We must speak as people who witness with power (Acts 1:8).

A second characteristic of a good introduction is brevity. Some of the short African folktales and proverbial sayings would serve this purpose very well. It happens that many of our people who live in the urban areas these days are losing touch with some of those stories and proverbs. For example, everyone wants to be rich quickly, and we all know the kind of problems that come along with such efforts. In Shona we have a saying, *Kumhanya sandikusvika,* which means "running or rushing does not necessarily mean reaching your destination." Such statements, packed with wisdom and culture, can serve as a wonderful introduction to a sermon.

Third, a good introduction is pertinent or relevant. It must take people from the familiar experiences into the sermon itself, without losing them. The preacher has to make sure that there is a relationship between the introduction and the main body of the sermon. Quite often in Africa, one hears an introductory story that is about Europe, the United Kingdom, or the United States, maybe because the preacher has been to those countries. The story may sound amusing to the congregation, but questions still have to be asked: Does the story introduce the subject? Do the people in the congregation find it easy to identify themselves with the story? Too many introductory stories are given in sermons as if the preacher simply wanted people to know where one has been lately. Let us keep our introductions relevant.

Fourth, a good introduction should be interesting in order to capture the attention of the congregation. People tend to think that preachers are too serious all the time. Some people think preaching is just a godly talk that is dry and makes one fall asleep. On the other hand, an interesting introduction does not necessarily mean a chain of jokes, nor should one lose sight of the subject to be introduced merely for an interesting story. We are not in the business of entertainment. The rule is that whatever introduction one chooses for a sermon, it should be interesting enough to capture the attention of the congregation, as well as introduce the subject.

Fifth, a good introduction is timely. In other words, a preacher should, by all means, use the latest materials to introduce a sermon. However, one could use a historical event that took place

181

twenty or more years ago if it illustrates what is happening today in the lives of people. Timeliness of events also means preachers should keep pace with the latest developments, including the interests and concerns of young people.

Sixth, a good introduction should be worthy of sharing with the congregation. Occasionally, we have heard stories told as sermon introductions that were embarrassing. Avoid using that kind of story, or mentioning some names that you, as the preacher, will regret. The last thing that a preacher would want to happen is to have one's parishioners ask one another after a worship service whether what the preacher said was worthy of saying.

One of the most important tasks in preparing a sermon is to establish the purpose of a sermon. In other words, why does the preacher want to preach that sermon? What has he or she heard from the Lord? If one were preaching from the text "For the Son of Man came to seek and to save what was lost" (Luke 19:10), one would assume that the purpose of the sermon was evangelistic. If a sermon was preached from Acts 13:1-3, one would assume that the purpose was to make people mission-conscious. A preacher needs to establish the purpose for every sermon that he or she preaches.

The Sermon Body

One of the things that every preacher must learn in sermon preparation is never to prepare a sermon on a sermon idea that he or she does not understand sufficiently. There are seven points that one should consider when drafting the outline of the main body of a sermon: unity, order, simplicity, proportion, imagination, movement, and climax.

First, the outline of a sermon should have unity. Unity means that the points should come from the subject of the sermon. The unity of the sermon outline, or main points of a sermon, should be seen as naturally as the unity of a tree's main branches and the trunk of a tree.

Second, a sermon outline should have order. That means the preacher should determine which point comes first, which one comes next, and which one should be the final point. Again, taking the analogy of a tree, let's assume we were asked to draw a mango tree as our subject. The presentation would lose its order if one started with the branches, then trunk, then fruit and leaves. The parts of the mango tree in their natural order would be the trunk, the branches, the leaves, and the fruit. To speak about the tree with an outline that has an order, one would have to start either with the trunk or the fruit, depending on what one would consider as the climax in that presentation. Since a mango tree is a fruit tree, I am persuaded to think that the mango fruit would be the climax of the presentation; therefore, my natural order of presentation would be trunk, branches, leaves, and fruit.

Third, an outline should have simplicity. Jesus of Nazareth is probably the greatest teacher who ever lived. If one is to understand the effectiveness of Jesus' preaching and teaching, one has to look at the sayings, parables, and miracles of Jesus. All these works that are attributed to Jesus strike us to this day because of their simplicity. It was partly because of this simplicity that, even decades after his death, those who wrote about the Christ of their faith could still recover some of his actual words. That was part of the reason his hearers were amazed with his teaching— they could understand everything that he said. Hence, the acclamation, "He taught them as one who had authority" (Mark 1:22). A simple sermon outline is easy for a preacher to use as a guide, and it will be a blessing to the congregation as they can easily follow the movement of the sermon and the message.

Fourth, an outline should have proportion. One should look at a sermon as an oral discourse in development. Assume one wanted to prepare an eight-page single-spaced sermon. If it were a three-point sermon, maybe the introduction would take half a page. The first point, which presents the problem of the sermon subject, would take one and a half pages. The second point which usually deals with alternative solutions to the problem, may take two and a half pages. The final point, which would give the gospel answer together with the conclusion and present the final appeal, could take three and a half pages. That is what is meant by a sermon that has proportion to its structure or outline.

Fifth, a good sermon outline is full of imagination. Preaching is an art—an art that thrives on glowing imagination, without which one cannot preach. It is, indeed, only a pastor with imagination who can preach. When a young pastor moves to his first appointment, in a circuit or in a parish, he or she has dreams and can easily imagine things happening. However, the pastoral imagination that we are talking about is imagination that is firmly entrenched in God's mission—the mission that causes unrest in the life of both the pastor and the congregation. It is like the imagination of the psalmist who lifts his eyes to the hills, and rightly believes that his help can come only from the One who created the towering hills—the Lord himself, "the Maker of heaven and earth" (Ps. 121:1).

Sixth, an outline should have movement. A sermon starts with the introduction. It gradually builds, picking up momentum as the preacher moves from one point to another, until it reaches the last point and its conclusion. That is a movement of presentation that should be reflected in the sermon outline itself. The preacher must be aware of that movement of a sermon in the construction of the sermon outline.

Finally, a sermon outline should have a climax. A sermon outline will have to be arranged in such a manner that the sermon moves progressively from the first toward the last point. We have already talked about the movement of a sermon outline. The movement of a sermon automatically leads a preacher toward the climax, which should be located in the last point of the sermon. The climax should be the most forceful, exciting, and decisive turning point of the message of the sermon.

The climax of a sermon is like traditional hunting in Africa. It is one of the greatest and most cherished experiences of my boyhood when I was growing up in our village. One day all the men and boys of the village went to a big forest to hunt wild pigs. There were about fifty of us all together, with about an equal number of dogs. Most of the older men had their nets and weapons, such as an ax, bow and arrows, and a spear. The boys generally carried a small ax or a *knob-kerrie* (used in Southern Africa). We left the village very early in the morning, as roosters crowed the first time—meaning around three to four o'clock in the morning. Having arrived at our destination long before sunrise, we were all gathered together for a traditional prayer, which was led by one of the elders of our village. The part of the prayer that I still remember was the acknowledgment of the fact that the hunters were now entering the forest with children. So the elderly man in his prayer first requested that the ancestral spirits protect every one, especially the children. Second, he requested the

184

ancestors to provide the meat that was so much needed by all—the men, women, and children in the village.

Quickly and quietly before sunrise, all the dogs had been tied by ropes so that they would be under control, and all the hunters had been positioned, surrounding the area where the elderly people believed the wild pigs spent most of their time at night. The nets had been set in a valley that led to a bigger mountain than the one where we were. The hunters knew that once attacked, the wild pigs would take that route to a bigger mountain. All the boys were asked to climb trees and wait for the signal, when they were to shout and hit the trees they had climbed. The older men moved in the thickets with their weapons and dogs under control to find the wild pigs. It took about two hours to locate them.

As soon as they located the wild pigs, a signal was given to everybody, and dogs were released to take the first offensive, driving the wild pigs toward the nets. There was a lot of shouting from the hunters, and the dogs and the wild animals. The boys in the trees started hitting not only the trees, but also tins that would make a louder noise. Naturally, the wild pigs ran in the direction opposite the noise, down through the valley that they knew so well. As the wild pigs approached the nets, there was no easy way to escape; they had to hit the nets. There were hunters hidden next to the nets, and with the dogs chasing the wild pigs, it was the greatest hunting excitement that I had ever witnessed in my whole life. Thank God I was up in a tree, safe. Although many of the wild pigs managed to escape, about twenty-three were killed. A number of dogs were killed by the pigs, but no human was lost or hurt.

Every sermon outline builds up progressively from the first point to the last point. It is in the last point where the climax of the sermon should be found or built in. Once the climax has been reached, quit preaching. The Holy Spirit can help a preaching-minded preacher in the planning of his or her sermon outline just as the Spirit guides the preacher in the pulpit.

The Conclusion

Bicycles were a scarce commodity in my village when I was growing up. As growing boys, we learned by riding other people's bicycles. When visitors came to our village or house we would either politely ask to ride their bicycles or simply take the bicycle when the visitor was in the house busy talking to our parents. One day a friend took a visitor's bicycle without first asking for permission. What my friend did not know was that the bicycle did not have brakes. He realized it when he tried to stop the bicycle as he was riding down a steep slope. The best option he had was to crash against a house wall. Although the bicycle was not damaged, which was his prayer, he was left with bruises on the forehead.

Like my friend who rode on a bicycle without brakes, a number of preachers have problems with concluding a sermon. They keep on going when the message has long been delivered and the climax reached. The unfortunate thing about it is that they end up losing the fun of good preaching. For a sermon to have a good conclusion, a preacher has to plan that conclusion. The purpose of the conclusion of a sermon is to refocus and reinforce the message of the sermon in such a manner that people will remember it. The conclusion of a sermon can come as a warning or judgment (one has to be careful that it is not personal opinion), or it can express the purpose of the sermon. The conclusion of a sermon is more effective if it is planned as part of the climax of the sermon. The following are the characteristics of a good conclusion: brevity, congruity, confrontation, and high seriousness.

First, the conclusion of a sermon must be brief. It should not sound like another point of the sermon. As the congregation realizes that the sermon is coming to an end, they expect that end to come. The more brief the conclusion of the sermon is, the more dramatic—and often more appealing—the message becomes.

Second, the conclusion must be congruous with the subject of the sermon. People often want to tell a story to conclude a sermon. There is nothing wrong with concluding a sermon with a brief story; however, one does not want to lose the congregation, who have followed the sermon all along only to be confused by a conclusion that was not well thought through by the preacher.

Third, the conclusion of a sermon can come in the form of a confrontation. This is where the element of judgment may come in. When one studies the pronouncement stories, or brief narratives that are meant to describe encounters between Jesus and the Pharisees, confrontation seems to be the approach that Jesus

186

used. His last words to the rich young ruler were, "Sell everything you have and give to the poor, and you will have treasure in heaven. Then come, follow me" (Luke 18:22). And to an expert in the law, after telling the story of the good Samaritan, Jesus concluded, "Go and do likewise" (Luke 10:37).

Finally, the conclusion of a sermon must be characterized by high seriousness. There is no room for jokes. At this stage of the sermon, the message is characterized by a great sense of intensity and seriousness. The seriousness of an effective conclusion is like the seriousness of a woman in labor pains: she knows that the time has come for the birth of her child, and in spite of the pain, it is the last push that she must give in order for the baby to be born. Yet, "when her baby is born she forgets the anguish because of her joy that a child is born into the world" (John 16:21). There is always great joy for a preacher after preaching, for he or she knows that the restlessness is now over, while still hoping and praying that the seed has been planted and that, in God's own time, it will germinate, grow, and bear fruit.

The Use of Illustrations

Words don't always express all that we want to say. Because of that limitation, people try to find other ways to express their inmost feelings and experiences. One way is to use words in a picturesque manner. As we have already noted, Jesus used similes and parables in order to get his message across to the people of his time. The function of illustrations is basically to throw light on the subject under consideration. One does not have to use an illustration for something that is straightforward. A preacher should use illustrations sparingly, lest they distort the message one is trying to convey. A sermon subject can easily become submerged under too many illustrations. We shall look at a few points about the use of illustrations in sermons: functions of illustrations, types of illustrations, and how to make use of illustrations.

First, let us just go over the functions of illustrations in sermons. William Sangster lists the following functions, which I believe are so clear that they do not need further elaboration: they make the message clear; they ease a congregation; they make the truth impressive; they make preaching interesting; they make sermons memorable; they help to persuade people; they make repetition possible without weariness.[11]

Second, there are at least seven different types of illustrations. They are: figures of speech, analogy, allegory, fable, parable, biographical incident, and personal experience. Here I would like to commend African fables, or folktales. Those fables are packed with wisdom and are part of the African culture. Each time a preacher tells a fable to an African congregation, whether in the urban or rural areas, it generates interest. Some of the fables make excellent illustrations, either as the introduction, in the body of a sermon, or as a conclusion. Equally important are the similes and proverbs that are also packed with meaning. For example, one pastor used this proverb in a sermon: *N'anga yemukadzi inorapa ichitarisa zuwa.* The meaning is that a woman traditional healer who has been invited to attend to a patient away from her village, does her job, and still makes sure that she will make it back home before it is dark. These are sayings that our African cultures and vernacular languages are fully enriched with. We need to feel proud of using them.

Finally, how should one make use of illustrations? (1) Illustrations are used primarily to throw light on the subject under consideration. Hearers of the Word may forget the sermon title, the sermon outline, or many elaborate statements that preachers make in a sermon. However, they are likely to remember the message of the preacher through an illustration the preacher has used effectively. (2) Illustrations must be relevant to the matter under consideration. One should not use an illustration just because it is interesting. (3) Illustrations have to be appropriate. An illustration may not be appropriate for every congregation. One may be appropriate for young people but not for adults. Another may be appropriate for an African congregation but not for an Asian congregation. (4) Some illustrations are interesting and others are very dry; some are short and others are long. Because preaching, in one sense, is an art, every preacher has to be careful about the use of illustrations. (5) One of the things a pastor wants to be absolutely certain to avoid is sharing confidences from the pulpit, or giving illustrations about people in the charge or parish. (6) As with written sources, one should acknowledge one's sources. (7) One should not use too many illustrations in a sermon. Experience will be the best guide here.

Gathering Materials

We have defined the sermon, the sermon idea, and the general sermon outline. Now we are ready to talk about gathering the materials in order to design or construct a sermon. This may not sound like an easy job, but if one has decided to be a preacher who will be in the pulpit almost every Sunday, one should be willing to do whatever it takes. Gone are the days when preachers said that once one gets in the pulpit the Holy Spirit will give him the words to say. The congregations that we serve today know very well that if the Holy Spirit does not give it to us in the study, where we are supposed to read, prepare sermons, and be on our knees, he is not likely to give it to us just because we are in the pulpit. Let us look at the steps we should follow in preparing sermons.

First, the preacher gets a sermon idea. The sermon idea may come from reading and studying the Bible, in which case one may already have a text. Or the sermon idea may come through a pastoral contact with a member of one's charge, circuit, or parish. It may be an idea that would then lead a preacher to look for a text in the Bible. Or the idea could have come from elsewhere.

The next step for the preacher is to refine the sermon idea into a subject of the sermon. Once that is done, the preacher would open a file for that sermon, and put it aside. As a matter of fact, if a pastor preaches every Sunday, he or she could have five folders of sermons marked Sunday No. 1, Sunday No. 2, Sunday No. 3, Sunday No. 4, and Sunday No. 5 for the sermons he or she would be preaching in the next four or five Sundays. That means one will have decided on the subjects one would be preaching on during four or more Sundays. One may have even arranged to preach a series of sermons on a subject matter; or one might have arranged to preach a sequence of sermons from one book of the Bible. For purposes of convenience, let's assume that we are planning for four Sundays in advance at all times, although it may happen once in a while that we have five Sundays in a month.

Second, once one has decided on a subject for the sermon, the idea continues to percolate in one's mind even while one is engaged in other tasks. This is a good time for the preacher to read on the subjects that she has decided to preach on. Any new ideas or illustrations that come can be filed in the appropriate

189

folder. Sermon outlines may begin to take form. One may want to write them down and file them, too. At this stage, one may want to consult theological word books and Bible dictionaries—though not commentaries—to have clarification of some biblical terms or theological ideas that may come out of the text. Again, all these ideas should be filed, until one is ready to sit down and work on the sermon. In cultivating one's preaching garden nursery, it is not unusual for a preacher to discover that one of the topics might not have matured enough for preaching, in which case some adjustments will have to be made. At the same time, a preacher does not need to be reminded that some sermon ideas fail to mature, because they have not been sufficiently fertilized, watered, or cleared of weeds. The preaching nursery needs ongoing attention to flourish.

Preparing the Preacher

In talking about the preacher's preparation, I have in mind primarily those pastors who serve more than one congregation; and often as many as ten or fifteen. This situation necessitates a lot of traveling by the pastors. Few African pastors own cars, so travel is primarily by bicycle and on foot. The assumption is that a significant amount of time would be spent not only on the road, but also away from the parsonage and family or the main congregation. As scripture reminds us, this time spent traveling can be the occasion for great insight, as it was on the road to Emmaus. By the time those travelers reached Emmaus, their hearts were burning within them because the Master had traveled with them (Luke 24:13-32).

The pastor's preparation includes his or her spiritual growth and development in the ministry. We might have learned about the subject of spiritual formation in seminary or college. It is indeed the task and responsibility of the pastor, and cannot be delegated. As Paul tells us, "No, I beat my body and make it my slave so that after I have preached to others, I myself will not be disqualified for the prize" (1 Cor. 9:27). Clearly, the pastor's spiritual disciplines, such as devotional reading of the Bible and regular prayer, contribute to his Christian formation and hence the formation of sermons. Often, the sermons that most touch others are the ones that also were particularly alive to the preacher.

190

A preacher does not read the Bible only when he or she is searching for texts for preaching. A preacher needs to read the Bible foremost for his or her own sake. It does not matter that one has been through a theological seminary or college where one might have spent three or four years studying the Bible. He or she needs to be continually nourished by the Word of God, as also by prayer. We have already discussed the importance of prayer in the life of every pastor, and in fact we can never talk enough about its importance. We have to pray always. We have to keep learning from Jesus himself. Time and again, Jesus sought solitude, time to be alone (Mark 1:33-37), so that he could talk to his Father in secret (Matt. 6:6). Devotional reading and studying of the Bible, the life of prayer and general spiritual discipline are all inseparably linked with the life of sermon preparation and the preaching career of a pastor—not necessarily in a mechanical and formal way, but "in spirit and truth" (John 4:23).

Preparing the Sermon

In order to look at the steps one has to follow to write a sermon for this coming Sunday, a preacher will have to learn to work within a given schedule. The one I offer is given as a guideline. If one can use Monday through Saturday diligently, one has plenty of time to prepare a sermon for the coming Sunday—a sermon that will make a preacher walk in that pulpit with confidence, and present oneself to God and God's people "as one approved, a workman [or workwoman] who does not need to be ashamed and who correctly handles the word of truth" (2 Tim. 2:15). We shall follow each day of the week and see how we are going to make use of it for sermon preparation.

Monday is a day that most pastors want to take as their day off. That is understandable when one realizes that Sunday is the busiest day for most pastors. Also Monday is a day when a pastor should not schedule any meetings, so that one is able either to rest or attend to personal and family matters that may even require him or her to travel.

Tuesday, Wednesday, and Thursday are three very important days for every pastor in terms of sermon preparation. Never wait to prepare your sermon on Friday or Saturday, because you may never get to do so. In general, a pastor should plan to spend

191

between two and four hours in the study, office, a quiet place, or even en route to another church. If one is an itinerant pastor with a big circuit of two or more preaching points or congregations, it still is important for one to have some quiet time alone for study, either in the corner of a church building, a classroom, or at some beautiful spot in nature—even en route to another congregation. Mornings are often the most productive times, but whatever time is chosen, the most important thing is to set aside that time for the particular task of sermon preparation and spiritual and intellectual replenishment.

Unless a pastor has another time for his or her personal devotions, one may want to choose the first hour of those four study hours for that purpose. This is the time when a pastor studies the Bible and other reading materials, and devotes some time to prayer for one's own sake and, of course, for his congregation—remembering the bereaved, praying for the sick, praying for co-workers, both clergy and laity, and so forth.

Tuesday morning would be the best time for a pastor to start working on the sermon for the coming Sunday. If preliminary preparation has been done, the folder for Sunday No. 1 would already at this point contain the sermon text, a tentative topic of the sermon, tentative outlines, supporting materials gathered as ideas, materials from reading some books, articles, and so on.

This is the time to affirm the topic on which one is going to preach. Some preachers entertain indecision on a number of topics as late as Saturday evening, the night before they preach. One preacher talked about going into the pulpit with two sermons, because he had not yet decided what topic he was going to preach on. This assertion or declaration on the part of the preacher in his or her study is essential. It is also good discipline on the part of a preacher, because one would spend one's energy on one topic instead of hopping from one topic to another. The topic that will have been affirmed may need to be narrowed or broadened.

It is also time to affirm or determine the text from which one is going to preach. At the outset, one has to be satisfied that the topic and the text are congruous—that they agree. Having established that, the next step is to determine the parameters of text. One may have selected a verse as the basis of one's sermon. However, originally, the Bible did not come to us in verses and chapters.[12] In other words, the preacher will have to look at the text, be it a verse or a part of a verse, in the context of a larger text. Or as Long puts it, one has "to reconsider where the text begins and ends."[13] The meaning of the larger scriptural text surrounding the text selected for preaching may determine the real meaning of the sermon text. Thus, what a preacher would be "looking for in a text is not a passage that can stand alone—all texts are linked to their surroundings—but rather a text that can stand as a reasonably coherent unit of thought."[14]

The next step is to read and listen to the text so that we understand its historical meaning. Recall from chapter 2 of this book that the school of Antioch rose to its importance in preaching because its approach to scriptural interpretation searched for the original historical meaning of the text, unlike the school of Alexandria, which followed the allegorical interpretation of the scriptures. In order for the preacher to get closer to the historical message of the text, three sets of questions must be asked.

1) *Historical questions.* Who wrote the text? To whom was the text written? What were the historical circumstances? What was the message? How was the message received?

2) *Questions about literary style.* For example, suppose one wanted to preach on the Lord's Prayer. According to Matthew (6:9-13) that prayer was part of the Sermon on the Mount; but according to Luke (11:2-4) the prayer comes as a request from one of the disciples to teach them to pray. The preacher may want to ask himself or herself: What is happening? Why is it that two reliable authors give two different contexts to their message? Therefore, we may want to know a little more about the approach and style of the author of the text that is chosen for preaching.

3) *Theological questions.* What was the theological thinking of the writer of the text? Craddock insists that it is only the theology of the writer that will illuminate the text.[15] In other words, Matthew and Paul may talk about the subject of "righteousness"; however, when it comes to preaching, one should not use Paul's understanding of the concept of righteousness to interpret Matthew's text, or vice versa. Thus, Craddock goes on to say, "Johannine texts are to be preached in a way consistent with the Johannine perspective, Pauline texts consistent with Paul's theology, and likewise with all others."[16] This is a very important

hermeneutic and homiletical principle for a preacher to follow if one is going to be faithful in the exposition of any biblical text. Further, such biblical exegesis in the pulpit will not only bring the original and historical meaning of the Bible, it will enable the message of the sermon to be heard by the congregation.

These are the questions that every preacher must wrestle with as he works on the text of his sermon on Tuesday morning. This is also the time when one should consult commentaries. The beauty of the delay in consulting commentaries is that often they endorse your discovery and efforts. After all these questions are raised and answered on Tuesday morning, then one is ready to make a draft of the sermon outline; and then, maybe put the sermon outline aside, until the next day.

Wednesday is the day when the sermon must be written. The first thing one should do when one comes to the study on Wednesday is to affirm the sermon outline that was drafted on Tuesday. There are often new insights and alterations to be made to the sermon outline that should be incorporated. Actually that is the reason why it is wise to lay aside one's sermon outline overnight, because as one moves away from it, subconsciously the mind will continue working at it, and often, illustrations or a better introduction may occur to one in the midst of life.

Now one is ready to write the sermon. Preachers write their sermons differently and according to how they are going to deliver them. Some preachers write a skeleton outline of the sermon. Others prefer writing a very full sermon outline, and still others write the whole sermon the way they are going to preach it. This last method of writing a sermon is not very common in Africa; but there are some who use it.

There are three things I would like to mention in relation to the writing of sermons.

1) When one sits down to write a sermon, one should avoid disturbances. This is the time when you need to stay at your desk until that sermon is finished. It's preferable to put phone calls and mail on hold, though obviously there may be some interruptions of an emergency nature that need to be attended to.

2) In writing the sermon, (a) write imagining your congregation in front of you. It will make the sermon more immediate and keep you honest; (b) write remembering a sermon is heard, not read; and (c) write in short and distinct sentences. Use imagery.

194

3) Writing down sermons allows for later printing and publishing, particularly outstanding sermons. It has other advantages too: (a) more African congregations today expect their preachers to keep to their time limit. If written down, a pastor can better time the sermon; (b) writing a sermon helps the preacher to clarify his or her own thoughts; and (c) writing a sermon helps the preacher to know if the objective of the sermon is fulfilled in the sermon outline itself.

Finally, remember that the sermon is for your people; therefore, start where the people are and move along with them. Also, never use the pulpit to attack your critics, be they members of your congregation or people outside of your congregation. Never make statements that make some people feel they are being attacked by the pastor personally. The pulpit is for the preaching of the gospel; and the gospel has its way of blessing as well as judging people when preached studiously and faithfully.

Thursday morning is the time when a pastor comes to his study and goes over the sermon once more. Above all, it is the time to reaffirm the nature and message of the sermon. One may make alterations here and there; but preparation of the sermon on paper and in the office is done, and should be completed by Thursday at noon. This leaves ample time for the preacher to go over the sermon several times until the sermon has become part of one's system, and leave Saturday open so that one is able to be with the spouse and family, knowing though that he or she is ready for the coming Sunday. Saturday is always a good day for social activities. The preacher may want to spend his or her time not only meditating about the sermon, but also continuously preparing oneself, offering one's body, gifts, and life "as living sacrifices, holy and pleasing to God" (Rom. 12:1). This is a very critical time in preparing for preaching. It is the time for blending the personality of the preacher and the message of the sermon.

Support from one's spouse always proves useful. This can be done through praying together, as well as avoiding unnecessary family quarrels, especially as Sunday arrives. In Zimbabwe, I have heard of couples who have made a covenant that once they are in their bedroom, there shouldn't be any quarrels or arguments. Surely, if such couples find it so important to respect and jealously guard their evening and romantic hours in their bedrooms, how much more so should it be when it comes to a preacher and his or her spouse whose thoughts are preoccupied with the preparation and meditation for the worship of the One who has blessed us with the abundant riches and pleasures of life.

The truth of the matter is that when a preacher has a message for his or her congregation, people can tell; but when the preacher has no message for them, or preaches like one who has been wounded, they can also tell. It is at this point that one may want to pay heed to John Knox's words: "The aim of preparation is clear; it is a man [or woman] prepared and not a sermon prepared."[17]

Delivering the Message

A preacher never has rest until the message that has been at the center of his or her heart and thoughts for the past seven days of the week has been delivered. One of the most satisfying feelings for a preacher is to walk into the pulpit on a Sunday morning knowing that he or she has a message to deliver to the people; and that he or she has put forth all the effort it takes to understand and deliver that message faithfully. As often is the case, God gives the message, and the preacher has to find the best way to deliver that message.

Methods of Delivery

There are many ways of delivering the message or of preaching a sermon; but every preacher will have to determine and develop his or her own style of delivery. One may have to change ways of preaching from time to time, depending upon the circumstances or the message one is preaching. Whatever method of preaching one chooses, one has to be authentically oneself and not imitate another preacher. We shall look at three basic methods of delivering a sermon; (1) impromptu preaching; (2) extemporaneous preaching; and (3) reading verbatim from a manuscript.

Impromptu preaching is delivered without any immediate preparation at all.[18] This means that one would be asked to preach an unrehearsed sermon.[19] The preacher is not given the chance to prepare. This practice is still very common in Africa.

A preacher gets into a number of situations where, because he or she is there, people ask him or her to preach the Word. For example, a preacher may go to a funeral of a relative, and because the pastor who happens to have several congregations did not get the message in good time to be present, the preacher present is therefore asked to take the place of the pastor. He or she must deliver the Word.

We find that this was the kind of practice that was also used in the early church. When Paul and his companions got to Perga, after the reading from the Law, they were asked, "Brothers, if you have a message of encouragement for the people, please speak" (Acts 13:15). That was the manner in which Jesus preached in his hometown, Nazareth. Both Jesus and Paul might not have prepared a sermon as such, but they were prepared preachers.

The advantage of impromptu preaching is that the preacher does not have to go through the painful experience of preparing a sermon. Often, such preaching that is "off the cuff" can be very effective. That is the reason why we must always remember that preparation for preaching also means the preparation of the preacher. One must be ready to be called upon to make a witness through preaching at any time. A word of warning must be made here; one does not plan to preach impromptu sermons. A preacher who uses an impromptu preaching delivery in his or her pulpit on Sunday morning because he or she expects the Holy Spirit to bring the message is abusing the pulpit of the church. As a matter of fact, that kind of preacher could be considered a lazy preacher. Impromptu preaching is delivered only when one is called upon at the spur of the moment. And one is always very limited in what one can accomplish under those circumstances.

Extemporaneous preaching is preaching in which one has had the opportunity to prepare a sermon, and has even had as much time as possible to go over the sermon several times before preaching the sermon extemporaneously. Stephen Lucas, professor of public speaking at the University of Wisconsin pointed out that "in popular usage, 'extemporaneous' means the same as 'impromptu.' But technically the two are different. Unlike an impromptu speech, which is totally off the cuff, an extemporaneous speech is carefully prepared and practiced in advance."[20] Some preachers have a spouse who is prepared and patient enough to listen to the preacher's whole sermon as a sounding board and even make some suggestions. Others will go in the pulpit in an empty church and pretend the congregation is already seated, listening to the message. Still many more preachers will preach in a car or on a bicycle or as they walk; with many others, they shout and jump behind bushes, preaching to birds of the air. In preaching the sermon, an extemporaneous preacher uses only a set of brief notes or a speaking outline to jog the memory.

In preaching the extemporaneous sermon, the preacher uses only a set of brief notes or a preaching outline. As a matter of both historical and homiletical interest, Martin Luther preached extemporaneously on three different lections for the day at the church of Wittenberg, where they had three Sunday worship services.[21] The points to remember about this method of preaching delivery are as follows: (1) the sermon is carefully prepared in advance; (2) the preacher goes over the sermon several times, until the sermon becomes part of one's system; and (3) at the point of preaching, one can deliver the sermon without notes, or one can use a brief sermon outline, or one can use a full sermon outline to preach the sermon, but without reading it. The brief notes or the full sermon outline are used simply to jog one's memory. The extemporaneous method of preaching has several advantages over the other methods of delivery, such as spontaneity and directness.

A third method of sermon delivery is reading *verbatim from a manuscript.* In our discussions about sermon preparation we talked about the importance of writing the whole sermon. Once in a while, it happens that there are sermons that may need to be carefully worded and articulated—maybe sermons on controversial doctrinal or social issues that may call not only for a well written sermon, but also for a particularly clear presentation. It is on such occasions that a preacher may want to preach by reading his or her sermon from a manuscript.

There are preachers who always choose to write the sermon in full and preach it this way. We do not seem to have many preachers who use this method in Africa today; but I suppose as preachers have greater access to the use of new electronic equipment such as computers, nothing will be impossible. It is certainly a method that instills confidence in preachers who do not have the gift of preaching extemporaneously.

Advantages of reading from a manuscript are: (1) that the preacher is able to deliver exactly what he or she has prepared. With other methods of delivery, the preacher may forget a sub-point, or something that could have made a difference in the sermon. That is not likely to happen with this method of delivery. (2) No one is likely to accuse the preacher of saying something in the sermon that may not be found in the manuscript. (3) Although written primarily to be heard, such sermons can also easily be printed and circulated for reading. At times, when a pastor has established a good rapport with his or her parishioners, no matter where the parishioners may be—in a hospital or nursing home, for instance—when they read the printed sermons of their pastor, they hear his or her voice again. However, should one choose to preach by reading verbatim sermons, just like those who choose extemporaneous preaching, one will have to go over the sermon several times so that the delivery sounds conversational and not studied.

Whatever method of sermon delivery a preacher chooses, people in the congregation want a preacher they believe is talking to them directly, who truly knows the subject of the sermon, and who, through the sermon has a message that challenges their lives.

The Preacher's Voice

Every preacher who has been called to preach has his or her own kind of voice. In spite of the kind of voice one may have, God chooses whom he wishes to have as his instrument. Therefore, when it comes to preaching, we have to start with the voice that we have, for it is God who gave us that voice and the mouth that we have (Exod. 4:11). I have a relative who, at the time of his call to the ministry, could have reiterated what Moses said: "O Lord, I have never been eloquent, neither in the past nor since you have spoken to your servant. I am slow of speech and tongue" (Exod. 4:10). Today, he is one of the preachers whom people want to hear in the Zimbabwe Annual Conference of The United Methodist Church. When he is preaching, one can hardly tell that he was a man of slow speech and tongue. In spite of all the human frailty, it is amazing what God does with men and women who become heedful to God's voice as he

199

begins to bring to our senses the many blessings that he has already endowed us with.

Yet, the voice, too, needs training. Christian Buehler and Wil Linkugel, both professors at the University of Kansas, suggest three standards for effective vocal delivery; the speaker must be heard, he must be understood, and he must be pleasing.[22] Let us look at each one of these standards for effective vocal delivery, relating them to the preacher.

First, the preacher must be heard. Today we witness the growth of large congregations in the urban areas of Africa. We have also seen large church buildings that have been constructed in order to accommodate all these people. It is not every church that can acquire a public address system to assist the voice of the preacher to be heard by all who come to worship. The situation is made even worse when large outdoor meetings are held without the assistance of an electronic sound system. Nevertheless, the standard for effective vocal delivery stands, namely, that the preacher in the pulpit must be heard. It reminds me of Reverend Chihota, who was pastor of Epworth Mission of the Methodist Church in Zimbabwe in the late 1950s and early 1960s. The old man enjoyed preaching the gospel to a packed church. There came a time when children would cry in the congregation, disturbing the preaching. So he used to stop and call to the women, *"Vana mai varikuseri uko; isai mazamu mukanwa mevana; vatitadzisa kuzwa Baiberi nevangeri kuno,"* suggesting that they breast-feed their children so that all could hear the reading of the Bible and the proclamation of the gospel. Reverend Chihota knew that if one was in the pulpit one had to be heard. The old man was a good and effective preacher.

Second, the preacher must be understood. In Africa, I have come across preaching where a pastor used two languages. A sermon would start in the vernacular language, and after ten minutes or so the preacher would switch to English (or French or Portuguese). At times this happened because of the presence of a missionary, who was not yet conversant with the local language. Often the pastor would be showing off. (In other countries, a parallel might be where a preacher uses inordinate amounts of Greek or Hebrew in a sermon, a tactic that is rarely enlightening to a congregation.) Every preacher ought to take pride in effectively speaking his or her vernacular language, using the cultural idioms, proverbs, and folktales, and reading the Bible in the vernacular. It certainly helps develop rhetorical skills in one's own language.

Third, the preacher must be pleasing. A preacher is a messenger of the good news—joy, hope, faith, love, and victory through Christ. In all circumstances, the messenger of God lives a life of celebration of victory in Christ over sin, because there is forgiveness (1 John 1:9), and over death, because through the resurrection of Jesus "death has been swallowed in victory" (1 Cor. 15:54). That message of joy and hope will temper the life of a preacher, helping him or her always to celebrate and to be pleasing to listen to.

In the pulpit, his or her voice will not lack a variety of pitch, rate, force, or melody.[23] Such a preacher will leave no room for monotony. He or she will not succumb to what people often complain about, such as the monotonous ministerial tone that many preachers fall into the moment they get in the pulpit. He or she is always pleasing and comforting, because he or she is a messenger of God. Hence the words of the Prophet Isaiah: "How beautiful on the mountains are the feet of those who bring good news, who proclaim peace, who bring good tidings, who proclaim salvation, who say to Zion, 'Your God reigns!' " (52:7).

* * * *

A father realized he was an old man and could die any time. He had six sons. The old man had always provided for his family. But he was concerned that his children had not learned to discipline themselves and work hard enough to support themselves. On the day he died, he told his six sons that he had a hidden treasure around the house. He was too weak to get up and try to locate where the treasure was. As a matter of fact, he told them that he had forgotten exactly where he had hidden the treasure. But the old man instructed his sons to dig around the house and in the fields as they looked for the treasure. After the father died, for the first time the six sons actually agreed on a strategy, which was to dig around the house, then into the fields. To their amazement, even after working harder in the fields than they had ever done before, they found no hidden treasure. As the rainy season approached the six sons decided to plant corn in the whole area they had dug, and to their surprise they had a bumper harvest. Even after that, the sons were still convinced that their father had a hidden treasure as he had told them. They started digging once more until another rainy season approached. Again, they had another bumper harvest. It dawned on the six sons that maybe they had already discovered the hidden treasure in cooperatively working hard together. From then on, the six sons were a new and changed people, who not only worked hard together each year, but who also started planning well ahead of time the preparation of the soil, so that it "produced a crop, multiplying thirty, sixty, or even a hundred times" (Mark 4:8).

So it is with a preacher who takes sermon preparation seriously. It may all start as a burden and hard work that one is tempted to avoid. But as one gets used to it, and realizes the manifold results for both the congregation and the preacher, one begins to understand both the mystery and secret of experiencing God—and preaching the gospel of his kingdom with a tone of love and faithfulness.

Chapter 10

A Charge for Preaching

S ome years ago, I was appointed as a student pastor to Grace United Methodist Church, Springfield, Illinois. My first Sunday worship service with that congregation included celebration of Holy Communion. I will always cherish the memories of that first Sunday: the singing, the responses to the reading of the Bible, the music of the Lord's Prayer, and other parts of the Holy Communion liturgy that were sung, not spoken. It was a moving experience. For a while I thought the experience I was going through was subjective, until I witnessed the same sense in the eyes of those who came forward to partake of Holy Communion. I then concluded we had the *Visitor* in our midst. That experience always reminds me of the promise of Jesus to his disciples: "I will not leave you as orphans; I will come to you" (John 14:18).

Christian worship at its best has a way of generating spiritual power that captures the worshipers' hearts and minds and raises them to a new level of awareness. The individual rediscovers the totality and unity of his or her own humanity and experiences a renewed awareness of God's presence. This awareness is like that of Isaiah, who "saw the Lord seated on a throne, high and exalted" (Isa. 6:1). One then becomes aware of the surrounding community within which one lives, and with that awareness is also a sense of belonging to something greater than just the individual (Isa. 6:5). Above all, the community is brought face-to-face with God's mission, "Set apart for . . . the work to which I have called them" (Acts 13:2). Often, that is what happens when God, who is Spirit, is worshiped "in spirit and in truth" (John 4:24).

It is always a joy for parishioners to look forward to Sunday, knowing that their hearts and minds will be blessed once more as they go to worship the Lord. In one of his letters to Timothy, his "true son in the faith" (1 Tim. 1:2), Paul wrote, "In the presence of God and of Christ Jesus, who will judge the living and the dead, and in view of his appearing and his kingdom, I give you this charge: *Preach the Word*" (2 Tim. 4:1-2, emphasis added). There is no greater responsibility and honor endowed upon an ordained preacher than being given the charge to preach the gospel of Jesus Christ to the people. This chapter will focus on the pastor's preaching responsibilities.

Liturgical Preaching

The word *liturgy* comes from the Greek word *leitourgia,* which literally means a service, mission, ministry, or public, common work or duty of the people. In worship service, worship or liturgy would mean people responding to God's revelation. That means liturgy would consist of the various acts of worship, including prayers, singing, and reading of scriptures. Another way of looking at liturgy is as a drama, with God in the center as he reveals himself through Christ, with the Holy Spirit uniting and guiding all present in their response to what God is doing and saying through his Son. For Christians, that drama is all about the salvation of humankind. Biblically speaking, it is the drama in which God began to reveal himself through the Law, the Prophets, and finally through his Son, Jesus Christ. The whole of Christian worship dramatizes that story repeatedly. As God has revealed himself, and continues to reveal himself, people respond by worshiping—"work of the people"—praying, singing, and giving offerings.

Therefore, liturgical preaching is preaching that takes place "during the liturgy or formal or public worship of God."[1] There are four points to emphasize under the rubric of liturgical preaching.

First, as in any other type of Christian worship, a liturgical worship service emphasizes the worship of God—doing service for God. "The Lord God Almighty, who was, and is, and is to come" (Rev. 4:8) is the only one worthy of our worship. "You are worthy our Lord and God, to receive glory and honor and power,

204

for you created all things, and by your will they were created and have their being" (Rev. 4:11). That is the attitude and spirit in which preachers approach liturgical preaching. In Shona we have a saying, *Mwana washe muranda kumwe,* meaning a son of a chief who goes into the land of another chief automatically becomes a servant. There are many preachers in Africa who come from royal families, that is, chieftainship families, who often receive great respect from their people for their social status in society. Nevertheless, it needs to be pointed out here that, as such pastors enter the house of the Lord or stand before God's people for purposes of worshiping, they are treading on foreign land. Like anyone else, they become servants; and there is only one living God to be worshiped.

Second, every part of the order of worship is important. The preaching act itself is as effective as the whole liturgy. That means the pastor needs to give just as much time to preparing the liturgy as he gives to preparing the sermon. That calls for a creative and meaningful call to worship; looking for appropriate hymns for the topic of the day; good scripture reading (not just to ask someone a few minutes before the service to read scripture); a well thought out pastoral prayer in terms of the needs and hopes of the congregation, community, and international affairs and disasters; good singing by the choir; and everything else related to the worship service. The pastor must prepare everything well ahead of time, for liturgical preaching is integral to the whole worship service experience.

Third, the pastor is the leading worshiper. He or she leads worshipers. The pastor is not there simply to conduct the worship service, but rather to participate in worship with the congregation through singing, prayers, responsive reading. He or she does not just stand in front of the congregation, waiting for the time to preach.

Fourth, liturgical preaching takes cognizance of the experiences of the worshipers. Worshipers are people who have come to worship—that is, to do God's work. One of the most difficult things for some parishioners is to listen to the same preacher every Sunday. A pastor is not a wandering preacher who can survive by repeating the best few sermons developed throughout the year, getting by with a few jokes. William Barclay has three points that are helpful to a pastor.[2]

PREACHING AND CULTURAL IDENTITY

1) The preacher must give his or her congregation *something to feel.* When I was about ten years old, a preacher at a revival meeting at my village church made people stand up and grouped them according to their extended families. The whole congregation sang, as part of his sermon, a song with an African tune that was composed by one of the earliest African pastor-teachers, Jonas Mandara Manjengwa. The preacher used that hymn, especially one of the stanzas that went as follows:

Madzinza ariyo
Kunyika ya Tenzi
Havachazochemi
Havana rusuwo

The meaning of the words is: "Even the families are in heaven, In the realm of the Lord, They will never mourn anymore, There is no grief anymore." I still remember how the people who came from the villages nearby ran back to their homes to bring in some of the people who were not even members of the church so that they could stand together as extended families. The preacher gave the people something to feel—a reunion with those who had gone before them to heaven. What a feeling, yet it is so true of the gospel.

2) The preacher must give the congregation *something to remember.* While feeling may be more of a message for the heart, the preacher must also feed and challenge the mind. Often, a good story will do it. People may forget the topic and the text of a sermon, but if one has a good story, they will always remember the message through that story. That was the way Jesus taught and preached. That was part of the reason why the early church remembered Jesus' parables. Whatever stories we use, they must be pregnant with the gospel truth about the human life situation.

A child five years old was allowed to visit her mother and a newborn baby brother in the hospital. Because the child had so much excitement about her little brother, she tried to talk to him, but with nothing much of a relevant response from him. She then made a remark to her mother, "she will be able to talk soon." That is the wish of God for each one of his children, that they become able to talk to him soon. Preaching the gospel to the

206

people opens opportunities for and encourages people to commune with God as their loving Mother or Father.

3) Finally, the preacher must provide *something to do*. Preaching is meant to motivate people for action. People are bound to ask the question at the end of the sermon: So what? What differences does it make? If a pastor knows his people well, liturgical preaching means doing God's work. People can be challenged to do something, and they expect the challenge to come. The preacher must always preach the gospel in such a manner that people make a definite decision for or against it. Every sermon has a purpose; one hopes that some of the purposes preachers set for their sermons are such that they help the congregation to do something. Many of our African congregations have not achieved much in the way of mission-awareness, because they have not been challenged enough to do something for others. We have been too much on the receiving end of mission-awareness. We can achieve great things if we are prepared to start, even with the little that we may have. Get your congregation to do something.

Unctuous Preaching

People who come to worship are sometimes hurting. They may be hurting because of grief, loneliness, anger, temptations, stress, or depression. So it is good for a pastor, realizing that people are often overburdened with such personal problems, to ask the members of the congregation to come forward to the altar to have some time of silent prayer. It provides psychological satisfaction, spiritual assurance, and nourishment when people of their own accord go to the altar and take "hold of the horns of the altar" (1 Kings 1:50) in sincere prayer. We all often have need of such moments.

How then should we preach to such a congregation with members who are hurting? James reminds us that the early church faced similar problems: "Is any one of you in trouble? . . . Is any one of you sick? He should call the elders of the church to pray over him and anoint him with oil in the name of the Lord. . . . If he has sinned, he will be forgiven. Therefore confess your sins to each other and pray for each other so that you may be healed" (James 5:13-16).

It will take unctuous preaching to communicate the gospel to people who are hurting. The word *unction* means the act of anointing, as in medical treatment or religious ceremony. Therefore, unctuous preaching is preaching that takes cognizance of those members of the congregation who have been crushed, bruised, wounded, and oppressed. It is preaching that seeks to convey a healing message. I suggest that the following three habits are vital to this kind of ministry.

First, a pastor needs to know his parishioners by name for preaching to be meaningful and unctuous. At times preaching is like a person who puts twenty empty glasses of water on a table, and then throws a bucket of water over the glasses, trying to fill all of them at one time. The result is likely to be that only one or perhaps none of the glasses will receive enough water to fill it. Most of the glasses end up with just a splash of water in them by this method, whereas, one could easily fill each one of the glasses individually and still have some water left in the bucket. Unctuous preaching does not begin and end in the pulpit; it begins with knowing the parishioner who sits in the pew. Knowing a parishioner by his or her name might also more broadly mean knowing the parishioner's home, the rest of the family, the kind of work he or she does, the person's strengths and weaknesses, hopes and ambitions as well as his or her deep fears. Preaching the gospel to persons one has taken the time to get to know is like filling each of their water glasses individually, although one is preaching to hundreds of people.

In a world that is becoming increasingly urbanized, industrialized, and secularized, the parishioners may not lavishly share personal information with the pastor as parishioners of past generations have done. Today we have young professionals and young couples who know where to go when they need a doctor, a lawyer, a marriage counselor, or a financial advisor. Because of the multiplicity of resources for assistance in the wider community, the pastor may feel he or she is not needed. Some doors may not easily open as a pastor goes round on her daily visits. Because of pressures of work, families begin to guard the rare moments they have at home to take care of their family affairs. It can take creativity to get to know one's congregation personally, but the bottom line is that people still appreciate the caring attention of a pastor in their lives.

The more parishioners the pastor gets to know closely, the more preaching becomes focused on communicating the gospel at the point of the parishioners' need. That is when preaching becomes unctuous. And sometimes it can happen that a parishioner may raise a question of clarification during a pastoral visit about the message preached the previous Sunday or a month ago, or by some other preacher. That is filling the glasses of water individually, and it is what Jesus meant when he said, "I am the good shepherd; I know my sheep and my sheep know me" (John 10:14).

Second, the pastor needs to have a big heart in order to be able to bind up the injured members of the congregation. It is not uncommon for a pastor to visit parishioners who have suffered heartbreak in some area of their lives. Today in Africa, some of the heartbroken people are elderly people who find themselves in nursing homes, either because they have no one to look after them, or because the children have deliberately decided that they should be kept in a nursing home. Equally brokenhearted could be the sons and daughters who may feel guilty for sending their parents to a nursing home, when traditional life tends to teach something different. Or it could be parents who have lost their sons and daughters to the cities, and they feel abandoned. An elderly widow with a piece of land she cultivated for years with her late husband might be heartbroken because, with no one to help her care for the land, it is usurped by another.

The Lord spoke to Ezekiel about such parishioners as the sick and the injured, those with broken limbs, and those scattered in the mountains (34:1-10). The Lord confronted the shepherds and says that none of them was searching for the sheep (34:6); and to Hosea the Lord said, "My people are destroyed from lack of knowledge" (4:6). The pastoral desire of the Lord is clearly manifested when he said to Ezekiel that he would rescue his sheep, tend them in good pasture, find them good grazing land, bind up the injured, and strengthen the weak—in short, "I will shepherd the flock with justice" (34:11-16). It is only the pastor who knows who is sick—who has a broken limb, who is weak, who has been unjustly treated—who is in a position to minister effectively to people and preach unctuously so that the word is good news indeed.

Third, a pastor should never be ashamed of leading healing

prayers. I recall that one morning, as a young pastor I heard the sound of footsteps fast approaching the parsonage. As I was wondering what was happening, there was a loud knock at the door. A man entered the house carrying a two-year-old child in his arms. The weeping mother followed. The man could hardly speak intelligible statements, except to repeat, "Pastor, Pastor, my child is dying!" I was quite shaken up. I asked the father, "Why didn't you go to the clinic? Let us rush there right now." But then came the answer from my parishioner, "I thought I should come to you first, as my pastor. Maybe you would want to pray for my child before we go to see the nurse at the clinic." My immediate reaction was like the man who confessed, "I do believe; help me overcome my unbelief" (Mark 9:24). I took the child in my arms as the three of us bowed our heads in prayer. As we came to the end of our prayer, the three of us looked at one another, because the child not only was already returning our gaze, but was even smiling. I handed the child back to the parents and asked them nonetheless to go to the clinic so that a nurse could check the child. What a lesson it was to a young pastor about the use of healing prayer.

The early church consistently used "anointing as a means of healing the sick."[3] The practice of anointing the sick with oil that James, the brother of Jesus, wrote about in his Letter (5:14), was a practice that came from the Jewish tradition. Barclay informs us that, when a Jew was ill, he went to a rabbi who would anoint him with oil, as well as pray over him.[4] Justinus, Irenaeus, Tertullian, and Clement all testify to this practice in the life of the early church. The significance of anointing the sick with oil was primarily "as a means of cure."[5] It was not until A.D. 852 that the sacrament of Extreme Unction was introduced in the church, not as a means of cure, but as "preparation for death as it now is in the Roman Catholic Church."[6] Protestantism does not regard unction or anointing with oil as a sacrament, but purely as a means of curing and healing. That is also our understanding of the practice of anointing with oil as the early church practiced it.

The church in Africa, especially the independent churches, practice healing services for the sick; anointing with oil is also administered. The majority of the mainline churches tend to remain aloof. In spite of this, a number of pastors in the mainline churches have drawn crowds as people claim that they have healing powers. There is no doubt that persons may be endowed with the gift of healing (1 Cor. 15:9). Yet it is also good to do as James says: if someone is sick, "He should call the elders of the church to pray over him and anoint him with oil in the name of the Lord" (5:14).

The Bible is full of stories about healing, and preachers are always preaching on these stories. So why should we be ashamed of leading healing services? Kathy Black, assistant professor of homiletics at the School of Theology at Claremont, points out that the unfortunate thing is that preachers tend to use the terms *cure* and *healing* interchangeably, yet in the English language the two words are different. Black says:

> Cure is the elimination of at least the symptoms if not the disease itself. Healing, on the other hand, has many meanings attached to it. Consider the phrases "healing presence," "healing moment," and "healing service." Each of these images elicits a sense of peace and of well-being, but they do not imply cure. While a healing worship service may include hope and even prayer for a cure for a particular individual, the intent of the service is to bring some sense of well-being into the person's life, a sense of comfort, support and peace. Linda is blind and will be physically blind for the rest of her life, but she can still experience much healing in the midst of her blindness.[7]

Because pastors are always preaching about the healing stories of the Bible, I have two proposals:

1) If a pastor is convinced about holding special healing services, one should do so, following the teaching of James (5:13-16). The power to heal the sick here is invested in the elders, which would also mean the church, or the community as a whole. It is not a one-man or one-woman show. One of the best things that could happen is that, as the church prays for such persons who are sick, the pastor and several lay people could together lay their hands on the sick. It is a corporate prayer and effort that also serves to unite the church.

2) Healing is always inclusive, involving the wholeness of the person as opposed to the specific focus of a cure. Paul reminds us of how he prayed three times for a thorn to be removed from his flesh, only to receive as the answer, "My grace is sufficient for you, for my power is made perfect in weakness" (2 Cor. 12:7-10).

211

A pastor is in a unique position to bring messages of healing to a congregation through preaching and solicitous care.

Evangelistic Preaching

In his charge to Timothy, his "true son in the faith" (1 Tim. 1:2), Paul gave him the charge to "Preach the Word" (2 Tim. 4:2). Paul makes another emphatic statement, "Do the work of an evangelist" (2 Tim. 4:5). The church in Africa is growing very fast today. However, it is often easier for all of us to comment on what is going on countrywide or continent-wide than it is to talk of how people's lives are changing in one's own locale because of the gospel.

My brother was appointed to a circuit that I had served before him. One day he told me about a dynamic woman of strong faith who had become the lay leader in that circuit. He recounted the great difference her election to that position had made in the life of the circuit. I had great satisfaction in sharing with my brother how that same woman had been converted to Christ during the time I was serving that circuit. Now she was glowing fervently in her new faith.

So, what is evangelism? *Evangelism is sharing with other persons one's knowledge and experience of the love and mercy of God as one has come to know God through Jesus Christ, and inviting those persons to put their lives in the hands of Christ, by confessing their sins, so as to receive forgiveness and the ensuing peace; and to continue being purified by the Holy Spirit from all unrighteousness, as one becomes an obedient and faithful disciple of Christ, and an instrument of God for God's mission.* That was what my brother and I were so glad to testify about in the life of the woman whose church we had both served. Her troubled life turned around when she committed her life to Jesus Christ and turned over a new leaf, so much so that she ended up as a circuit lay leader with fervent testimony of her new faith. Each time she gave her testimony, she described her life before she met Christ as hell; she was fond of saying that after meeting Christ (and being born again or being born from above), she, her husband, and her neighbors were all new persons.

One of the blessings of a pastor charged with the responsibility of preaching the word is to see lives transformed by the power of the gospel. To see what it takes for that kind of experience to happen, I would like us to look at three ways a pastor, especially in the African situation, could fulfill Paul's charge to Timothy to "do the work of an evangelist" through pulpit evangelism, house church evangelism, and visitation evangelism.

First, the pulpit provides a tremendous opportunity for every pastor to do *pulpit evangelism*. For example, most of the church buildings in African urban areas and cities are filled to capacity on Sunday morning worship services. It might be a different thing if there was a soccer match, especially for those who worship on Sunday afternoon, or whose worship service goes beyond the noon hour. In the rural areas, the attendance again is still good, but it also depends on how close the church building is to the people. Attendance at worship service is not anything a pastor would complain about in Africa yet. Often, the people who attend the Sunday worship service can be put into three groups: the committed members, the inactive members, and the noncommitted members.

While one would have no problem with the first group, certainly there is still work to be done with the second and third categories. In the second group, the pastor often finds people who have good intentions; they are baptized, they were married in church, a spouse and children may attend more regularly, or they all come once in a while. They do participate, but only if they are asked. Yet they are not always there when their services are needed. With the third category, we have people who feel that they are too busy elsewhere to commit regular time to the church. They come to church once in a while. They may have been baptized, but may not have been married in church, or attend church regularly. In other words, they are not quite convinced that that is what they should be doing. Consequently, they attend church only when it is convenient.

When one looks at all these people on a Sunday morning in the urban churches, such as those in Zimbabwe, one would say, if church membership was at 300, chances are that your church attendance would be 300 to 400 people. This would be more true with urban than rural congregations. For example, let us pick out three congregations of The United Methodist Church in Harare at random. Congregation A has a total membership of 2,340, of whom 974 are full members and 1,366 probationary members.

Congregation B has a total membership of 967, of whom 576 are full members and 391 are probationers. Congregation C has a total membership of 959, of whom 348 are full members, 595 are probationary members, and 16 are affiliated and associate members.

Given this typical situation, the pastor has an opportunity to preach the gospel in such a manner that the worshipers commit their lives to Christ. This is the challenge that the churches in Africa must take seriously. A pastor who takes pulpit evangelism seriously must remember that preaching for conviction and decision will not yield anything without harvesting. The good thing about evangelistic preaching is that the pastor's function is only to preach the Word faithfully and persuasively and extend the invitation; that is, removing oneself from the scene, and like John the Baptist, simply point to Jesus—"Look, the Lamb of God!" (John 1:36). Conviction is not the work of the preacher; rather, that is the work of the Holy Spirit (John 16:8, 2 Thess. 1:5). Neither do preachers bring about conversion or new birth. Again, that is the work of Christ to those who turn and confess that "Jesus is Lord" (Rom. 10:9) of their life.

Second, one of the ways the African church has shown its capacity to grow is through *house church evangelism.* In the last two years, while I worked at Africa University, my wife and I associated ourselves with Tsvingwe circuit, a small circuit that has five preaching points. It is only the main church of Tsvingwe that has a church building; at the preaching points, members still meet in their homes. Paul wrote to the "holy and faithful brothers in Christ at Colosse," sending his greetings "to Nympha and the church in her house" (Col. 4:15). That makes a lot of sense to the African church. The pattern, according to our experience in the Zimbabwe Annual Conference of The United Methodist Church, is that, in a circuit, some people may live five kilometers or more from the church building of their own church. There could be two or more families in the same area. The pastor may arrange for such persons to meet in one of the houses. As the group grows bigger and there is no longer a big enough house for them in which to meet, they look for a school classroom, or any other public building where they can be authorized to meet. If such a small congregation is in a growing community, then eventually they will have a church building of their own. If it is on a farm, then chances are that it remains a small congregation.

During the war of liberation, especially in the 1970s, the house church became a very strong feature of the churches in Zimbabwe. As traveling around became increasingly difficult and dangerous, people still met in their homes. The only thing that was important was to be sure that the people who met as a house church knew and trusted one another. The house churches became intimate groups that prayed for and shared with one another what they would not normally share in a larger group, especially in the presence of strangers. However, what came out of all that experience was the emergence of strong Christians as true disciples of Christ; though they realized there was danger, they never failed to come together for prayer and testimonies, often strengthening one another, as many of the families lost loved ones during that war. These small communities were also able to bring in new members to the Christian faith in spite of the hostile circumstances. So these house churches are potential points of growth for the church; they are not preaching points where only lay preachers are to be assigned. The pastor must take just as much interest in those small communities as he or she would with the larger congregations of the circuit or parish.

The phenomenon of house churches has taken on a new dimension in the Zimbabwe Annual Conference, where congregations are divided into geographical sections of the charge or circuit. While this practice could also apply to other denominations, in the case of the United Methodists, this system of organizing people seems to have taken the place of the traditional practice of Methodist class meetings. Each section meets for prayers, witnessing for Christ in the community where they are located, as well as supporting one another in times of joy, such as weddings and dedications of new homes. They invite speakers to talk on developmental topics and support one another in difficult times of illness, natural disasters, and death. Wherever a section has a particularly good program, it can become an effective arm of the church in reaching out to new people. The sections are frequently in a position to know the new people who are coming into their community. Often, the section leaders make contacts with such persons even before the pastor does. The section leaders and their people decide where the weekly prayers are to be held. Because they sometimes even schedule such prayer meetings in the homes of persons new to the area or the church, it is not surprising that some people join the church because of the witnessing of the sections in their community.

It may also happen that all that the sections can do is to invite the new people to attend their church. This is again where the pastor must never be relaxed when it comes to evangelistic preaching. If the pulpit and the sections work hand in hand, with each one doing what one is supposed to do, the church will continue to grow in Africa. My hope and prayer is that as people come to church for worship services on Sundays, preachers intensify their evangelistic efforts, both from the pulpit and through the house churches. We can never do enough for Christ.

Third, churches have been growing in Africa partly through the use of *visitation evangelism.* Due to the prevailing social system of extended families, which still makes it easy for family members to pay each other unannounced visits, pastoral visitation and visits by members of the church in homes of church members and nonchurch members alike are still most welcomed. A pastor who is interested in evangelism would do well to exploit the method of visitation evangelism. As a small village boy, I enjoyed hunting the traditional way. We used bows and arrows, but we also used dogs, and some of the dogs had become well trained in the task of hunting. The moment we killed the first rabbit or deer, we would bring all the dogs together to smell the kill, but we never allowed them to take a bite. From that point on, the dogs became more excited and went wild in their search for another kill. They would enter the thickets of the forests and the caves, and often any animal that would be hiding there would be exposed to those dogs.

That is what happens to a church that has caught the imagination and vision of what visitation evangelism can do. If properly introduced and trained, members of the church would feel like going out to every house in their community, and would have a share of the experience when Jesus sent his disciples out to the various homes, two by two (Mark 6:6-13; Luke 9:1-9). Visitation evangelism works fairly well in most of the two-thirds world countries—and both urban and rural congregations could be trained to use it. This method of evangelism has several advantages:

1) Visitation evangelism involves every member of the congregation in the work—both full members and those not yet full members, old and young, clergy and laity, men and women. All will have to work together as a family. Visitation evangelism unites the congregation.

2) Visitation evangelism is personal and very communicative. Earlier we likened unctuous preaching to filling glasses of water individually. That illustration could equally well suit visitation evangelism. There could be some people out there who really want to know what it means "to put one's life in the hands of Jesus Christ," or whether "the peace" Christians talk about amidst all the problems and pressures of life problems is real. Often, it takes another person, one who has experienced the love and mercy of God through Christ to say, "Whether he is a sinner or not, I don't know. One thing I do know. I was blind but now I see!" (John 9:25). That is how visitation evangelism can be personal and communicative.

3) In order for personal evangelism to be successful, both the congregation and the pastor must see the need for it. Members must receive training, and, above all, there must be time to pray about the undertaking.

4) Finally, the goal of personal evangelism is to share with another person the love and mercy of God through Christ, so as to introduce him or her to Jesus Christ with the purpose of becoming a disciple of Christ for the rest of one's life. Visitation evangelism is incomplete without emphasis on evangelistic pulpit preaching that sets the tone for those who visit the homes of their relatives, friends, and neighbors and openly extends the invitation to those who come to church for worship and to seek to make a commitment to Jesus Christ as Lord of their life.

Indeed, there are many other ways of doing evangelism; but in this chapter we are saying that a pastor who takes evangelism seriously through the pulpit, house church, and visitation in the homes through the use of the congregation, will have started well.

Preaching That Equips for Mission

A pastor and congregation who are aware of the mission context help preaching thrive, for that kind of preaching is not only evangelistic but touches on social needs and pastoral concerns of the people and the communities in which the congregations are situated. The thrust of such preaching is to engage congregations in God's mission, for mission is the very heart of the living church; it is its very conscience that makes it restless,[8] and without it a congregation is dead. Jesus had an awesome sense of mission. As "he saw the crowds, he had compassion on them, because they were harassed and helpless, like sheep without a shepherd" (Matt. 9:36). Daily, he saw those people hungry and thirsty. He saw the strangers lacking hospitality. He saw the naked, the sick, and the prisoners who all needed caring attention (Matt. 25:37-39).

The African churches still see many of these people in our African villages, mining towns, and cities. We see people who are jobless and homeless in our urban centers on a daily basis. We have also seen people who either lost their jobs or are at the end of the working career and are sent home with no pension to sustain them. We have seen many who have no one to take care of them, because they do not have children or extended families. Such people often become lonely and desperate. They are people who have no one to give them a sense of hope in life. Consequently, they feel rejected by society. They also feel rejected and cursed by God, for they believe in God's existence. We have also seen many people who go without food, medical and dental attention, shelter, and clean water in spite of the fact that their countries have had political independence for decades. Some of these people are still dying like flies because of ethnic wars, refugee camps, hunger, and diseases such as AIDS, malaria, and others.

Every church denomination in Africa has its own polity and traditions, especially in relation to how it operates its churches and congregations. Most of our systems, methods, and traditions of mission have disregarded the African cultural context in which we operate. Often, what happens is that the parent denominational bodies in Europe, America, Australia, or New Zealand, which always seem to be changing their ways of doing things to fit their own cultural situation, insist that the African churches of the same denomination follow suit despite the vast cultural differences. If they start talking about merging with another church in Europe or America because that is what suits their situation overseas, the churches of the same denomination in Africa will also start similar discussion. If the parent churches break the talks, those in Africa will do the same, even if such merger talks were going to strengthen the witness of the African churches. If the mother churches decide on different committees in the church in order for their congregations to respond to their social issues more effectively in their cultural context, often those changes are imitated in Africa. At times one feels that the churches in Africa spend more of their valuable time learning exported systems of doing things and trying to make some of those systems work in their own African situation than they do engaging in mission. Thus, knowing how to operate under those foreign traditions unfortunately is considered an achievement on the part of the African church in becoming more Christian and mature. Meanwhile, the mission that extends the compassion of Jesus is neglected.

Maybe the time has come for the African church, through its denominations, ecumenical groupings, or congregations, to find new ways of meeting needs in their communities as an engagement in mission. One of the most innovative systems introduced by two pastors of the Zimbabwe Annual Conference of The United Methodist Church was the introduction of "sections" as a geographical unit of membership of a congregation under a leader. That was a great improvement on the Wesleyan idea of class meetings. Many churches have made similar innovations; we certainly emulate such efforts and express a strong word of encouragement to the church leadership that is always motivated by the sense of mission, rather than falling prey to unnecessary "denominational trappings" that hinder mission.

Jesus identified the mission of his Father with the people. Hence, as he went through all the towns and villages he saw only the people. In the crowds he saw real people, not mere social fabric. He saw who they were, where they came from, and what their needs were. Indeed, he saw them as "harassed and helpless, like sheep without a shepherd" (Matt. 9:36). Jesus still sees the mission of his church as ministering to the people his Father loves (John 3:16). He still sees the mission of his church as the harvest that is "plentiful" (Matt. 9:37). A congregation situated in a community similar to what Jesus saw then and still sees today cannot remain unmoved. An African congregation that has the

219

conscience of mission and sees Africa today the same way Christ sees it is bound to be moved by deep compassion for the people every day. God's mission is not to be found in the biblical text, but in the discernment of and service to God's people—those who are hungry, thirsty, naked, homeless, jobless, sick, power-less, and rejected. Every African congregation knows some people who are rejected in their community or town, but the question is: What have our congregations done for such people that Christ would have done for them if he visited them?

It is interesting to see how Jesus identified his mission among the people in the lowest social stratum of his society, people who were excluded from temple worship, as Kathy Black reminds us.[9] Thus, Jesus preached the good news to the poor who had been neglected. He proclaimed freedom to the people (such as prisoners) to whom no one would normally pay any attention. He proclaimed and restored sight to the blind (Luke 4:18), and he healed the lame, deaf, mute (Mark 2:1-5; 7:31-37), and those who had leprosy (Mark 1:40-45).

It is sobering to remember that earlier, things had been very different when God spoke to Moses:

> Say to Aaron: "For the generations to come none of your descen-dants who has a defect may come near to offer the food of his God. No man who has any defect may come near: no man who is blind or lame, disfigured or deformed; no man with a crippled foot or hand, or who is hunchbacked or dwarfed, or who has any eye defect, or who has festering or running sores or damaged testicles. No descendant of Aaron the priest who has any defect is to come near to present the offerings made to the LORD by fire. He has a defect; he must not come near to offer the food of his God. He may eat the most holy food of his God, as well as the holy food; yet because of his defect, he must not go near the curtain or approach the altar, and so desecrate my sanctuary. I am the LORD, who makes them holy." (Lev. 21:16-23)

It was among such people, and from that lowest social class of people, that the preaching of the kingdom of God became *good news* to Jesus' hearers. It was from that lowest social stratum that the church of Jesus was established. It worked its way up to engulf people of all social strata until there were saints who belonged "to Caesar's household" (Phil. 4:22); and after three centuries of preaching the gospel, to Constantine, the emperor himself.

At times I feel that the church in Africa has done a good job of propagating the gospel. I have attended a few national and international ecumenical church conferences, and it is so good to dine with heads of state or presidents among the guests at such church events. The upward movement seems to have been accomplished. But has the church in Africa equally dined with the poor, the blind, the lame, the lepers, and others typically cast out? All people are God's mission, both in our own community and beyond. They are all our neighbors.

The Church in Africa has a mission to which Christ is leading us all. In his letter to the saints in Ephesus, Paul wrote to them that Christ had already apportioned the gifts to the church in general, and to Ephesus in particular. He gave some to be apostles, some to be prophets, some to be evangelists, and others to be pastors and teachers—all for mission (Eph. 4:11-13). If it is important for a congregation to identify God's mission in its own community and beyond, it is equally important for a congregation to know with what gifts, talents, and skills God has already endowed the members of the congregation.

Today we are obsessed with the idea of looking at happiness as the ultimate goal in life. One gets education or a position that offers more money, or skills that enable one to be elevated more quickly than others, and we behave as if we are entitled to such life. Worse still, we view the blessings of life as "a right." Paul is reminding us that actually those talents, gifts, and skills have been apportioned to us through the grace of Christ and for the purpose of God's mission. All we are and have is because of the love and mercy of God, and these very talents and skills are to be used for the building up of the people of God in the community, and assisting those to whom Christ leads us in our communities.

We may never know the gifts or talents that we already possess until a challenging situation arises in life. In other words, a congregation never realizes its potential until it has received a sense of mission for God's people. Moses never thought he would be a leader of Israel. Probably he was preoccupied with the idea that he was slow of speech and tongue. Yet when the Lord sent Moses back to Egypt, the Lord did not give him new weaponry; rather, the Lord asked Moses, "What is that in your hand?" (Exod. 4:2).

It had never occurred to Moses that God could use the staff in his hand. The native talents that Moses already possessed were means through which God performed miracles for the liberation of Israel from slavery in Egypt. Preaching that equips a congregation for mission will prayerfully concentrate on discerning God's mission and discovering the talents and skills already endowed within its congregation. The task will have to be a team effort.

If a congregation is seriously planning to be involved in God's mission, it will have to know its community. It must know how many people are living in that community. The community may be a village or villages, a mining town, or a section of a city. The congregation must also know the type of people who reside in their community. Above all, the congregation would have to know the community's stories of success and failure, its blessings and problems, its fears, anxieties, and social problems.

It is always gratifying to remember that there are people in our congregations who are endowed with gifts to be used through the life and ministry of their congregations to meet the needs of those who are suffering. Preaching that equips the people of God for mission always works as a catalyst in enabling persons with talents and skills to come out, while at the same time challenging the whole congregation to investigate needs of the people of their own communities. In urban congregations there are typically doctors and nurses, lawyers, business executives, teachers, and many other professionals—all dedicated people. A small group of such persons could identify a need in the community and challenge their congregation to do something about alleviating that need. That same dynamic was certainly true of Jesus, for as he walked in the villages and towns of Galilee, he was always attracted or pulled by people's needs. Doctors and nurses could quickly identify people who are suffering from AIDS. What is the ministry of African churches to such persons? Business executives have knowledge and experience that could help people (particularly women) who are trying to manage small businesses. What if such businesspeople organized to train fledgling small business managers? We can all be creative in similar ways in sharing our talents. Preaching that equips for mission challenges people to rediscover their talents, which often are realized only when they are used for the good of other people. Whether we preach the gospel to equip the congregation for such mission, or preach through pulpit evangelism, house evangelism, or visitation evangelism, the goal is always salvation. The gospel "is the power of God for the salvation of everyone who believes" (Rom. 1:16). It has the power to save the total person, soul and body. The gospel is strong enough to bring good news to individuals, communities, cities, and all our African nations. Our people have been waiting for peace, justice, freedom, and prosperity of their nations for too long. These will come more readily if we learn to work together as "the body of Christ" (Eph. 4:12).

A story is told about the animals of the jungle. Once upon a time, there was severe drought in the land. They all came together to consider how they would survive the drought. They decided to dig a well. All the big animals like the elephant, rhinoceros, hippopotamus, and lion took turns stamping the ground on the spot they thought they would get water. But there was no water to be seen. They went deep enough so that they had to use ladders to go down and come back out; but they produced dust instead of any sign of water. Eventually, the tortoise requested he take a turn. All the other animals laughed at the tortoise. Nevertheless, since everybody was tired, they threw the tortoise down into the well. While down in the well the tortoise started singing a song that made the other animals begin to dance. The song went like this:

> Chaka, chaka, chakandye mataka!
> Chaka, chaka, chakandye mataka!

The meaning is simply that wherever the tortoise is, it eats mud. Therefore, water had to come out. When the other animals saw that water was indeed forming, they quickly took the tortoise out and took over the digging. All they succeeded in doing was digging the well deeper, and again, producing a lot of dust. No doubt they wanted to receive the credit. Eventually, they decided to put the tortoise back into the well, and not to disturb it until the water they so badly needed came out. The other animals then believed that the tortoise was endowed with the secret of creating water. Again, the tortoise asked the rest of the animals not to dig anymore, but to sing along with it as it danced in the well. Soon water started forming until it filled the well that had been dug.

What a mission the animals of the jungle had! Yet, all they

needed was to recognize each other's talents and skills in order to get the water. Their mission was mammoth, like a "harvest that is plentiful." They also had the animal resources to do all that needed to be done. They demonstrated and accomplished what Paul was talking about to the saints in Ephesus, regarding "unity in the body of Christ."

The charge to preach the gospel should bring meaning to worship, and healing to the whole person. It should challenge people to be reconciled with God, and it should equip the saints to work together in the mission of God.

Notes

1. African Cultural Background

1. Kenneth Scott Latourette, *A History of Christianity*, Vol. 1: To A.D. 1500, rev. ed. (San Francisco: HarperCollins Publishers, 1975), 77.
2. G. S. P. Freeman-Grenville, *The New Atlas of African History* (New York: Simon and Schuster, 1991), 52.
3. John Ernest Leonard Oulton, Henry Chadwick, ed., *Alexandrian Christianity* (Philadelphia: Westminster, 1954), 15.
4. Roland Oliver and J. D. Fage, *A Short History of Africa*, 6th ed. (Harmondsworth: Penguin Books, 1990), 2.
5. Ibid.
6. Ibid.
7. Ibid.
8. Ibid., 31.
9. Ibid.
10. *Time* (March 30, 1998), 46.
11. John S. Mbiti, *African Religions and Philosophy* (New York: Praeger, 1970), 7.
12. Geoffrey Parrinder, *Religion in Africa* (Baltimore: Penguin Books, 1969), 67.
13. George B. N. Ayittey, *Africa Betrayed* (New York: St. Martin Press, 1992), 1.
14. Ibid., 23.
15. *Christianity Today* (September 7, 1998), 32-33.
16. Africa–Church Growth and Development Report, General Board of Global Ministries of The United Methodist Church (December 1994), 1.
17. David Barrett, ed., *World Christian Encyclopedia: A Comparative Study of Churches and Religions in the Modern World 1900–2000* (Oxford: Oxford University Press, 1982), table 21.
18. *The United Methodist Reporter* (January 1, 1999).
19. Oliver and Fage, *A Short History of Africa*, 2.

2. Preaching in the Early Church

1. Ralph G. Turnbull, *Baker's Dictionary of Practical Theology* (Grand Rapids: Baker Book House, 1967), 50.
2. In this section, I will expand on what I have written in my publication *Biblical Proclamation for Africa Today* (Nashville: Abingdon Press, 1995).
3. Gerhard von Rad, *Old Testament Theology*, Vol. 1 (New York: Harper & Bros., 1962), 71.

4. Ibid., 72.

5. Turnbull, *Dictionary of Practical Theology*, 31.

6. *The Interpreter's Dictionary of the Bible*, Vol. R-Z (Nashville / New York: Abingdon Press, 1962), 478-79.

7. C. S. C. Williams, *The Acts of the Apostles* (New York: Harper and Bros., 1957), 99.

8. Turnbull, ed., *Baker's Dictionary of Practical Theology*, 50; see also Kurewa, *Biblical Proclamation for Africa Today*, 22.

9. *The Interpreter's Dictionary of the Bible*, Vol. K-Q (Nashville / New York: Abingdon Press, 1962), 868.

10. William Bancraft Hill, *The Apostolic Age* (New York: Fleming H. Revell, 1922), 13.

11. Bruce Manning Metzger, *The New Testament: Its Background, Growth, and Development* (Nashville / New York: Abingdon Press, 1965), 179.

12. Hill, *Apostolic Age*, 13.

13. Metzger, *The New Testament*, 179.

14. Ibid., 184.

15. Ibid.

16. Ibid.

17. G. S. P. Freeman-Grenville, *The New Atlas of African History* (New York: Simon and Schuster, 1991), 18.

18. Ibid., 36.

19. W. H. C. Frend, *The Rise of Christianity* (Philadelphia: Fortress Press, 1984), 1915.

20. William Barclay, *Acts of the Apostles*, rev. ed. (Philadelphia: Westminster Press, 1975), 98.

21. William Barclay, *The Letters to Timothy, Titus, Philemon*, rev. ed. (Philadelphia: Westminster, 1975), 98.

22. Henry Bettenson, *Documents of the Christian Church*, 2nd ed. (London: Oxford University Press, 1963), 27.

23. Ibid., 71.

24. Ibid., 68-69.

25. Ibid.

26. Ibid., 68.

27. Ibid.

28. Ibid., 11.

29. Ibid., 9.

30. Ibid., 68.

31. Ibid., 67.

32. J. Stevenson, ed., *A New Eusebius: Documents Illustrative of the History of the Church to A.D. 337* (London: S.P.C.K., 1957), 139.

33. Henry Bettenson, *Documents of the Christian Church*, 6.

34. J. Stevenson, *A New Eusebius*, 202.

35. Edwin Charles Dargan, *A History of Preaching*, Vol. 1 (New York: Hodder & Stoughton, George H. Doran Co., 1905), 40.

36. Roland H. Bainton, *Christendom: A Short History of Christianity and Its Impact on Western Civilization*, Vol. 1 (New York: Harper & Row, 1964), 79.

37. Yngve Brilioth, *A Brief History of Preaching* (Philadelphia: Fortress Press, 1965), 24.

38. William H. Willimon and Richard Lischer, eds., *Concise Encyclopedia of Preaching* (Louisville: Westminster/John Knox Press, 1995), 189.

39. Bainton, *Christendom*, 92.

40. Brilioth, *A Brief History of Preaching*, 26.

41. Ibid.

42. Willimon and Lischer, *Concise Encyclopedia of Preaching*, 190.

43. Dargan, *A History of Preaching*, 87.

44. Brilioth, *A Brief History of Preaching*, 26.

45. Dargan, *A History of Preaching*, 89.

46. Ibid.

47. Ibid., 58.

48. Brilioth, *A Brief History of Preaching*, 42.

49. Dargan, *A History of Preaching*, 96.
50. Ibid.
51. Williston Walker, *A History of the Christian Church*, rev. (New York: Charles Scribner's Sons, 1959), 128.
52. S. L. Greenlade, trans. *Early Latin Theology*, Vol. V (Philadelphia: Westminster), 19.
53. Dargan, *A History of Preaching*, 99.
54. Ibid.
55. Brilioth, *A Brief History of Preaching*, 44.
56. Walker, *A History of the Christian Church*, 161.
57. Brilioth, *A Brief History of Preaching*, 47.
58. Ibid.
59. Ibid., 48.
60. Walker, *A History of the Christian Church*, 162.
61. Brilioth, *A Brief History of Preaching*, 50.
62. Ibid., 51.
63. Ibid., 50.
64. Ibid., 55.
65. Ibid., 57.
66. Dargan, *A History of Preaching*, 109.

3. Preaching of the Middle Ages and Reformation

1. William H. Willimon and Richard Lischer, eds., *Concise Encyclopedia of Preaching* (Louisville: Westminster/John Knox Press, 1995), 195.
2. Edwin Charles Dargan, *A History of Preaching*, Vol. 1 (New York: Hodder & Stoughton, George H. Duran Co., 1905), 106.
3. Kenneth Scott Latourette, *A History of Christianity* (New York: Harper & Bros., 1953), 273.
4. Ibid.
5. Latourette, *A History of Christianity*, 269.
6. Ibid.
7. Paul Tillich, *A History of Christian Thought* (New York: Harper & Row, 1968), 134.
8. Ibid., 135.
9. Ibid.
10. Ibid., 137.
11. Ibid.
12. Hubert Cunliffe-Jones, *A History of Christian Doctrine* (Philadelphia: Fortress Press, 1978), 183.
13. Ibid.
14. Ibid., 184.
15. Latourette, *A History of Christianity*, 524.
16. Ibid.
17. Dargan, *A History of Preaching*, 109.
18. Latourette, *A History of Christianity*, 524ff.
19. Yngve Brilioth, *A Brief History of Preaching* (Philadelphia: Fortress Press, 1965), 70.
20. Willimon and Lischer, *Concise Encyclopedia of Preaching*, 195.
21. Latourette, *A History of Christianity*, 527.
22. Gustaf Aulen, *The Faith of the Christian Church* (Philadelphia: Muhlenberg Press, 1962), 366.
23. Dargan, *A History of Preaching*, 110.
24. Ibid.
25. Latourette, *A History of Christianity*, 441.
26. Willimon and Lischer, *Concise Encyclopedia of Preaching*, 198.
27. Ibid.
28. Dargan, *A History of Preaching*, 135.
29. Ibid., 136.

30. Ibid., 137.
31. Ibid., 136.
32. Brilioth, *A Brief History of Preaching*, 70.
33. Ibid.
34. Ibid., 71.
35. Roland H. Bainton, *Christendom: A Short History of Christianity and Its Impact on Western Civilization*, Vol. 1 (New York: Harper & Row, 1964), 162.
36. Latourette, *A History of Christianity*, 425.
37. Williston Walker, *A History of the Christian Church*, rev. (New York: Charles Scribner's Sons, 1959), 219.
38. Brilioth, *A Brief History of Preaching*, 77.
39. Latourette, *A History of Christianity*, 427.
40. Brilioth, *A Brief History of Preaching*, 94.
41. Daniel R. Lesnick, *Preaching in Medieval Florence* (Athens: University of Georgia Press, 1989), 63.
42. Brilioth, *A Brief History of Preaching*, 94.
43. Willimon and Lischer, *Concise Encyclopedia of Preaching*, 201ff.
44. Tillich, *A History of Christian Thought*, 110.
45. Dargan, *A History of Preaching*, 433.
46. Ibid., 462.
47. Ibid., 464.
48. Philip S. Watson, *Let God Be God* (Philadelphia: Fortress Press, 1970), 92-93.
49. Ibid., 74.
50. Ibid., 94.
51. Ibid.
52. Ibid., 149.
53. Ibid.
54. Willimon and Lischer, *Concise Encyclopedia of Preaching*, 204.
55. Donald K. McKim, *The Bible in Theology and Preaching* (Nashville: Abingdon Press, 1994), 31.
56. Willimon and Lischer, *Concise Encyclopedia of Preaching*, 205.
57. Ibid.
58. Ibid.
59. Brilioth, *A Brief History of Preaching*, 116.
60. Dargan, *A History of Preaching*, 448.
61. F. A. Burkill, *The Evolution of Christian Thought* (London: Cornell University Press, 1971), 253.
62. Georgia Harkness, *John Calvin: The Man and His Ethics* (New York: Henry Holt and Co., 1931), 63.
63. Hugh T. Kerr, ed., *A Compend of the Institute of the Christian Religion by John Calvin* (Philadelphia: Westminster, 1939), 3.
64. Wilhelm Niesel, *The Theology of Calvin* (Philadelphia: Westminster, 1956), 23-24.
65. Ibid., 24.
66. Hugh T. Kerr, *A Compend*, 171-72.
67. Niesel, *The Theology of Calvin*, 104-5.
68. Burkill, *Evolution of Christian Thought*, 252.
69. T. H. L. Parker, *Portrait of Calvin* (Philadelphia: Westminster, 1954), 80.
70. Ibid.
71. Ibid., 30.
72. Ibid., 84.
73. Harkness, *John Calvin*, 72.
74. Niesel, *The Theology of Calvin*, 160.
75. Ibid., 163.
76. Willimon and Lischer, *Concise Encyclopedia of Preaching*, 209.
77. Ibid., 210.
78. John McManners, ed., *The Oxford History of Christianity* (Oxford: Oxford University Press, 1990), 274.

79. Roland Oliver and J. D. Fage, *A Short History of Africa* (Harmondsworth: Penguin Books, 1990), 118.

4. Defining Preaching in the African Context

1. *The Interpreter's Dictionary of the Bible*, Vol. K-Q (Nashville / New York: Abingdon Press, 1962), 868.
2. Ibid.
3. Ralph G. Turnbull, *Baker's Dictionary of Practical Theology* (Grand Rapids: Baker Book House, 1976), 50.
4. R. F. Kennell, *Communication Contracts in Contemporary American Protestant Homiletics* (unpublished Ph.D. dissertation), 18.
5. Alan Walker, *The Whole Gospel for the Whole World* (1957), 51.
6. This is a definition of preaching that was given by Philip Whitmer, who was a doctoral student at Garrett-Evangelical Theological Seminary, Evanston, Illinois, in 1965.
7. Kennel, *Communication Contracts*, 18.
8. W. E. Sangster, *The Craft of Sermon Construction* (Philadelphia: Westminster, 1950), 14.
9. Phillips Brooks, *The Joy of Preaching* (Grand Rapids: Kregel Publications, 1889), 9.
10. This definition was given by Philip Whitmer, who was an assistant instructor in Homiletics at Garrett Theological Seminary, 1964–65.
11. Jean-Jacques van Allmen, *Preaching and Congregation* (Richmond: John Knox Press, 1962), 7.
12. Ibid.
13. Bishop Gerald Kennedy, *His Word Through Preaching* (New York: Harper & Bros., 1947), 9.
14. Allmen, *Preaching and Congregation*, 7.
15. *Preaching, A Journal of Homiletics*, Vol. 111, No. 3 (May–June, 1968): 18.
16. Ilion T. Jones, *Principles and Practices of Preaching* (Nashville / New York: Abingdon Press, 1964), 11.
17. Reginald H. Fuller, *Preaching the Lectionary*, rev. ed. (Collegeville: Liturgical Press, 1984), xviii.
18. Jones, *Principles and Practices of Preaching*, 11.
19. Philip Whitmer, who was an assistant instructor in Homiletics at Garrett Theological Seminary, 1964–1965, gave this definition.
20. William H. Willimon and Richard Lischer, *Concise Encyclopedia of Preaching* (Louisville: Westminster/John Knox Press, 1995), 487.

5. Using the Bible in Preaching

1. William H. Willimon and Richard Lischer, *Concise Encyclopedia of Preaching* (Louisville: Westminster/John Knox Press, 1995), 487.
2. William Barclay, *The Gospel of John*, Vol. 1 (Philadelphia: Westminster, 1975), 21.
3. G. Waddy Polkinghorne, *The Canon of the New Testament* (London: Charles S. Kelly, 1914), 112.
4. Bruce Metzger, *The Canon of the New Testament* (Oxford: Clarendon Press, 1987), 251ff.
5. Alan Richardson, ed., *A Theological Word Book of the Bible* (New York: Macmillan, 1966), 156.
6. John Wesley Zwomunondiita Kurewa, *Biblical Proclamation for Africa Today* (Nashville: Abingdon Press, 1995), 49.
7. Van A. Harvey, *A Handbook of Theological Terms* (New York: Macmillan, 1964), 131.
8. Metzger, *The Canon of the New Testament*, 254ff.
9. Ibid.

10. L. Harold DeWolf, *A Theology of the Living Church* (New York: Harper and Bros., 1953), 76.

11. Donald K. McKim, *The Bible in Theology and Preaching* (Nashville: Abingdon Press, 1985), 32.

12. Gustaf Aulen, *The Faith of the Christian Church* (Philadelphia: Muhlenberg Press, 1962), 75.

13. C. F. D. Moule, *The Birth of the New Testament* (New York: Harper and Bros., 1957), 179.

14. Dwight E. Stevenson, *In the Biblical Preacher's Workshop* (Nashville / New York: Abingdon Press, 1967), 18.

15. Barclay, *The Gospel of John*, 27.

16. Ibid.

17. Ibid.

18. Robert Nelson, *The Realm of Redemption*, 7th ed. (London: Epworth Press, 1964), 106.

19. Philip Watson, *Let God Be God* (Philadelphia: Fortress Press, 1947), 149.

20. Ibid.

21. *The Interpreter's Dictionary of the Bible*, Vol. R-Z (Nashville / New York: Abingdon Press, 1962).

22. Stevenson, *In the Biblical Preacher's Workshop*, 42.

23. Ibid., 146.

24. Thomas G. Long, *The Witness of Preaching* (Louisville: Westminster/John Knox Press, 1989), 48.

25. Stevenson, *In the Biblical Preacher's Workshop*, 150.

6. African Spirituality for Preaching

1. Phillips Brooks, *On Preaching* (New York: Seabury Press, 1964), 14ff.

2. Minutes of the East Central Africa Mission Conference (1910), 50.

3. Thomas G. Long, *The Witness of Preaching* (Louisville: Westminster/John Knox Press, 1989), 12-13.

4. Henry H. Mitchell, *The Recovery of Preaching* (San Francisco: Harper & Row, 1977), 6-7.

5. G. S. P. Freeman-Grenville, *The New Atlas of African History* (New York: Simon and Schuster, 1991), 23.

6. Howard Hanchey, *Church Growth and the Power of Evangelism* (Cambridge: Cowley Publications, 1990), 130.

7. Oscar Cullmann, *Prayer in the New Testament* (Minneapolis: Fortress Press, 1995), xiv.

8. M. Robert Mulholland, Jr., *Shaped by the Word* (Nashville: Upper Room, 1985), 47.

9. Minutes of the East Central Africa Mission Conference (1906), 6.

10. J. F. Ade Ajayi, *Christian Missions in Nigeria 1841–1891* (Evanston: Northwestern University Press, 1965), 206.

11. E. A. Iyandele, *The Missionary Impact on Modern Nigeria 1842–1914* (New York: Humanities Press, 1967), 182.

12. Ibid., 118.

13. Minutes of the East Central Africa Mission Conference (1908), 51.

7. African Characteristics of Preaching

1. Minutes of the Rhodesia Mission Conference (1919), 39.

2. Minutes of the Rhodesia Mission Conference (1924), 35.

3. Ronald Sleeth, *Biblical Proclamation* (Nashville / New York: Abingdon Press, 1962).

4. *Christianity Today* (July 13, 1998), 22.

5. William Barclay, *The Letter to the Romans*, rev. (Philadelphia: Westminster, 1975), 21-22.

8. Planning for Preaching

1. Reginald H. Fuller, *Preaching the Lectionary* (Collegeville: Liturgical Press, 1984), xxv.
2. Ibid.
3. Henry Bettenson, *Documents of the Christian Church*, 2nd ed. (Oxford: Oxford University Press, 1981), 67.
4. Ibid.
5. Oscar Cullmann, ed., A. J. B. Higgin, trans., *The Early Church* (Philadelphia: Westminster, 1956), 31.
6. Ibid., 33.
7. Ibid.
8. Fuller, *Preaching the Lectionary*, xxv.
9. *Webster's New World Dictionary* (Cleveland: World Publishing Company, 1956), 834.
10. William Willimon and Richard Lischer, *Concise Encyclopedia of Preaching* (Louisville: Westminster/John Knox Press, 1995), 304.
11. Fuller, *Preaching the Lectionary*, 1.
12. Ibid., 14.
13. Ibid., 28.
14. John Wesley Zwomunondiita Kurewa, *Biblical Proclamation for Africa Today* (Nashville: Abingdon Press, 1995), 99.
15. Ibid., 102.
16. Ibid.

9. Preparing Sermons for Preaching

1. Martin Luther King, Jr., *Strength to Love* (Philadelphia: Fortress Press, 1963), x.
2. Fred B. Craddock, *Preaching* (Nashville: Abingdon Press, 1985), 31.
3. Ilion Jones, *Principles and Practice of Preaching* (Nashville: Abingdon Press, 1984), 20.
4. John Knox, *The Integrity of Preaching* (Nashville / New York: Abingdon Press, 1957), 76.
5. Ibid.
6. Henry Glady Davis, *Design for Preaching* (Philadelphia: Fortress Press, 1958), 20-21.
7. Ibid., 43-44.
8. Thomas G. Long, *The Witness of Preaching* (Louisville: Westminster/John Knox Press, 1989), 92.
9. Ibid.
10. David Bosch, "The Question of the Mission of Today," *Journal of Theology for Southern Africa* (December 1972), 121.
11. William Sangster, *The Craft of Sermon Construction* (Philadelphia: Westminster, 1950), 13ff.
12. Craddock, *Preaching*, 110.
13. Long, *Witness of Preaching*, 64.
14. Ibid.
15. Craddock, *Preaching*, 115.
16. Ibid., 15.
17. Knox, *Integrity of Preaching*, 67.
18. Stephen E. Lucas, *The Art of Public Speaking* (New York: Random House, 1983), 222.
19. Clark S. Carlie and Arlie V. Daniel, *Project Text for Public Speaking* (New York: Harper & Row, 1987), 35.
20. Lucas, *The Art of Public Speaking*, 222.
21. Willimon and Lischer, *Concise Encyclopedia of Preaching* (Louisville: Westminster/John Knox Press, 1995), 205.
22. E. Christian Buehler and Wil A. Linkugel, *Speech Communication* (New York: Harper & Row, 1968), 87.
23. Ibid., 89.

10. A Charge for Preaching

1. William H. Willimon and Richard Lischer, *Concise Encyclopedia of Preaching* (Louisville: Westminster/John Knox Press, 1995), 311.

2. William Barclay, *In the Hands of God* (New York: Harper & Row, 1965), 22-23.

3. William Barclay, *Letters of James and Peter,* rev. (Philadelphia: Westminster, 1976), 130.

4. Ibid., 129.

5. Ibid., 130.

6. Ibid.

7. Kathy Black, *A Healing Homiletic: Preaching and Disability* (Nashville: Abingdon Press, 1996), 51.

8. David Bosch, "The Question of the Mission of Today," *Journal of Theology for Southern Africa* (December 1972), 14.

9. Black, *A Healing Homiletic,* 48-49.